Transforming Food and Agricultural Policy

Western democratic welfare states often featured sectoral governance arrangements where governments negotiated policy with sectoral elites, based on shared ideas and exclusive institutional arrangements. Food and agriculture policy is widely considered an extreme case of compartmentalized and 'exceptionalist' policy-making, where sector-specific policy ideas and institutions provide privileged access for sectoral interest groups and generate policies that benefit their members. In the last two decades, policy exceptionalism has been under pressure from internationalization of policy-making, increasing interlinkage of policy areas and trends towards self-regulation, liberalization and performance-based policies. This book introduces the concept of 'post-exceptionalism' to characterize an incomplete transformation of exceptionalist policies and politics which preserves significant exceptionalist features. Post-exceptional constellations of ideas, institutions, interests and policies can be complementary and stable, or tense and unstable. Food and agriculture policy serves as an example to illustrate an incomplete transformation towards a more open, contested and networked politics. Chapters on agricultural policy-making in the European Union and the United States, the politics of food in Germany and the United Kingdom, transnational organic standard setting and global food security debates demonstrate how 'post-exceptionalism' helps to understand the co-existence of transformation and path dependency in contemporary public policies.

The chapters in this book were originally published as a special issue of the *Journal of European Public Policy*.

Carsten Daugbjerg is Professor of Food and Agricultural Policy in the Department of Food and Resource Economics, University of Copenhagen, Denmark, and an Honorary Professor in the Crawford School of Public Policy, The Australian National University, Australia.

Peter H. Feindt is Professor of Agricultural and Food Policy in the Albrecht Daniel Thaer-Institute of Agricultural and Horticultural Sciences, Humboldt-University Berlin, Germany.

Journal of European Public Policy Series
Series Editors
Jeremy Richardson is Emeritus Fellow at Nuffield College, Oxford University, UK, and an Adjunct Professor in the National Centre for Research on Europe, University of Canterbury, New Zealand.

Berthold Rittberger is Professor and Chair of International Relations at the Geschwister-Scholl-Institute of Political Science, University of Munich, Germany.

This series seeks to bring together some of the finest edited works on European Public Policy. Reprinting from Special Issues of the *Journal of European Public Policy*, the focus is on using a wide range of social sciences approaches, both qualitative and quantitative, to gain a comprehensive and definitive understanding of Public Policy in Europe.

For a complete list of books in this series please visit https://www.routledge.com/Journal-of-European-Public-Policy-Special-Issues-as-Books/book-series/JEPPSPIBS.

Transforming Food and Agricultural Policy

Post-exceptionalism in Public Policy

Edited by
Carsten Daugbjerg and Peter H. Feindt

Routledge
Taylor & Francis Group

LONDON AND NEW YORK

First published 2018
by Routledge

2 Park Square, Milton Park, Abingdon, Oxfordshire OX14 4RN
52 Vanderbilt Avenue, New York, NY 10017

Routledge is an imprint of the Taylor & Francis Group, an informa business

First issued in paperback 2020

British Library Cataloguing in Publication Data
A catalogue record for this book is available from the British Library

ISBN 13: 978-0-8153-6036-0 (hbk)
ISBN 13: 978-0-367-53073-0 (pbk)

Typeset in Myriad Pro
by RefineCatch Limited, Bungay, Suffolk

Publisher's Note
The publisher accepts responsibility for any inconsistencies that may have
arisen during the conversion of this book from journal articles to book chapters,
namely the possible inclusion of journal terminology.

Disclaimer
Every effort has been made to contact copyright holders for their permission to
reprint material in this book. The publishers would be grateful to hear from any
copyright holder who is not here acknowledged and will undertake to rectify
any errors or omissions in future editions of this book.

Contents

Citation Information

The chapters in this book were originally published in the *Journal of European Public Policy*, volume 24, issue 11 (2017). When citing this material, please use the original page numbering for each article, as follows:

Chapter 6

'Feeding 9 billion people': global food security debates and the productionist trap
Eve Fouilleux, Nicolas Bricas and Arlène Alpha
Journal of European Public Policy, volume 24, issue 11 (2017), pp. 1658–1677

Chapter 7

Global organic agriculture policy-making through standards as an organizational field: when institutional dynamics meet entrepreneurs
Sandra Schwindenhammer
Journal of European Public Policy, volume 24, issue 11 (2017), pp. 1678–1697

Chapter 8

The resilience of paradigm mixes: food security in a post-exceptionalist trade regime
Carsten Daugbjerg, Arild Aurvåg Farsund and Oluf Langhelle
Journal of European Public Policy, volume 24, issue 11 (2017), pp. 1698–1715

For any permission-related enquiries please visit:
http://www.tandfonline.com/page/help/permissions

Notes on Contributors

Gerry Alons is Assistant Professor of International Relations at the Institute for Management Research, Radboud University, Nijmegen, the Netherlands; and Marie Curie Fellow at the Frederick Pardee School of Global Studies, Boston University, USA.

Arlène Alpha is a Cirad senior researcher in Ougadougou, Burkina-Faso. She is a member of MOISA, which is associated with the University of Montpellier, France.

Nicolas Bricas is a Cirad senior researcher at MOISA, which is associated with the University of Montpellier, France.

Carsten Daugbjerg is Professor of Food and Agricultural Policy in the Department of Food and Resource Economics, University of Copenhagen, Denmark, and an Honorary Professor in the Crawford School of Public Policy, The Australian National University, Australia.

Arild Aurvåg Farsund is Professor of Political Science at the University of Stavanger, Norway.

Peter H. Feindt is Professor of Agricultural and Food Policy at the Albrecht Daniel Thaer Institute of Agricultural and Horticultural Sciences, Humboldt-University Berlin, Germany.

Eve Fouilleux is a CNRS research director at Lisis, University of Paris-Est, France. She is associated to the French Agricultural Research Centre for International Development (Cirad) in Montpellier, France.

Alan Greer is Associate Professor of Politics and Public Policy at the University of the West of England (UWE), Bristol, UK.

Oluf Langhelle is Professor of Political Science at the University of Stavanger, Norway.

Bob Martin is Senior Lecturer at the Johns Hopkins Bloomberg School of Public Health, USA.

Keeve Nachman is Assistant Professor of Environmental Health and Engineering at the Johns Hopkins Bloomberg School of Public Health, USA.

Allysan Scatterday is a graduate student at the Johns Hopkins Bloomberg School of Public Health, USA.

Sandra Schwindenhammer is Assistant Professor of International Relations at Justus-Liebig-University Giessen, Germany.

Adam Sheingate is Professor of Political Science at Johns Hopkins University, USA.

Jale Tosun is Professor of Political Science at the Institute of Political Science at Heidelberg University, Germany.

Post-exceptionalism in public policy: transforming food and agricultural policy

Carsten Daugbjerg ⓘ and Peter H. Feindt ⓘ

ABSTRACT
Framing the special issue on the transformation of Food and Agricultural Policy, this article introduces the concept of post-exceptionalism in public policies. The analysis of change in agri-food policy serves as a generative example to conceptualize current transformations in sectoral policy arrangements in democratic welfare states. Often these arrangements have been characterized by an exceptionalist ideational framework that legitimizes a sector's special treatment through compartmentalized, exclusive and producer-centered policies and politics. In times of internationalization of policy-making, increasing interlinkage of policy areas and trends towards self-regulation, liberalization and performance-based policies, policy exceptionalism is under pressure to either transform or give way to (neo-)liberal policy arrangements. Post-exceptionalism denotes a partial transformation of exceptionalist ideas, institutions, interest constellations and policy instruments. It reflects the more complex, open, contested and fluid nature of contemporary policy fields that nevertheless still maintain their policy heritage. Discussing stability, the authors distinguish between complementary and tense post-exceptionalism.

Introduction

The Western democratic welfare states of the twentieth century were often marked by sectoral governance arrangements where governments nego-tiated policy with sectoral élites. Since the 1980s, such arrangements have experienced increasing pressure from governments who wanted to exercise a higher degree of control over policy outcomes and the efficiency of public expenditure (Capano 2011; Capano et al. 2015; Richardson 2017). While these relatively closed and self-referential modes of governance and the attempts to submit them to the discipline of performance review and financial discipline have received much attention, one dimension of struggle has not been systematically explored: the tension between ideas that claim the need for special treatment for a sector, or what we term policy exceptionalism, and the generalized ideas of market-oriented and performance-based steering often associated with neoliberalism. In this special issue, we take agricultural policy as an example to develop the concept of policy post-exceptionalism which characterizes the compromise outcome of struggles between policy exceptionalism and attempted (neo-) liberalization.

Over the years, political scientists and policy scholars have repeatedly taken a significant interest in studying agricultural-policy making as a generative empirical example in the theoretical development of policy studies. What made the agricultural-policy sector attractive was that it could be considered an extreme case of a compartmentalized and 'exceptionalist' policy-making process. The agricultural-policy sector was characterized by a distinct set of sector-oriented institutions and ideas, well-organized and well-resourced sectoral interest groups, substantial government intervention in the market, and the potential for a significant redistribution of economic assets from the whole population (through taxes and higher consumer prices) to a relatively small group of producers and landowners. Consequently, these studies have contributed to theoretical developments in the policy and political sciences within a number of research fields that were concerned with the explanation of policy outcome, policy stability and change. These include: interest groups (e.g., Lowi 1969; Olson 1965; Sheingate 2003), government-interest group relations (e.g., Browne 1988; Jordan et al. 1994; Marsh and Smith 2000; Smith 1993), the role of ideas and paradigms in explaining policy change and stability (Coleman et al. 1996; Feindt 2010; Skogstad 1998), policy feedback and path dependency (Coleman and Grant 1998; Daugbjerg 2003; Hooghe and Oser 2016; Kay 2003; Zhu and Lipsmeyer 2015) and more recently, policy layering (Chou 2012; Daugbjerg and Swinbank 2016; Feindt and Flynn 2009; Jackson and Deeg 2012) and internationalization of public policy (Daugbjerg and Swinbank 2009, 2015; Skogstad 2008). Indeed, some of the classic studies on these concepts were grounded in agricultural policy, and often examples were drawn from this area to illustrate theoretical points (see Daugbjerg and Swinbank [2012] for a review of the literature).

The new developments in the food and agriculture sector pose new questions about the nature of policy-making and how we should approach this analytically, not only in the food and agriculture sector, but also in other policy sectors with exceptionalist features. In particular internationalization of policy-making, the growing and new role of self- and co-regulation (which is particularly sensitive in the food sector), concerns about policy efficiency and performance and the interlinkage with other policy domains, such as the rising environmental state (Duit et al. 2016), challenge existing policy arrangements.

Against this background, we propose policy post-exceptionalism as a diagnostic concept to characterize simultaneous continuity and change in a policy arena. Policy (post-)exceptionalism is unavoidably policy specific but has some more general features. Post-exceptionalism denotes a partial departure from compartmentalized, exclusive and exceptionalist policies and politics which, however, preserves some exceptionalist features and has not led to a complete transformation to market-oriented and performance-based policies. It is an incomplete transformation of ideas, institutions, interest constellations and policies with a significant legacy from past policy.

Through an analysis of food and agricultural policy, this article defines policy exceptionalism, reviews its challenges since the 1980s, introduces the concept of 'post-exceptionalism' and characterizes its developments over the last two decades. Based on the key findings of the contributions to this special issue, we discuss the stability of post-exceptionalist arrangements and argue for the broader value of the concept for understanding change in other policy sectors as well.

Defining policy exceptionalism

Exceptionalism is a political belief system that assigns special status to a group, a sector or a country, often on the basis of a historical narrative, to justify special treatment, to claim the validity of special rules or to mobilize group pride or particular efforts for a group's alleged mission (cf. Lipset 1997). Apart from agricultural policy, exceptionalism is a rarely used concept in public-policy studies. The notion of policy exceptionalism describes the special treatment of a sector by governments and international organizations and the belief system that provides cognitive justification and political legitimation. The concept was introduced by Grant (1995) and juxtaposed to attempts to liberalize agricultural markets in line with more general trends towards market liberalism. It was deployed by Skogstad (1998) to explain different policy reforms across the Atlantic in the 1990s and has informed later discussions about paradigm shifts in agriculture policy. Policy exceptionalism is likely also to exist in other policy sectors that are significant for the welfare state, such as housing, energy, higher education, health and care, or pensions, to support calls for, e.g., price controls, producer privileges or state-backed modes of provision. Abstracting from the earlier works on agricultural exceptionalism, we understand policy exceptionalism to comprise four dimensions: ideas; institutions; interests; and policy (instruments and implementation). The core of the concept is a set of exceptionalist *ideas* which shape and legitimize compartmental *institutions* that provide a dedicated policy space for a *policy community* to adopt and implement *policy instruments and programs* that serve their interests and comply with their ideas. We briefly discuss each dimension in turn, using agricultural exceptionalism to illustrate the broader concept.

Ideas

Public policies are shaped by cognitive and normative beliefs which are communicated through policy ideas that provide meaning to situations (Béland and Cox 2011) and set standards for appropriate behavior and desirable outcomes (Skogstad and Schmidt 2011: 8–9). Exceptionalist ideas explain the unique nature of a particular sector which renders it unsuitable and/or inappropriate to be governed by market forces and highlight how the sector contributes to broader societal values. Agricultural exceptionalism, for example, is based on the assumption that agriculture is different from other economic sectors in modern societies and requires and deserves special policy treatment for three reasons. First, the claim that unlike other sectors, agricultural producers are faced with unpredictable natural risks: unstable weather, changing climatic factors, unpredictable plant and animal diseases and pests impact on farms and frequently result in sharp fluctuations in market prices, and thus farm incomes, often exacerbated by the ensuing adjustments because collectively agricultural markets tend to over-react to price oscillations (the proverbial pork cycle). Second, it has often been argued that in a growing economy farm incomes may be chronically low ('the farm income problem'). Low income elasticity of food demand implies that an increase in consumer income will only result in limited growth in demand for farm products. To keep up with rising incomes in the rest of the economy, farmers will have to expand production. If not enough farmers are able and willing to exit the farm industry and earn more elsewhere, their income may be depressed (Daugbjerg and Swinbank 2009). Therefore, as Skogstad (1998: 468) emphasizes: 'The first rationale for treating agriculture as an exceptional sector is tied to the *specific interests and needs* of farmers.' The third defining rationale of agricultural exceptionalism is that the farming sector provides an indispensable contribution to the national interest, in particular food security (Skogstad 1998: 468) and the welfare state, i.e., employment, income and safe and affordable food. Occasionally, agriculture or farmers are also linked to values of the polity, e.g., when rural farm communities are presented as models of local grassroots democracy or democracy more generally (Griswold [1948] 1952) or agriculture is stylized as the embodiment of national values (Browne *et al.* 1992). A variation is to claim a special position of farmers in rural communities or society at large (e.g., the policy-mission statement of the German government stresses that family farms 'are of great importance for the development of rural regions and for social cohesion', BMEL 2015: 8). Overall, the agricultural exceptionalist view holds that their special nature means that agricultural production and markets, if left unregulated, will fail to deliver a secure and safe food supply at stable and reasonable food prices, which will lead to decline of farm incomes and possibly rural communities and, more recently, natural resources and ecosystems.

Institutions

Exceptionalist ideas co-develop with a set of institutions and often provide the blueprint for tailor-made institutional design (Blyth 2002) that reflects the perceived uniqueness of the policy sector and at the same time serves to reproduce the exceptionalist ideas (cf. Béland and Cox 2011: 9). In agriculture, the perceived distinctive character of the sector is used to justify institutional compartmentalization, which in turn has helped to further entrench exceptionalist ideas (Grant 1995: 168). In most industrialized countries, until fairly recently, special ministries have been dedicated to serving agriculture (Halpin 2005: 10). At the political level, the ministers often defined their role as the minister *for* agriculture rather the minister *of* agriculture (Daugbjerg and Swinbank 2009: 9). At the administrative level, special administrative bodies integrating farm associations have been formed to administer agricultural policies. These often led to the formation of closed networks of agricultural civil servants and farm-group officials, resulting in a compartmentalized and corporatist policy style. The core of the compartment is often surrounded by a plethora of auxiliary and satellite institutions, such as extension services, agricultural colleges and semi-state chambers of agriculture that tie farmers into the dominant policy and thinking (Rieger 1996). The compartmentalized sectoral institutions exercise ideational power through persuasion, exclusion of alternative ideas or by shaping the terms of debate (Feindt 2017).

Interests

Exceptionalist ideas and institutions shape the formation of interests and the patterns of interaction between government and interest groups, in particular by affecting the distribution of policy costs and benefits. Exceptionalist policies tend to provide benefits to specific groups while costs are dispersed to broad groups, such as consumers and taxpayers, who find it difficult to counter-mobilize. The beneficiaries are likely to develop a strong interest in upholding compartmentalized institutions which give them a privileged position to defend the exceptionalist policy. For example, agricultural exceptionalism supports the interests of agricultural producers but also benefits other groups, such as landowners, suppliers of agricultural inputs, financial institutions, food processors and retailers. Agricultural exceptionalism can be linked to the promotion of specific farming models, typically a productivist focus on high-input and high-yield agriculture (Clunies-Ross *et al.* 1994). For political success, the exceptionalist ideas must resonate with broader audiences and need to be adopted by influential political parties (Roederer-Rynning 2003).

Policy

Exceptionalist policy ideas typically precipitate in exceptional policy instruments which are designed to regulate or mitigate market forces and to achieve specific policy outcomes. Exceptionalist instruments are often sector specific and therefore do not usually travel easily across policy sectors. For example, exceptionalist agricultural policies regulate domestic production through a set of specific instruments, such as intervention buying by state agencies to stabilize producer prices, farm input subsidies, production-linked direct payments, production quota to limit surplus production and maintain price levels or programs to enhance predefined environmental and conservation practices (Greer 2005). To protect farmers from international competition exceptionally high tariffs have been imposed on imports while agricultural exports have received various types of direct and indirect subsidies (Daugbjerg and Swinbank 2009).

As in many other entrenched policy areas, exceptionalism has made any attempt at policy reform a high-stakes game. The policy field has been surrounded by high entry barriers in terms of its arcane technical regulations and diffuse costs to taxpayers, consumers and the environment – not dissimilar to other highly complex policy areas.

Challenges to policy exceptionalism

Given their redistributive implications, policy exceptionalisms are vulnerable to challenges to their cognitive and normative foundations. Agricultural exceptionalism, for example, has always been contested. Already Bismarck's price support policies for cereal producers or the establishment of a special common agricultural policy in the EC were the object of long and hard-fought struggles (Tracy 1989). Nevertheless, in Western democracies agricultural exceptionalism was fully established as part of the post-war welfare consensus and constituted the equivalent of the welfare state for the farm sector (Knudsen 2009; Sheingate 2003).

However, the rise of neoliberalism in the 1980s increasingly challenged policy sectors based on exceptionalist ideas. By the mid-1990s Grant (1995: 167) asked whether agricultural policy was still exceptional. Following his article, agricultural policy research has directly or indirectly addressed the issue of exceptionalism in agricultural policy. New agendas in the agri-food sector followed ideational and institutional changes of the broader context within which the exceptionalist farm policies were embedded. Market liberal ideas gained political force in agricultural policy in the early 1980s, in step with the ascent of neo-liberalism in the age of Thatcherism and Reaganomics. New OECD indicators made the degree of government intervention and costs of agricultural support and protection visible (Legg 2003) and strengthened the arguments of reform advocates. The idea of sustainability entered the agricultural policy debate in the 1990s. Environmentalists used the concept to promote policy measures encouraging transformation to more sustainable forms of agriculture (Feindt 2010). Within the farming industry, various segments welcomed the sustainability debate. For instance, organic farming movements reinforced the sustainability discourse and attempted to position organic farming as the best practical expression of the idea of sustainable farming. Similarly, bio-energy policies were launched as contributions to sustainable development and corresponded well with farm and land-owner interests in increased demand for biomass and agricultural land respectively.

Emphasis on sustainability and consumer concerns can form a combined challenge to policy exceptionalism. In agri-food policy, the rising sustainability discourse coincided with the ascent of a 'new consumerism' in which food represents and embodies certain values to the purchaser as a result of the method or place of their production (Darby and Karni 1973: 68–9). These attributes are often associated with environmentally friendly production, animal welfare, social sustainability, geographical origin and perceived healthiness (often based on the precautionary principle in relation to personal health). Capitalizing on these concerns, the food market became more differentiated. The new consumerism resonated with attempts to create premium markets against a background of deflated producer prices.

Single events can redefine struggles over policy exceptionalism. In agri-food policy, the food price spikes of 2007/2008 rattled the agenda and reinvigorated the food-security debate (Grafton et al. 2015). Though this debate has been dominated by an advocacy coalition that focused on increased production, the engagement of new actors added nutrition, sustainability, social and a range of other concerns to food security, making it a contested concept (Candel et al. 2014). Long-term food security might require giving priority to conservation of soils, ecosystem services and biodiversity along with dietary change rather than increasing yield. These complex public concerns often challenge agricultural policies which rest on a narrow productionist foundation.

The emergence of these new ideas in agri-food policy-making was associated with the activation of international institutions. In particular the World Trade Organization (WTO) and the World Bank, that hitherto had little involvement in agricultural policy, gained power in the policy arena on the back of the new ideas which they at the same time effectively helped to reinforce. With the exception of Australia, New Zealand and the United States in the mid-1990s, the market liberal critique of exceptionalism had limited direct impact on domestic policy reforms. However, influenced by market liberal ideas, the General Agreement on Tariffs and Trade (GATT) and later the WTO became key institutions in the adoption and implementation of international disciplines on agricultural support and protection (Daugbjerg and Swinbank 2009).

Exceptionalist policies are characterized by significant self-regulation. In agricultural policy this was institutionalized primarily at the level of primary producers. Farm commodity associations (e.g., dairy boards) were delegated authority to administer government regulations and subsidy schemes (Grant 1987). While this type of self-regulation is in decline, new types have emerged with the rise of consumerism and business concentration in the retail sector. Retailers, increasingly in association with civil society (and in some instances producer) associations, have established self-regulatory schemes (Havinga and Verbruggen 2017), shaping production standards and controlling their implementation. Retailer-led standards such as Global-G.A.P. (a global certification scheme for good agricultural practice) or national sector-led management and traceability systems have gained significant authority over the definition of good practice relating to health, food safety and environmental concerns. Some private standards are increasingly tied into governmental regulatory compliance regimes, adding a co-regulatory layer to an already complex set of public and private regulations. While self-regulation continues to be significant, the authoritative power has dissipated away from producer organizations to the retailer end of increasingly transnational value chains.

Overall, the emergence of new ideas affecting the agricultural-policy debate and the involvement of new institutions have brought new actors into the agri-food policy arena. Internationalization has changed the setting of domestic-policy making to varying extents. The integration of agriculture into the WTO regime has significant implications for domestic policy. The concerns of both developed and developing countries' trading partners must now be considered to avoid domestic policy measures being challenged in the WTO. Within the trade arena, coalition formation among developing countries and emerging economies has tipped the power balance away from the EU and the US in the WTO. Across all levels, and often competing with free-trade interests, sustainability concerns have drawn environmental authorities and a range of animal welfare and green advocacy groups as well as new farm groups (e.g., organic farmers) into the agricultural policy domain, albeit they have not usually been admitted to the core of agricultural policy networks. While consumer groups to varying extents have sought influence on agricultural policy, the increased emphasis on consumer concerns has enabled retailers, often in collaboration with various NGOs, to gain a hold in the broader agri-food policy space through self-regulation and a self-appointed role as representatives of consumer values (Botterill and Daugbjerg 2015; Marx et al. 2012). The increased corporatization and financialization of the agricultural industry (cf. Lawrence et al. 2015) have brought a wide array of upstream (e.g., financial institutions, machinery, seeds and chemical produ-cers) and downstream (processors and distributors of food commodities) interests into the food value chain. While we know relatively little about the extent to which these actors attempt to influence agricultural and food policy, financial institutions clearly exert strategic influence on entire sub-sectors (e.g., Rabobank on the Dutch pig sector).

Characterizing policy post-exceptionalism

We propose the term 'policy post-exceptionalism' to capture the combination of a less compartmentalized policy arena (institutions and interests) with an updated set of policy ideas that retain at its core claims that a policy sector is special, albeit with updated arguments that relate to the problems on the evolving policy agenda and which trigger novel policy instruments. Post-exceptionalism denotes a partial transformation in which an exceptionalist policy sector has not been completely 'normalized' and in which old and new ideas, institutions, interests and policy instruments coexist. The concept of post-exceptionalism highlights that exceptionalist legacies on all dimensions have been maintained over extended periods despite significant changes to one or more of the four dimensions, resulting in a layered mixture of old and new policy elements, either in a symbiotic or in a contested relationship.

Post-exceptionalism can clearly be observed in the agri-food policy sector as a result of agricultural policy reforms adopted over the recent three decades. The underlying trends and pressures – internationalization, financia-lization, cross-policy linkages, sustainability concerns, new consumerism – suggest that similar developments are likely in other policy domains with an exceptionalist past. The concept can help us diagnose such transformation processes from a longitudinal perspective and to understand their dynamics.

Agriculture was once an archetypical exceptional policy sector but policies have been transforming over the last two or three decades. Therefore, if post-exceptionalism as defined in this article can be demonstrated to be relevant for understanding the transformation process, we suggest that it could be successfully applied as an analytical concept in other policy domains with exceptionalist features.

Agricultural policy communities, responding to the external pressures out-lined above, as well as to major structural change in the agriculture sector and in relevant value chains, have adapted their positions and strategies without abandoning their policy heritage. In the ideational dimension, new lines of argument appear. On the one hand, these respond to the significant chal-lenges to legitimacy and acceptance of agricultural exceptionalism under neo-liberal doctrines and from neo-liberal institutions (WTO, patent law and so on). On the other, they link agricultural policy to new overarching discourses such as sustainability and globalization, and cross-cutting concerns such as the environment, climate change and food security. Old and new discourses are integrated to build new exceptionalist arguments. This is eased by the fact that the proponents of these new policies are often critical towards the dominant, neo-liberal regime and therefore sympathize with exceptionalist approaches (e.g., Lang and Heasman 2015; Tansey and Rajotte 2008). The overall outcome is a transformed, post-exceptionalist belief system that has integrated new discourses to justify novel, but still special, policies and institutions for the agricultural sector. Since the 1990s, agricultural support has been increasingly presented as important for policy aims such as rural development and demographics, maintenance of cultural landscapes, natural resource management and provision of ecosystem services, or more recent attempts to embed agricultural policy in a broader food policy (Lang and Barling 2013; Sonnino *et al.* 2014).

In the institutional dimension, post-exceptional policies are integrated into more general regimes. In agri-food, these are trade, consumer safety, public health and environmental protection, and in this sense the policy has become less exceptional. However, within these broader regimes, food and agriculture often receive special attention due to the sensitivities surrounding food intake and the specifics of biologically based production processes (Feindt 2012; Ge *et al.* 2016). However, while agricultural policy has been increasingly embedded in broader arenas of decision-making, the sector has maintained a privileged position. Governments still feature agricultural ministers or state secretaries, mirrored by a specialist parliamentary committee. The European Union still has an Agriculture Council, a Directorate-General for Agriculture and Commissioner for Agriculture and Rural Development and the US still has a Farm Bill and a distinct Department and Secretary of Agriculture. Within the WTO, agriculture continues to be treated as a special sector with its own trade agreement and the UN maintain their Food and Agriculture Organization. New institutions such as agro-environmental regulations and food security or nutrition councils are layered on top of these older institutions, often creating on-going tensions between old and new institutional layers. An indication is the multiplying struggles over exceptions, e.g., in trade law, patent law or the implementation of environmental regulations. The increasing role of self-regulation and private standards can potentially undermine exceptionalism because control moves from farmers to retailers who claim to act on behalf of consumers (Busch 2011).

In step with processes of institutional layering, post-exceptionalist actor constellations are more complex and contain players from a wider range of backgrounds. In agricultural policy, these include consumer, environmental and animal-welfare groups, slow-food activists, certification bodies, corporate actors, financial institutions and retailers. Importantly, many coalitions emerge around post-exceptionalist ideas, e.g., the loose coalition between farmers and environmentalists in EU agricultural policy reform (Swinnen 2015), often in an attempt to fend off market-liberalism or to capture a share of entrenched budgets for new farm-related purposes. Couching new interests in post-exceptionalist terminology has also been instrumental in gaining access to the policy arena. Such discursive strategies stabilize the exceptionalist idea-tional framework, but also change it towards more post-exceptionalism. Farm policy-makers have tended to treat these new coalitions in an instru-mental way, which has frustrated environmental and food-security NGOs (Hart 2015). The integration of the farm sector into often transnational value chains has raised concerns about (small) farmers' lack of market power, in particular *vis-à-vis* large retailers and food processors (Sexton 2013). But while calls for price regulation and/or quota to avoid ruinous com-petition can also be heard in other sectors with either low entry barriers (e.g., taxi-drivers) or high exit barriers (e.g., steel industries), in agricultural post-exceptionalism they are systematically linked to non-producer concerns, such as environmental sustainability, animal welfare or consumer health.

New, post-exceptional policy ideas can trigger a range of policy innovations. Examples in agri-food policy are the move from price support through market intervention to income support through less production and trade-distorting direct payments and the introduction of agro-environmental policies. Under the influence of market liberalism, the general direction has been a move away from market-distorting instruments (guaranteed floor prices, pro-duction-linked direct payments and comparatively high tariffs), making agricul-ture less exceptional in this regard. Though reformed, the instruments remain sector-specific but are increasingly linked to public interest concerns. For instance, direct payments have been linked to specific conservation practices ('greening') or to compliance with established or new regulations ('cross com-pliance'), and agro-environmental programs that incentivize specific farming practices have been introduced. Sector-specific exemptions from general regu-latory requirements or taxation reinforce the overall pattern that the agricul-tural sector continues to enjoy special treatment, albeit legitimized differently from three decades ago. Similarly, while proliferation of self-regu-lation is not limited to the food and agriculture sector, the specific concerns and sensibilities in this area have created a very specific set of private standards and public–private co-regulation, e.g., traceability regimes, organic standards or animal welfare labeling which have institutionalized broader concerns within the food sector. These trends in the design of policy instruments reinforce the post-exceptionalist nature of agri-food policy.

Reflecting on the contributions to this special issue

The contributions in this special issue analyze whether and how agricultural and food policies have moved away from their old exceptionalist (and predominantly productivist) character. Overall the articles validate the post-exceptionalism concept for this specific policy sector. They find significant persistence of exceptionalist ideas and institutions, although the ideational framework is often broadened.

Alan Greer's analysis of recent developments on the EU's CAP concludes that the new institutional structures after the Lisbon Treaty strengthened the role of the Parliament, in particular its agriculture committee. While more civil-society actors were probably involved than in the past, their influence was limited to the margins of the policy. Consequently, new ideas were adopted by core actors but in ways that mostly served to justify the continuation of a redistributional policy benefitting the farm sector and to stabilize the entrenched exceptionalist and productivist agricultural policies. The attempt by new actors to embark on and then transform exceptionalist ideas in order to re-orient the budget delivered little policy change because the institutional setting worked in favor of the old actors. The result can be termed 'shallow' post-exceptionalism: inclusion of some novel ideas to legitimize special treatment under new circumstances, access of new actors to negotiations and adoption of some new policy instruments, but neither the ideational framework nor the policy nor the institutional core are significantly affected.

Gerry Alons elaborates what post-exceptionalism means for environmental policy integration (EPI) in agricultural policy and beyond. Her analysis of the CAP finds that environmental interests and concerns are now regularly included, albeit often strategically to secure sectoral income policies. The policy process remains tilted towards producer interests. Accordingly, adoption of environmental policy instruments is widely conditional on them serving producer interests. Consequently, positive environmental effects are limited. Moreover, the productivist discourse was stronger in the 2013 CAP reform debate than it had been for decades, while a public good discourse is now pervasive either as goal or as instrumental justification. This suggests layering of new exceptionalist ideas on top of old ones rather than a full transformation of the CAP's ideational foundations. Overall, Alons argues that domain-specific, i.e., (post-)exceptional, policy paradigms will affect EPI trajectories since EPI has to connect to dominant policy concerns.

Jale Tosun stresses the importance of member-states in European policy processes and looks at statements about agri-food policy in party manifestos in Germany and the UK. She finds that all parties – albeit to different degrees – place agri-food policies in the context of a broad actor network, but also acknowledge special needs of the farm sector, in particular *vis-à-vis* the market power of supermarkets. The findings suggest that post-exceptional approaches, which combine ideas about agriculture being special with a de-compartmentalized vision of the relevant actors, are prevalent in both countries across the political spectrum. While the relatively high compartmentalization of the CAP continues and prevents an immediate realization of party manifesto statements into actual policy, the findings suggest that future policy shifts may move towards post-exceptionalism rather than market liberalism.

Adam Sheingate, Allysan Scatterday, Bob Martin and *Keeve Nachman* discuss how the patterns of influence around the US Farm Bill have moved from compartmentalized policy-making that privileged farm producer groups to a more pluralist policy-making style which has resulted in a significantly expanded policy complex. Their analysis of recent data on lobbying patterns demonstrates that participation in the Farm Bill has broadened considerably to include resourceful corporate actors, most notably the chemical and seed industry, manufacturers of agricultural inputs, food processors and retailers, financial industries and infrastructure and transport providers. However, this has not undermined the exceptionalist features of the Farm Bill. The new corporate actors in US agricultural policy-making share an interest with farmers in maintaining agricultural support but could potentially voice concerns which diverge from those of farmers. While policy-making has become less compartmentalized, policy exceptionalism is upheld as a result of the shared interests in maintaining subsidies, including food stamps.

Eve Fouilleux, Nicolas Bricas and *Aléne Alpha*'s analysis shows that since the 2007/2008 food crisis, caused by price spikes, the global debate on food security has become more exceptionalist. The debate is characterized by a return to a stronger focus on a productionist approach to food security which views the challenge as mainly a question of availability of food. This change came after three decades in which the World Bank and a number of NGOs had promoted a more liberal approach to food security that emphasized individual access to food, poverty and trade-based solutions. In the aftermath of the 2007/2008 food crisis, an institutional consolidation took place around the UN's Food and Agriculture Organization (FAO) as the champion of productionism. The G8/G20 also became involved and sided with the FAO's productionist approach. This privileged trans-national agro-industry and farm export interests and compartmentalized policy-making, laying the ground for agriculturally centered policies.

Sandra Schwindenhammer analyses the development of organic farming as an organizational field. Several stages of structuration, homogenization and calibration (balancing of internal and external pressures) have created a distinct regulatory regime that embodies post-exceptionalism within the broader food and agriculture regime. It is based on a discrete set of post-exceptionalist ideas that connect agricultural production as something special with environmental, health, social, developmental and trade concerns. The co-regulatory institutions in global and regional standard-setting have resulted in a decompartmentalized policy arena providing access to a set of actors from the state, business and civil-society spheres.

Carsten Daugbjerg, Arild Aurvåg Farsund and *Oluf Langhelle* analyze the resilience of the international food trade regime which is characterized by post-exceptionalism. The Agreement on Agriculture, adopted in 1995 and forming part of the WTO's legal framework, sets the direction towards trade liberalization, but includes significant exceptionalist components from the old GATT regime as the Agreement allows comparatively high levels of agricultural protectionism and support. Daugbjerg and associates show that despite being a mixture of two contradictory paradigms, the food-trading regime has proven resilient. During the ongoing Doha Round negotiations the regime has been sufficiently flexible to accommodate changing power relations and preferences for exceptionalist food-security policy measures and at the same time enable further liberalization. This indicates that a post-exceptionalist policy regime can be a relatively robust institutional arrangement despite its internal tensions.

Perspectives: policy post-exceptionalism and policy stability

The articles in this collection demonstrate the analytical utility of the concept of post-exceptionalism. They show that in agri-food policy, to varying degrees, changes have taken place in at least two of the four dimensions of policy exceptionalism (ideas, institutions, actors and policy). They also indicate that such partial transformation of policy means that in some situations post-exceptionalism can be a stable constellation while in others it may be a fragile and contested arrangement which can potentially move towards a 'normalization' of the policy sector or reverse to a more classical exceptionalist mode. The concept of post-exceptionalism provides a broader and more nuanced perspective on policy transition processes than typically found in studies of policy change. Since the developments in the food and agriculture policy sector reflect an increasingly complex and fluid broader policy environment, similar developments may be observed in other policy fields where attempts at normalization become entangled with technical complexities, professional norms, vested interests and entrenched sectoral institutions (Capano 2011).

The way in which the transition process from exceptionalism to post-exceptionalism unfolds and the specific resultant policy arrangements influence its degree of stability. Transition processes may involve *simultaneous* changes on more than one dimension, for example when policy change is combined with institutional change and engagement of new actors. The transition can also be *sequential* when change on one dimension leads to subsequent changes in some or all other dimensions. This occurs when for instance a change in institutions sets in motion policy changes which subsequently activate new actors whose involvement in turn leads to reformulation of the ideational underpinning of the policy sector.

A key factor influencing the degree of stability of post-exceptionalism relates to the ways in which changes in the four dimensions are lined up. When the ambition of change across the four dimensions is well aligned and the changes complement each other, post-exceptionalism can become an enduring third option between market liberalization and 'old' policy exceptionalism with a relatively stable constellation of mutually reinforcing ideas, institutions, interests and policies. Such *complementary post-exceptionalism* requires that the post-exceptional ideas are accompanied by policy reform in which the reformulation of exceptionalism is matched with either redesigned policy instruments and/or layering of new policies on top of the existing policy complex to address the wider set of concerns. To obtain legitimacy within the broadened community of stakeholders, a decompartmentalization of the institutions is necessary to allow new policy actors to participate in policy formulation and implementation. The expanded policy network needs to provide real inclusion of the new policy actors in decision-making rather than merely positioning them at the margins of the network.

When such an alignment of ambitions on the four dimensions is lacking, *tense post-exceptionalism* is likely to result. In this case, post-exceptionalism will more likely be a transitional constellation in which a mixture of old and new ideational, institutional, interest group and policy components co-exists in an unbalanced way, which undermines its political viability. If for example the ideational underpinning of the policy sector is reformulated or expanded to include broader concerns but the institutional arrangements remain compartmentalized without meaningful inclusion of new actors, policy changes are likely to be modest or even mostly symbolic. Hence, policy will disappoint expectations and the ideational reformulation will be perceived as mere rhetoric added to sugar-coat the entrenched exceptional policy core without systematic integration of new ideational aspects. This might result in loss of credibility and legitimation and increase the pressure for genuine policy reform and decompartmentalization of institutions. Similarly, if the institutions of a policy are decompartmentalized but the new actors remain relatively powerless at the margins of the policy network with little influence on the ideational and policy development, ensuing tensions between old incumbents and disappointed newcomers might undermine the post-exceptionalist arrangement. It will render it vulnerable to the forces of normalization through further reform driven by actors in the broader policy environment – which might either support or sideline the new post-exceptionalist minded actors. Hence, inconclusive reform under tense post-exceptionalism can create openings for the forces of 'normalization' – read: market liberalization or performance-based policy – doing away with most of the exceptionalist legacies.

Another possible scenario resulting from tense post-exceptionalism is reversal back to old exceptionalism. In this scenario, post-exceptionalist reforms are adopted in which new actors gain neither an institutional foothold nor influence on policy development, but time works in favor of dissatisfied old client groups and provides opportunities for reversing the incomplete reform. The attention of policy-makers, the media and the general public is likely to shift elsewhere after post-exceptionalist changes have taken place; and watchdog groups (e.g., consumer and environmental NGOs) may lack incentives or resources to monitor policy developments in the post-enactment phase (Patashnik 2003: 211). Further, political circumstances often change. New personalities may take control and old concerns may come to the fore again (Daugbjerg and Swinbank 2016). In such circumstances, reversal back to exceptionalism is a real possibility.

Overall, the concept of policy post-exceptionalism provides a diagnostic lens to understanding the interplay of ideational, institutional, interest and instrumental change in policy sectors characterized by exceptionalism. The concept of post-exceptionalism could also add a novel twist to current discussions about changing modes of governance. For example, further application of the concept could focus on the ways governments shape patterns of interaction with interest groups under exceptionalist and post-exceptionalist arrangements (Capano 2011; Richardson 2017). The contributions to this special issue have demonstrated the usefulness of this concept for understanding change in agricultural and food policies. We hope that future research will prove the value of the concept for other policy areas and for cross-policy comparison.

Acknowledgements

Earlier versions of the articles of this special issue were presented at the general conferences of the European Consortium for Political Research (ECPR) in Glasgow, 2014, Montreal, 2015 and Prague, 2016; and at the International Conference of Public Policy (ICPP) in Milan, 2015. We thank the Editors of this journal for support and helpful suggestions.

Disclosure Statement

No potential conflict of interest was reported by the authors.

ORCID

Carsten Daugbjerg ⓘ http://orcid.org/0000-0003-3869-6034
Peter H. Feindt ⓘ http://orcid.org/0000-0002-5978-5944

References

Béland, D. and Cox, R.H. (2011) 'Introduction: ideas and politics', in D. Béland and R.H. Cox (eds.), *Ideas and Politics in Social Science Research*, New York: Oxford University Press, pp. 3–20.

Blyth, M.M. (2002) *Great Transformations: Economic Ideas and Institutional Change in the Twentieth Century*, Cambridge: Cambridge University Press.

BMEL. (2015) *Agrarpolitischer Bericht der Bundesregierung 2015*, BMEL: Berlin.

Botterill, L.C. and Daugbjerg, C. (2015) 'Commensalistic institutions and value conflicts: the World Trade Organization and global private food standards'. *European Political Science Review* 7(1): 23–42.

Browne, W.P. (1988) *Private Interests, Public Policy, and American Agriculture*, Lawrence: University Press of Kansas.

Browne, W.P., Skees, J.R., Swanson, L.E., Thompson, P.B., and Unnevehr, L.J. (1992) *Sacred Cows and Hot Potatoes: Agrarian Myths in Agricultural Policy*, Boulder, Co: Westview Press.

Busch, L. (2011) 'The private governance of food: equitable exchange or bizarre bazaar?' *Agriculture and Human Values* 28(3): 345–52.

Candel, J.J., Breeman, G.E., Stiller, S.J. and Termeer, C.J. (2014) 'Disentangling the consensus frame of food security: the case of the EU common agricultural policy reform debate', *Food Policy* 44: 47–58.

Capano, G. (2011) 'Government continues to do its job: a comparative study of governance shifts in the higher education sector', *Public Administration* 89(4): 1622–44.

Capano, G., Howlett, M. and Ramesh, M. (2015) 'Bringing governments back in: governance and governing in comparative policy analysis', *Journal of Comparative Policy Analysis: Research and Practice* 17(4): 311–21.

Chou, M.-H. (2012) 'Constructing an internal market for research through sectoral and lateral strategies: layering, the European Commission and the fifth freedom', *Journal of European Public Policy* 19(7): 1052–70.

Clunies-Ross, T., Cox, G., Lowe, P., Marsden, T. and Whatmore, S. (1994) 'Challenging the productivist paradigm: organic farming and the politics of agricultural change', in P. Lowe, T. Marsden and S. Whatmore (eds.), *Regulating Agriculture*, London: CAB, pp. 53–74.

Coleman, W.D. and Grant, W. (1998) 'Policy convergence and policy feedback: agricultural finance policies in a globalizing Era', *European Journal of Political Research* 34(2): 225–47.

Coleman, W.D., Skogstad, G.D. and Atkinson, M.M. (1996) 'Paradigm shifts and policy networks: cumulative change in agriculture', *Journal of Public Policy* 16(3): 273–301.

Darby, M.R. and Karni, E. (1973) 'Free competition and the optimal amount of Fraud', *Journal of Law and Economics* 16(1): 67–88.

Daugbjerg, C. (2003) 'Policy feedback and paradigm shift in EU agricultural policy: the effects of the MacSharry reform on future reform', *Journal of European Public Policy* 10(3): 421–37.

Daugbjerg, C. and Swinbank, A. (2009) *Ideas, Institutions, and Trade: the WTO and the Curious Role of EU Farm Policy in Trade Liberalization*, Oxford: Oxford University Press.

Daugbjerg, C. and Swinbank, A. (2012) 'An introduction to the 'new'politics of agriculture and food', *Policy and Society* 31(4): 259–70.

Daugbjerg, C. and Swinbank, A. (2015) 'Globalization and new policy concerns: the WTO and the EU's sustainability criteria for biofuels', *Journal of European Public Policy* 22(3): 429–46.

Daugbjerg, C. and Swinbank, A. (2016) 'Three decades of policy layering and politically sustainable reform in the European Union's agricultural policy', *Governance* 29(2): 265–80.

Duit, A., Feindt, P.H. and Meadowcroft, J. (2016) 'Greening Leviathan: the rise of the environmental state?' *Environmental Politics* 25(1): 1–23. doi:10.1080/09644016. 2015.1085218

Feindt, P.H. (2010) 'Policy-learning and environmental policy integration in the common agricultural policy, 1973–2003', *Public Administration* 88(2): 296–314.

Feindt, P.H. (2012) 'The politics of biopatents in food and agriculture, 1950–2010: value conflict, competing paradigms and contested institutionalisation in multi-level governance', *Policy and Society* 31(4): 281–93.

Feindt, P.H. (2017) 'Agricultural policy', in H. Heinelt and S. Münch (eds.), *Handbook of European Policy: Formulation, Development and Evaluation*, London: Edward Elgar.

Feindt, P.H. and Flynn, A. (2009) 'Policy stretching and institutional layering: British food policy between security, safety, quality, health and climate change', *British Politics* 4 (3): 386–414.

Ge, L., *et al.* (2016) 'Why we need resilience thinking to meet societal challenges in bio-based production systems', *Current Opinion in Environmental Sustainability* 23. doi:10.1016/j.cosust.2016.11.009

Grafton, Q., Daugbjerg, C. and Qureshi, E. (2015) 'Feeding more than 9 billion by 2015: challenges and opportunities', *Food Security* 7(2): 179–83.

Grant, W. (ed) (1987) *Business Interest, Organizational Development and the Private Interest Government: An International Comparative Study of the Food Processing Industry*, Berlin: Walter de Gruyter.

Grant, W. (1995) 'Is agricultural policy still exceptional?' *The Political Quarterly* 66: 156–69.

Greer, A. (2005) *Agricultural Policy in Europe*, Manchester: Manchester University Press.

Griswold, A.W. ([1948] 1952) *Farming and Democracy*, New Haven: Yale University Press.

Halpin, D. (2005) 'Agricultural interest groups and global challenges: decline and resilience', in D. Halpin (ed.), *Surviving Global Change? Agricultural Interest Groups in Comparative Perspective*, Aldershot: Ashgate, pp. 1–28.

Hart, K. (2015) 'The fate of green direct payments in the CAP reform negotiations', in J. Swinnen (ed.), *The Political Economy of the 2014–2020 Common Agricultural Policy. An Imperfect Storm*, Brussels/London: Centre for European Policy Studies (CEPS)/Rowman and Littlefield International, pp. 245–76.

Havinga, T. and Verbruggen, P. (2017) 'Understanding complex governance relationships in food safety regulation: The RIT model as a theoretical Lens', *The Annals of the American Academy of Political and Social Science* 670(1): 58–77.

Hooghe, M. and Oser, J. (2016) 'Trade union density and social expenditure: a longitudinal analysis of policy feedback effects in OECD countries, 1980–2010', *Journal of European Public Policy* 23(10): 1520–42.

Jackson, G. and Deeg, R. (2012) 'The long-term trajectories of institutional change in European capitalism', *Journal of European Public Policy* 19(8): 1109–25.

Jordan, G., Maloney, W.A. and McLaughlin, A.M. (1994) 'Characterizing agricultural policy making', *Public Administration* 72(4): 505–26.

Kay, A. (2003) 'Path dependency and the CAP', *Journal of European Public Policy* 10(3): 405–20.

Knudsen, A.-C.L. (2009) *Farmers on Welfare. The Making of Europe's Common Agricultural Policy*, Ithaca and London: Cornell University Press.

Lang, T. and Barling, D. (2013) 'Nutrition and sustainability: an emerging food policy discourse', *Proceedings of the Nutrition Society* 72(01): 1–12.

Lang, T. and Heasman, M. (2015) *Food Wars: The Global Battle for Mouths, Minds and Markets*, London: Routledge.

Lawrence, G., Sippel, S.R. and Burch, D. (2015) 'The financialisation of food and farming', in G.M. Robinson and D.A. Carson (eds.), *Handbook on the Globalisation of Agriculture*, Cheltenham: Edward Elgar, pp. 309–27.

Legg, W. (2003) 'Presidential address agricultural subsidies: measurement and use in policy evaluation', *Journal of Agricultural Economics* 54(2): 175–201.

Lipset, S.M. (1997) *American Exceptionalism: A Double-Edged Sword*, New York: WW Norton & Company.

Lowi, T.J. (1969) *The end of Liberalism: Ideology, Policy, and the Crisis of Public Authority*, New York: WW Norton & Company.

Marsh, D. and Smith, M. (2000) 'Understanding policy networks: towards a dialectical approach', *Political Studies* 48(1): 4–21.

Marx, A., Maertens, M., Swinnen, J. and Wouters, J. (eds) (2012) *Private Standards and Global Governance: Economic, Legal and Political Perspectives*, Cheltenham: Edward Elgar.

Olson, M. (1965) *The Logic of Collective Action: Public Goods and the Theory of Group*, Cambridge, Ma: Harvard University Press.

Patashnik, E. (2003) 'After the public interest prevails: the political sustainability of policy reform', *Governance* 16(2): 203–34.

Richardson, J. (2017) 'The changing British policy style: from governance to government?'. *British Politics*. doi:10.1057/s41293-017-0051-y

Rieger, E. (1996) 'The common agricultural policy', in H. Wallace and W. Wallace (eds.), *Policy-Making in the European Union*. Oxford: Oxford University Press, pp. 97–123.

Roederer-Rynning, C. (2003) 'From 'talking shop' to 'working parliament'? The European parliament and agricultural change', *JCMS: Journal of Common Market Studies* 41(1): 113–35.

Sexton, R.J. (2013) 'Market power, misconceptions, and modern agricultural markets'. *American Journal of Agricultural Economics* 95(2): 209–19.

Sheingate, A.D. (2003) *The Rise of the Agricultural Welfare State: Institutions and Interest Group Power in the United States, France, and Japan*, Princeton and Oxford: Princeton University Press.

Skogstad, G. (1998) 'Ideas, paradigms and institutions: agricultural exceptionalism in the European Union and the United States', *Governance* 11(4): 463–90.

Skogstad, G. (2008) *Internationalization and Canadian Agriculture: Policy and Governing Paradigms*, Toronto: University of Toronto Press.

Skogstad, G. and Schmidt, V.A. (2011) 'Introduction: policy paradigms, transnationalism, and domestic politics', in G. Skogstad (ed.), *Policy Paradigms, Transnationalism, and Domestic Politics*, Toronto: University of Toronto Press, pp. 3–35.

Smith, M.J. (1993) *Pressure, Power and Policy: State Autonomy and Policy Networks in Britain and the United States*, New York: Harvester Wheatsheaf.

Sonnino, R., Moragues Faus, A. and Maggio, A. (2014) 'Sustainable food security: an emerging research and policy agenda', *International Journal of Sociology of Agriculture and Food* 21(1): 173–88.

Swinnen, J. (ed) (2015) *The Political Economy of the 2014–2020 Common Agricultural Policy: An Imperfect Storm*, London: Rowman & Littlefield International.

Tansey, G. and Rajotte, T. (2008) *The Future Control of Food*, London: Earthscan.

Tracy, M. (1989) *Government and Agriculture in Western Europe 1880–1988*, New York/London: Harvester Wheatsheaf.

Zhu, L. and Lipsmeyer, C.S. (2015) 'Policy feedback and economic risk: the influence of privatization on social policy preferences', *Journal of European Public Policy* 22(10): 1489–511.

Post-exceptional politics in agriculture: an examination of the 2013 CAP reform

Alan Greer ⓘ

ABSTRACT

A core claim about agricultural policy making is that it is 'compartmentalized' and 'exceptional'. In this picture, the policy process is insulated from other policy concerns, has a distinctive system of actors and institutional structures, and is rooted in extensive governmental intervention in the market and the redistribution of resources from taxpayers to food producers. Recently there have been suggestions that a 'post-exceptional' agricultural politics has emerged, which is more market-driven, has reduced state intervention, and where policies reflect influences relating to non-food issues such as the environment. This contribution discusses the concepts of compartmentalization and exceptionalism and then applies 'indicators of change' to a case study of the 2013 reform of the Common Agricultural Policy (CAP). It concludes that the reform provides evidence for 'shallow' post-exceptionalism where a historically persistent agricultural policy subsystem has opened up to new actors, incorporated some programme change but left the ideational framework largely intact.

Introduction

A central element in the historically dominant picture of agricultural policy is that decision making takes place in a subsystem with a distinctive set of actors and institutional structures that is insulated from other policy concerns (a 'compartmentalized' policy *process*) and that policy *instruments* and *programmes* reflect a particular form of state intervention that differs from rules that generally apply to other major sectors of the economy ('exceptionalism'). The agricultural policy subsystem has been underpinned by ideational congruence, a consensus over values that marginalizes some non-farm actors, and which produces policy outcomes that favour privileged interests. In recent years, attention has turned to the possibilities for a 'de-compartmentalized' and 'post-exceptional' agricultural politics (see Daugbjerg and Feindt 2017). In terms of process, this would mean that policy concerns relating to issues such as the environment and climate change (all 'messy' problems that tend to cut across the traditional boundaries of policy making) have become increasingly important; in relation to instruments and programmes, that the highly interventionist role of government has weakened.

This contribution uses four indicators of change that relate to institutions, actors, ideas and programmes to assess whether the 2013 reforms of the Common Agricultural Policy (CAP) provide evidence for post-exceptional agricultural politics. Broadly the contribution considers the impact of inter-institutional policy making and examines the tensions between the persistence of a strong agricultural policy heritage (which strongly emphasizes food security and production), and a more open, contested and networked politics that reflects a broader range of issues. It concludes that the reform provides evidence for what may be termed 'shallow' post-exceptionalism – some movement from a historically persistent agricultural policy subsystem involving the inclusion of some new actors and some programme change but which leaves the ideational framework largely intact.

Exceptionalism and post-exceptionalism

Much of the academic literature on agricultural policy has emphasized 'compartmentalization', 'exceptionalism' and the dominance of a 'state-assisted' paradigm (see Coleman *et al.* 1996; Rieger 2000; Roederer-Rynning 2010; Skogstad 1998). Writing on the CAP, for example, Grant noted that while the circle of actors involved in the policy process had widened in the early 1990s, agricultural policy remained 'highly compartmentalized', with a 'high political entry barrier into the policy community' (1997: 148). In this picture, the institutional configuration – at national and European Union (EU) levels – has been made up of distinctive actors that are contained within relatively impermeable boundaries. The agricultural policy subsystem – centred on food production – is highly insulated from other policy subsystems such as the environment, and the influence of actors who are not central to the core of the subsystem is limited.

'Exceptionalism' highlights a durable interpretive framework, how policy ideas, values and norms are embedded within institutional structures, and shape policy programmes. As defined by Skogstad, it is the 'idea that agriculture is a sector unlike any other economic sector, and, as such, warrants special government support'. This in turn provides the underpinning for the development of the 'state-assisted paradigm' with its associated government intervention in relation to regulation and expenditure (1998: 468). The concept of agricultural exceptionalism therefore 'describes the special treatment of the agricultural sector by governments and international organizations, and the belief system that provides cognitive justification and political legitimation' (Daugbjerg and Feindt 2017).

22

Bringing compartmentalization and exceptionalism together, Daugbjerg and Feindt note that the agricultural policy subsystem has been characterized 'by a distinct set of sector-oriented institutions and ideas', 'substantial government intervention in the market' and the redistribution of resources to a 'relatively small group of producers and land owners' (2017). A key part of this picture is the emphasis on policy networks, an approach well suited to established policy subsystems such as agriculture where the status quo is reinforced by ideational consensus around the nature of food production (for a summary, see Greer 2005: 23–30; Marsh and Smith 2000). Agriculture policies and associated institutions have been protected by established decision rules and dominant policy communities. The idea of closed policy communities has been especially prevalent, drawing attention to stable interactions and bargaining over time between state 'agriculture' departments and well-resourced groups representing farmers, based on consensus around values, with largely incremental policy outcomes (Smith 1992).

What then would 'post-exceptional' agricultural policy look like? In the first instance, it would involve the weakening of the historically dominant closed policy communities centred on farmers and the emergence of more 'open' network governance involving a wider range of actors, struggles between competing interests, and corresponding shifts in the nature of policy interventions. There is some evidence for this over the last 25 years, indicating that policy crisis and exogenous pressures (relating for example to trade liberalization) can be crucial factors. In the context of bovine spongiform encephalopathy (BSE) and other food crises in the UK for instance, some analysts identified the emergence of an issue network type structure with a wider range of pressure participants in addition to the historically dominant farmers' organizations (see Grant 2004; Jordan *et al.* 1994; Smith 1991). Certainly, there has been a broadening of the policy agenda, with the inclusion within the agriculture subsystem of issues such as environmental sustainability, rural development and climate change, alongside the traditional focus on food security and production. However, such issues can be absorbed into an agricultural paradigm, as is shown in the creation of the Department of the Environment, Food and Rural Affairs (Defra) in the UK (Winter 2003: 51), and there is disagreement over whether the configuration of institutions and actors has been substantially reshaped. So while Woods (2005) referred to the 'collapse' of the agricultural policy community, for others the policy process on the 2001 outbreak of foot-and-mouth disease (FMD) in the UK provided 'little evidence for the emergence of an issue network' and the outcomes 'exhibited a degree of continuity far more consistent with a policy community' centred on the historically powerful farmers' organizations (Wilkinson *et al.* 2010: 337–8).

A second element relates to a weakening of the 'state assistance paradigm' and the historically high degree of government intervention in the policy subsystem. In Skogstad's argument, paradigm change 'is indicated by deregulation of agricultural markets, the termination or substantial restraint of government expenditures for agriculture, and a discourse antithetical to government intervention' (1998: 471). Here there is also disagreement. For some, cumulative change to the CAP – including under the MacSharry reforms (1992) and the Fischler package (2003) – represents a decisive ideational shift in policy values and instruments that has substantially weakened the producer interest, illustrated for example by the move away from direct support for production to decoupled area payments. Burrell (2009) charts a pattern of continuous reform from a highly centralized protectionist policy focused on farm incomes to one that is more market sensitive and environmentally sustainable. For others, continuity is emphasized within the framework of the state-assisted paradigm (although it may include the incorporation of new objectives), exemplified in stable budgets and patterns of redistribution, persisting institutional settings and path dependence. As Daugbjerg and Feindt note, 'we almost face a paradox with much change in policy instruments, ideas and discourses while farm income remains the unaffected "policy core" with relatively stable redistribution of resources into the farm sector' (2017).

Yet policy change should not be viewed as a one-way process. The notion of 'sequencing' shows how changes to the CAP are not necessarily in the same direction and that each reform event opens possibilities for further 'reform' (Daugbjerg 2009). A reversal to older institutional logics is also possible. While Erjavec et al. (2008) argue that the policy discourse of (Agriculture Commissioners) Fischler and Fischer-Boel reflected a neoliberal rhetoric, others claim that the tenure of Cioloş saw a shift back to the state-assisted position in which subsidies are defended as a way to ensure a fair and efficient European agriculture (Rutz et al. 2014).

In this context, 'post-exceptionalism' can be used as a diagnostic concept that highlights both continuity and change in the agricultural policy subsystem. For Daugbjerg and Feindt, the value of the concept is that it captures 'the combination of a less compartmentalized policy arena' with ideas that 'retain claims that a policy sector is special, albeit with updated arguments that relate to the problems on the evolving policy agenda (e.g., sustainability, climate change) and which trigger novel policy instruments' (2017). As they summarize, there is 'a set of exceptionalist *ideas* which legitimize a set of compartmental *institutions* that provide a dedicated policy space for a *policy community* to adopt and implement *policy instruments and programmes* that serve their interests and comply with their ideas' (Introduction to this collection: 4; original italics). Drawing on these insights, there are four dimensions that can be used to develop indicators for the emergence of a post-exceptional agricultural politics:

(1) changes to the institutional structure of the policy subsystem;
(2) the incorporation of 'new' actors and interests;

(3) a weakening of the dominant ideational structure, with the introduction of conflicting values, new policy areas and ideas; and

(4) a weakening of policy stability, with policy change reflected in instruments and programmes.

In what follows, these four 'indicators of change' are applied to an analysis of the 2013 reform of the CAP.

CAP reform 2013

There is considerable disagreement about whether agricultural policy reform can be viewed as radical and extensive, or minimal and incremental. Proponents of the latter emphasize the obstacles in the way of CAP reform, sometimes using ideas about historical institutionalism and path dependence (Kay 2003). Incremental policy change leaves the 'state-assisted' paradigm largely intact. This is the result of bargaining between actors in which the key factors are the preferences and institutional structures of member states (brought together in the Agriculture Council), with the EU Commission playing a crucial role in setting the agenda, both buttressed by closed producer-dominated agricultural policy communities. Nonetheless, change does happen, often as a result of wider policy ideas and exogenous factors such as trade liberalization and budget reform, which may be important in weakening the compartment from the outside (Daugbjerg and Swinbank 2009; Lynggaard and Nedergaard 2009). Moreover, incremental policy change can have substantial cumulative effects over time (see Ackrill 2000; Cunha and Swinbank 2011; Keeler 1996; Swinbank 1999; Swinnen 2009).

Following initial consultations in spring 2010 about the CAP after 2014, the EU Commission's Directorate General for Agriculture and Rural Development (DG Agri) published legislative proposals in October 2011 (European Commission 2010, 2011b, 2011c; Swinbank 2012). After protracted negotiations, a political deal was reached on 26 June 2013, with everything finalized in the autumn. As one contemporary report put it, agreement came 'after months of haggling over how ambitious the policy would be on overhauling direct payments, ending quotas, and making farmers more environmentally accountable' (Spence 2013).

Wider negotiations about the Multiannual Financial Framework (MFF) for 2014–2020 were an important influence on the CAP reform debate. Here there were pressures for a radical reorientation of priorities and for lower spending in the context of austerity, which would inevitably mean a reduction in the agriculture budget (Greer 2012, 2013). Matthews (2015) identifies three linkages between the MFF and CAP negotiations: (1) the reform was shaped 'by the need to create a narrative to legitimise and defend the share of the CAP budget' in the MFF (2015: 169); (2) there was a condensed negotiation window because the key actors delayed finalizing their positions on CAP reform until the budget proposals were agreed in early 2013; and (3) some aspects of CAP reform – relating to convergence and greening, for example – were included in the MFF itself (with a subsequent impact on the decision-making process).

In essence, the broad lines of the reform were set out in the MFF, leaving the Agriculture Council to fill in the specific details. While there were disagreements between austerity-minded countries (Germany and the UK wanted a squeeze on the total budget) and those who wanted to keep agricultural spending at the existing level (e.g., France, Italy and Spain), the outcome of the MFF was that as a percentage of the budget, spending on the CAP will decrease slowly to around a third of the total by 2020 (the absolute figures remain relatively stable). As the Commission noted, this showed 'continued strong support for an ambitious agricultural policy' (2013: 3), and it also 'surprised and delighted farm groups' (Matthews 2015: 171). Crucially, the MFF maintained the 75:25 spending ratio between pillar 1 and pillar 2, which was a setback for countries such as the UK who wanted a reorientation of funds from direct payments to rural development programmes; indeed, the negotiations resulted in a reduction on the original plans of around 2 per cent for pillar 1 but nearly 8 per cent for pillar 2.

Key objectives for the Commission were to combine a 'greener and more equitably distributed' first pillar alongside a second pillar 'more focussed on competitiveness and innovation, climate change and the environment' (2011a: 16). As well as making the CAP more efficient and effective, a core aim was for a fairer distribution of payments – across pillars, between farmers (from larger to smaller enterprises) and between 'old' and 'new' member states. To do this, the approach had three main elements – convergence, capping and greening – and combined compulsory requirements with voluntary options. The extent to which this approach can meet the objectives set is still unclear (especially in relation to redistribution), but what is clear is that the reform has substantially extended the ability of member states to tailor the CAP to their own conditions (e.g., for regionalizing the basic payment, continuing 'coupled' support, providing assistance for small farmers, 'capping' and the reduction of payments, and environmental sustainability).

In the distribution of resources, member states can strike different balances between pillar 1 and pillar 2. For most countries, up to 15 per cent of national envelopes can be transferred in either direction and are not restricted to increasing funding for rural development (some are allowed to transfer up to 25 per cent). Eleven member states have decided to transfer funds to pillar 2, mostly at a rate of less than 5 per cent each year (only the UK and Estonia will apply relatively high rates of transfer at 10.8 and 15 per cent respectively). Five member states (mainly in eastern Europe) opted to transfer funds to pillar 1, with Poland transferring the maximum 25 per cent. Overall, the net funding gain for pillar 2 will be €3bn over six years (European Commission 2016: 4), a very small amount in relation to the total funding.

Within the suite of direct aid schemes, the Basic Payment Scheme (BPS), young farmers' scheme and the greening payment are compulsory; countries (and regions within them) also have flexibility to implement a 'redistributive payment', introduce voluntary coupled support schemes (VCS), and support measures in areas with natural constraints (ANC). Only Denmark has chosen to implement the ANC payment, whereas all countries except Germany have opted to use VCS, covering a whole range of production sectors but especially beef and dairy (11 member states have allocated the maximum 13 per cent, 9 have allocated less than 8 per cent). Fifteen 'countries' have decided to adopt the new simplified 'small farmers' scheme' (which replaces all of the other direct payment schemes for the beneficiaries concerned). The overall impact of this enhanced flexibility (or 'renationalization') is that both the structure of the CAP in member states and the share of funding allocated to different schemes can 'vary significantly throughout the EU' (European Commission 2013: 7; 2016: 20).

A central reform aim for the Commission was *convergence* to narrow variations in direct payments across countries, particularly between old and 'new' Europe ('external' convergence), and between producers with 'fairer treatment of farmers performing the same activities' ('internal' convergence) (European Commission 2011a: 16). French and Spanish ministers had strong reservations about this because they feared that redistribution would reduce the benefits received by their own farmers (a Commission estimate put this as high as a 7 per cent reduction for French farmers). Consequently, they wanted a more careful phasing in of convergence and complained that the 'magnitude' and 'pace' proposed by the Commission was 'not acceptable' (Euractiv.com 2012b).

The restructuring of the architecture for direct payments is the principal mechanism for achieving convergence. For external convergence, national envelopes are adjusted to bring them closer to the EU average: increased for those where the average payment is below 90 per cent of the EU average, correspondingly adjusted downwards for those member states receiving more than the average. A minimum average national or regional payment (at least 75 per cent of the EU average) will be achieved by 2019. For 'internal convergence', the intention is that payments under the BPS within member states become more uniform. For example, countries may decide to introduce a flat rate at either national or regional level from 2015, or to achieve this by 2019, or to increase the payments to those farms receiving less than 90 per cent of the average (with each payment entitlement normally reaching a minimum of 60 per cent of the average by 2019). No farmer receiving payments above the average will lose more than 30 per cent of their entitlements (European Commission 2015). Among the 18 member states implementing the BPS (ten 2004 entrants continue to apply the flat rate Single Area Payment until 2020), six opted for regionalizing the payments (including Germany and the UK), four countries/regions (including Germany and England) introduced the flat rate from 2015, five (including both Scotland and Wales) will apply the flat rate from 2019, and the others will apply a partial convergence by 2019 (European Commission 2015: 7).

A hotly disputed element of the reform was the proposal for 'capping' – the introduction of a maximum ceiling on payments – which had been fiercely resisted in previous reform episodes by countries with efficient and large-scale enterprises such as the UK and France. The Commission proposed that payment levels should 'progressively converge' and payments to large beneficiaries should be subject to 'progressive capping' to improve the distribution of payments between farmers (2011b: 3). Reductions (degressivity) would start at 20 per cent for entitlements between €150,000 and €200,000, gradually increasing in three stages to a 100 per cent reduction at a maximum ceiling for payments of €300,000. The final compromise reform allowed substantial flexibility to member states across a range of decisions. While all are required to reduce payments above €150,000 at a minimum rate of 5 per cent, member states have the choice about whether to cap payments. Fifteen 'countries' (only England in the UK) will apply the minimum reduction, whereas nine will apply a cap at different rates on amounts ranging from €150,000 (including Ireland and Poland) to €600,000 in Scotland. Italy introduced a 50 per cent reduction at €150,000 and 100 per cent at €500,000; Wales opted for the most graduated system, starting at 15 per cent over €150,000, increasing in stages to a 100 per cent reduction at €300,000. It is estimated by the Commission that these decisions will transfer over €500 m to rural development between 2015 and 2019 (European Commission 2016: 8, 21).

Within direct payments, countries can adopt a voluntary 'redistributive payment' to favour smaller holdings by diverting up to 30 per cent of the national envelope to farmers on the first 30 hectares of land (European Commission 2016: 10). Countries that introduce a redistributive element at a rate of at least 5 per cent are not required also to reduce payments. Nine countries/regions (but only Wales in the UK, and Wallonia in Belgium) introduced the redistributive measure, of which six (including France) coupled this with no reduction of payment. Poland, Bulgaria and Wales decided to introduce the redistributive payment alongside the reduction of payments mechanism (European Commission 2016: 8).

The greatest controversy surrounded the proposals for 'greening', in which 30 per cent of direct payments within pillar 1 are conditional on 'environmentally supportive practices' with farmers receiving payments to deliver public goods (European Commission 2011a: 16). These practices were to include crop diversification (the 'three crop rule'), maintenance of permanent grass-land, and the preservation of ecological reserves and landscapes. However, the original proposals were considerably altered in the negotiations (see below). Here also, member states have considerable flexibility in relation to policy choices, for example about the ratio of permanent grassland, whether to adopt the 'equivalence mechanism', the number and types of designated ecological focus areas (EFA), and the rules for making the payment (European Commission 2016: 14–18).

In other areas, the desire to foster market competitiveness was reflected in the removal of remaining production limits and the introduction of measures to facilitate co-operation between producers. Although market intervention remains as a safety net, and the last remaining export subsidies are reduced to zero, the force of renewed arguments about food security under-pinned decisions to retain some production quotas – for sugar until 2017 (two years later than their planned abolition) and a new vine planting scheme after 2016 was introduced.

A 'post-exceptional' CAP?

Four indicators for assessing the extent of movement to a post-exceptional agricultural policy were identified above, so how does the 2013 CAP reform fare in relation to these?

New institutions and structures

Compartmentalization has been a central feature of agricultural exceptional-ism, but constitutional change provides one avenue for 'institutional broaden-ing' (for example, the integration of agriculture into other regimes such as environmental protection). An important factor in the CAP reform process was the new institutional structure brought in by the Lisbon Treaty, in which 'co-decision' was extended to the CAP (see Greer 2013; Greer and Hind 2012). The European Parliament (EP) is now a formal co-actor in the agri-cultural policy process, sharing legislative power with the Council of Ministers. The 2013 CAP reform was the first major agricultural policy dossier to be subject to co-decision. Between April and June 2013, more than 40 'trialogue' discussions took place – informal tripartite bargaining between the three main institutions before the opening of formal conciliation negotiations. An inter-institutional deal was reached in June 2013 and the Agriculture Council then adopted the reform package without discussion following a first reading agreement with the EP.

For Swinnen and Knops, the entry of the EP as a 'new player' in decision making resulted in 'a reshuffle of the rules of the game, with new coalition opportunities and inter-institutional transfers of power' (2014: 73). However, the parallel negotiations on the MFF restricted the EP's room for manoeuvre and 'set the overall framework' within which it negotiated with the Council (2014: 17). Co-decision certainly prolonged the policy process – with agreement reached around two years after the Commission published its legislative proposals – and the implementation of most of the reforms was delayed until 2015, rather than 2014 as planned.

In advance of the reform, Greer and Hind (2012) sketched out some scenarios for how inter-institutional relationships might be reconfigured under co-decision. These included the possibility that the EP would gain influence at the expense of both Commission and Council (the 'conventional' scenario), and that a dominant Council-EP axis would develop. Some observers conclude that inter-institutional bargaining weakened the influence of the Commission and enhanced that of the Council Presidency (Matthews 2013), but there is no clear consensus among actors and commentators about which scenario best summarizes the 'reality'. As reported in a study by the Centre for European Policy Studies (using an interview sample of 34 actors composed mainly of those working in the EP, but also including some working in the Commission, the Council and from civil society), 40 per cent favoured the conventional scenario, 30 per cent believed that the other institutions gained power, and a quarter said that none of the scenarios described the process particularly well (Swinnen and Knops 2014: 74).

Overall, the evidence indicates that the policy process on CAP reform has been substantially altered in terms of its institutional structures at the EU level, and that new patterns of inter-institutional policy making have emerged. The question, however, is whether this has been accompanied by the entry of new actors and ideas in the policy subsystem.

New actors and interests

Agricultural exceptionalism buttresses the interests of food producers, structured in dominant policy communities. Post-exceptionalism would see the emergence of actor constellations of a more 'issue-network' type that include 'players from a wider range of backgrounds' such as consumer, environmental and animal welfare groups, and slow food activists. However, conflict is not inevitable and coalition building – e.g., between farmers and environmentalists – may form around exceptionalist ideas. Paradoxically, while this can help to stabilize the ideational framework, it may also indicate a movement towards post-exceptionalism (Daugbjerg and Feindt 2017).

Despite the institutional changes around the CAP, it is not clear that the policy subsystem has substantially opened up to a wider range of actors and interests. Certainly, the EP has a greater formal role in CAP decision making, but the extent to which this indicates a post-exceptional agricultural politics is debatable. Importantly, the work of the EP is itself 'compartmenta-lized', with a crucial role for functional committees such as the Agriculture and Rural Development standing committee (COMAGRI). Although its member-ship reflects the political balance of the Parliament as a whole, it is dominated by farming, landowning and rural interests (Greer and Hind 2012). So co-decision may actually have strengthened farmer bias insofar as the political centre of gravity of COMAGRI lies around 'centre to-right farmer-friendly parties', its geographic orientation 'around a group of countries traditionally favouring an interventionist interpretation of the CAP' (Roederer-Rynning 2015: 354).

While the Commission conducted what it presented as an 'inclusive' public consultation and debate at the beginning of the reform process in 2010, it is not clear that 'new' actors and interests had much influence on the outcome. Overall, the influence of civil society actors was limited; environmental actors, for example, believe that their influence was at best marginal and that farm interests dominated the debate. However, this view is not universally shared. Co-decision did intensify contacts between the EP and stakeholders generally, so it may have opened up the relatively closed subsystem to some degree, albeit in an indirect way. Indeed, the 'broadening of interests', which some observers such as Greer and Hind (2012) had speculated about in relation to COMAGRI, 'might have actually happened via the emergence of a European civil society' (Swinnen and Knops 2014: 72).

New values and ideas

The importance of a changed constellation of actors depends partly on the assumption that this will bring with it new values and policy ideas. As Richard-son has noted, new ideas pose a particular threat to established policy com-munities because they can 'disrupt existing policy systems, power relationships and policies' (2000: 1017–8). In agricultural policy, this usually has been taken to mean a challenge to the preferences of the established pro-ductivist policy community, and to core ideas such as the notion that support-ing the farm sector is vital to the broader national interest, especially in relation to food security and the role of stable farm incomes in underpinning rural communities (Skogstad 1998: 468).

In ideational terms, post-exceptionalism might be indicated by greater influence for market liberal ideas, but these may be absorbed and reinter-preted in a way that preserves the notion that the sector is special. While in previous CAP reforms, policy windows were forced open by developments in relation to trade liberalization and enlargement, the 2013 version was rela-tively insulated from wider exogenous pressures. For example, Daugbjerg notes that the World Trade Organisation (WTO) is only referred to briefly in the Commission's original CAP reform communication, that domestic concerns were prioritized, and that pressure from the WTO 'vanished' when the Doha Round stalled in late 2008 (2017: 487). On the other hand, exceptionalism may be strengthened by connecting agriculture to 'new overarching discourses such as sustainability and globalization, and cross-cutting concerns such as the environment, climate change and food security' (Daugbjerg and Feindt 2017). In the 2013 CAP reform, there is some evidence of collaboration between groups representing farmers and environmentalists in resisting the extension of market liberalism and in protecting budgets. Overall, however, analysis suggests that the EP's formal role in decision making buttressed the established policy subsystem and that the changed institutional structure around the CAP did not facilitate the introduction of new values and ideas. Swinnen and Knops remark, for example, that most policy ideas within the EP were 'little more than a return to the market regulation instruments of the past', influenced by agricultural exceptionalism and 'justified by arguments relating to food security and economic crisis' (2014: 14, 95). As Matthews (2013) further notes, the notion that the EP 'would bring new ideas to the debate and help to widen the range of interests that could influence agricultural policy also proved to be hopelessly naïve'.

Policy change

The fourth indicator for the emergence of post-exceptional agricultural policy making relates to policy instruments and programmes. Exceptionalism was characterized by some specific policy mechanisms such as payments for production, tariffs and quotas, and intervention buying to stabilize prices. Certainly, there has been a move away from these instruments over the last 30 years, indicated by the removal of many 'trade distorting' market support mechanisms, the introduction of 'decoupled' direct payments, and pillar 2 measures such as agri-environment schemes, often justified using rhetoric about the provision of public goods. In the 2013 CAP reform, the Commission placed particular emphasis on promoting market competitiveness, convergence and capping to promote fairer distribution of resources, and the 'greening' of a substantial element of direct payments. While this may be viewed as consistent with a post-exceptional direction of travel, the retention of some market intervention instruments and the introduction of voluntary coupled support schemes (which have been adopted by over 20 countries), seem to suggest the persistence of older logics around food security. In convergence and capping, some countries have also exploited the flexibility allowed to reinforce more traditional exceptionalism. The ideas for 'greening' in particular were the subject of much debate and controversy. While environmentalists were sceptical about the impact of the 'limited greening' proposed by the Commission, for farmers the proposals undermined the EU's capacity to meet food security objectives, and some governments including those of

France and Spain argued for a 'flexible' system in which it would be possible to have 'agriculturally sustainable use of areas of ecological interest' (Euractiv.com 2012a).

The agreed reform markedly watered down the Commission's proposals on greening; indeed, some even suggest that the outcome was 'a step backwards for the integration of environmental concerns into the CAP' (Hart 2015: 246). According to a spokesperson for the European Environmental Bureau (EEB), while the proposals sowed 'some green shoots of hope', these were 'quickly cut down' in the inter-institutional bargaining. By 'trying to exempt as many farmers as possible from the most basic agronomic practices, they diluted the content of the greening measures and added dozens of grounds for exemption to already very weak rules' (Defossez 2014). There are no EU-wide performance standards, member states have flexibility in implementation, and a range of exceptions relating to water pollution, ecological focus areas, crop diversification and environmental sustainability were introduced. So, although a core principle of the original proposals was that greening should apply to all farms, nearly half of all farmland and 89 per cent of farmers will not be covered by the rules (for a full discussion of the greening outcomes, see Hart [2015]: 263–9).

This 'greenwashing' was largely a result of the inter-institutional bargaining between the EP and the Council, although the interplay between them was complex. Both were concerned about the impact of greening on competitiveness, production and food security, and supported plans to introduce 'greater flexibility', reflecting concerns expressed by farming stakeholder groups about 'being locked into standardised environmental rules despite the diverse landscape of European agriculture' (Spence 2013). Within COMAGRI, environmental considerations 'were drowned out by concerns about agricultural production effects' and there were few environmental interests in the EU institutions 'that saw much to be gained from a protracted defence of proposals whose environmental delivery looked likely to be disappointing' (Hart 2015: 271–2). As a spokesperson for BirdLife Europe complained, 'Europe is offered a budget that scales back investment in the environment and caters for the usual fat cats that have been milking the system' (Harrabin 2013). So, while environmental groups helped to fend off some proposals – such as paying farmers twice for carrying out the same activity in pillar 1 and pillar 2 – their influence overall was weak.

Post-exceptional agricultural policy?

In this analysis, four indicators for assessing whether agricultural policy can be described as post-exceptional have been applied to the 2013 CAP reform. The evidence is mixed. It is plausible to argue that (1) new institutional structures apply to agricultural policy, (2) as a result of the Lisbon Treaty some new actors and interests are involved in the decision process, and (3) there has been some further (if weak) extension of programmes and instruments in a direction consistent with post-exceptionalism. On the other hand, this has not been accompanied by substantial change in the ideational and value framework.

For Commissioner Cioloş, the reform was a 'paradigm shift' with its focus on greening, a fairer system of redistribution, and the reinforcement of the concept of public money for public goods (quoted in House of Commons 2013: 6). Certainly, it is possible to identify an aim for some radical change, even if the Commission saw its proposals as striking a mid-position between gradual adjustment and far-reaching reform. However, while some important policy changes were introduced, these arguably fit better with an incremental shift in the established policy direction rather than a radical redesign. For critics such as the UK Environment Secretary, Owen Patterson, the agreement did not even advance the reform trajectory started by MacSharry and continued by Fischler, or reinforce the emphasis on public goods; indeed, there were some areas 'where we definitely go backwards', for example with the reintroduction of coupled payments (House of Commons 2013: 6). Greening also was markedly watered down, and how extensive any redistribution of resources will be as a result of capping and convergence remains unclear.

Essentially, the changed institutional and actor context did not go hand-in-hand with ideational and more extensive policy change because the decision rules and institutional structures around the CAP, plus the balance of forces between member states – most of whom like the CAP – still work as a barrier against radical change (see Greer [2013] for a discussion of the preferences of member states). Co-decision, and the MFF agreement (as well as the weak influence of exogenous factors such as trade liberalization), reinforced the existing policy subsystem rather than opening it up to new influences and ideas. So, despite the changed context, policy ideas and programmes were not affected in a way that substantially weakened the preferences of the established policy subsystem. As Matthews argues, once the threat of a budget cut in the MFF had receded, the institutional structure favoured those such as farm groups who took 'a status quo position on the reform proposals' while disadvantaging those 'who sought a more radical change' (2015: 178). For Erjavec et al., the rhetoric around the reforms hid the desire of a conservative block 'to extend the re-distributional logic of the CAP within a still comprehensive budget while implementing as few paradigmatic changes as possible' (2015: 236).

It seems clear then, in terms of the ideational underpinnings of those actors who were influential in the reform process, that the dominant motivation was the desire to support farm production and farm incomes. As Erjavec et al. suggest, although the Commission's core aims emphasized the environment and climate change (for example, at least 30 per cent of spending in pillar 2 rural development programmes must be reserved for such measures), they were reinterpreted in ways that preserve the CAP (2015: 232). So, while an alternative discourse about environmental sustainability and climate change was present, this was heavily outweighed by productivist objectives and a traditional discourse that emphasized food production and food security.

Issues about rural development, environmental sustainability and climate change have all been integrated to some degree within the CAP in recent years, and there is some evidence to support post-exceptionalism in terms of changed institutional structures and actors. Overall, however, the policy impact has been weak and the ideational framework little altered. The analysis of the 2013 CAP reforms in this contribution views them as consistent with a sequencing in which an older policy heritage around food production and security is reasserted, rather than a substantial shift to reflecting non-productivist concerns. Indeed, farm incomes arguably continue to be the main driving force underpinning the CAP, as illustrated by trade disputes between the EU and Russia, a result of the conflict in Ukraine (the EU response to a Russian embargo on agricultural products was to provide a €500 m relief package for farmers hit by falls in prices as a result of the loss of export markets) (European Commission 2015).

It is important to note, however, that with greater flexibility for countries, different national patterns may emerge, with some moving at a faster rate than others towards post-exceptionalism in agriculture. After the 2013 reforms, what exists in relation to the CAP is still an 'agricultural' policy subsystem, albeit one that exhibits both continuity and change. The CAP reform illustrates what might be described as 'shallow' post-exceptionalism, insofar as there has been some shift from a historically persistent agricultural policy subsystem with the inclusion of new institutions and actors/interests, some limited change in policy programmes and instruments, but leaving the ideational framework around redistribution and farms subsidies largely intact.

Disclosure statement

No potential conflict of interest was reported by the author.

ORCID

Alan Greer http://orcid.org/0000-0003-2526-5892

References

Ackrill, R. W. (2000) 'CAP reform 1999: a crisis in the making?' *JCMS: Journal of Common Market Studies* 38(2): 343–53.

Burrell, A. (2009) 'The CAP: looking back, looking ahead', *Journal of European Integration* 31(3): 271–89.

Coleman, W. D., Skogstad, G. D. and Atkinson, M. M. (1996) 'Paradigm shifts and policy networks: cumulative change in agriculture', *Journal of Public Policy* 16: 273–301.

Cunha, A. with Swinbank, A. (2011) *An Inside View of the CAP Reform Process: Explaining the MacSharry, Agenda 2000, and Fischler Reforms*, Oxford: Oxford University Press.

Daugbjerg, C. (2009) 'Sequencing in public policy: the evolution of the CAP over a decade', *Journal of European Public Policy* 16(3): 395–411.

Daugbjerg, C. (2017) 'Responding to non-linear internationalization of public policy: the world trade organization and reform of the CAP 1992–2013', *JCMS: Journal of Common Market Studies* 55: 486–501. doi:10.1111/jcms.12476.

Daugbjerg, C. and Feindt, P. H. (2017) 'Post-exceptionalism in public policy: transforming food and agricultural policy', *Journal of European Public Policy*, doi:10.1080/13501763.2017.1334081.

Daugbjerg, C. and Swinbank, A. (2009) 'Ideational change in the WTO and its impacts on EU agricultural policy institutions and the CAP', *Journal of European Integration* 31 (3): 311–27.

Defossez, F. (2014) 'Environment group condemns EU "greenwashing" of CAP reform', *The Parliament Magazine*, 18 June, available at https://www.theparliamentmagazine.eu/articles/news/environment-group-condemns-eu-greenwashing-cap-reform).

Erjavec, K., Erjavec, E. and Juvancic, L. (2008) 'New wine in old bottles: critical discourse analysis of the current common EU agricultural policy reform agenda', *Sociologia Ruralis* 49(1): 41–55.

Erjavec, E., Lovec, M. and Erjavec, K. (2015) 'From "greening" to "greenwash": the drivers and discourses of CAP 2020 "reform"', in J. Swinnen (ed.), *The Political Economy of the 2014–2020 Reforms of the Common Agricultural Policy: An Imperfect Storm*, Brussels: Centre for European Policy Studies/Rowman & Littlefield International, pp. 215–44.

Euractiv.com (2012a) 'France, Germany in joint call to freeze EU farm budget', 11 October, available at http://www.euractiv.com/cap/france-germany-agree-keep-eu-far-news-515325.

Euractiv.com (2012b) 'Spain joins France in bid to ring fence CAP budget', 15 February, available at http://www.euractiv.com/cap/spain-joins-france-bid-ring-fenc-news-510824.

European Commission (2010) 'The CAP towards 2020: meeting the food, natural resources and territorial challenges of the future', *COM(2010) 672 final*, 18 November, Brussels: Commission of the European Communities, available at http://eur-lex.europa.eu/LexUriServ/LexUriServ.do?uri=COM:2010:0672:FIN:en:PDF.

European Commission (2011a) 'Communication from the Commission to the European Parliament, the Council, the European Economic and Social Committee and the Committee of the Regions, A Budget for Europe 2020', *COM(2011) 500 final, Part I*, 29 June, Brussels: Commission of the European Communities, available at http://ec.europa.eu/health/programme/docs/maff-2020_en.pdf.

European Commission (2011b) 'Proposal for a regulation of the European Parliament and of the Council on the financing, management and monitoring of the

Common Agricultural Policy', *COM(2011) 628/final/2*, 19 October, Brussels: Commission of the European Communities, available at http://eur-lex.europa.eu/legal-content/EN/TXT/PDF/?uri=CELEX:52011PC0628R(01)&from=EN.

European Commission (2011c) 'Impact assessment: common agricultural policy towards 2020: assessment of alternative policy options', Commission Staff Working Paper, *SEC(2011) 1153 final/2*, 20 October, Brussels: Commission of the European Communities, available at http://ec.europa.eu/agriculture/sites/agriculture/files/policy-perspectives/impact-assessment/cap-towards-2020/report/full-text_en.pdf.

European Commission (2013) 'Overview of CAP reform 2014–2020', *Agricultural Policy Perspectives Brief no. 5*, Brussels: Commission of the European Communities, available at http://ec.europa.eu/agriculture/policy-perspectives/policy-briefs/05_en.pdf.

European Commission (2015) *Direct Payments: The Basic Payment Scheme from 2015. Convergence of the Value of Payment Entitlements ('Internal Convergence')*, available at http://ec.europa.eu/agriculture/sites/agriculture/files/direct-support/direct-payments/docs/internal-convergence_en.pdf.

European Commission DG Agri (2015) *The Russian Ban on EU Agricultural Products – 12 Months on*, Press Release 7 August, available at https://ec.europa.eu/agriculture/newsroom/218_en.

European Commission (2016) *Direct Payments 2015–2020 Decisions Taken by Member States: State of Play as at June 2016 - Information Note*, available at https://ec.europa.eu/agriculture/sites/agriculture/files/direct-support/direct-payments/docs/simplementation-decisions-ms-2016_en.pdf.

Grant, W. (1997) *The Common Agricultural Policy*, Basingstoke: Palgrave.

Grant, W. (2004) 'Pressure politics: the changing world of pressure groups', *Parliamentary Affairs* 57(2): 408–19.

Greer, A. (2005) *Agricultural Policy in Europe*, Manchester: Manchester University Press.

Greer, A. (2012) 'Reform of the EU budget: implications for the common agricultural Policy', in G. Benedetto and S. Milio (eds.), *European Union Budget Reform: Institutions, Policy and Economic Crisis*, Basingstoke: Palgrave Macmillan, pp. 103–21.

Greer, A. (2013) 'The common agricultural policy and the EU budget: stasis or change?' *European Journal of Government and Economics* 2(2): 119–36.

Greer, A. and Hind, T. (2012) 'The Lisbon treaty, agricultural decision-making and the reform of the CAP: an analysis of the nature and impact of "co-decision"', *Politics and Society* 31(4): 331–41.

Harrabin, R. (2013) 'EU budget deal for farmers raises wildlife concerns', *BBC News*, 12 February, available at http://www.bbc.co.uk/news/science-environment-21424957.

Hart, K. (2015) 'The fate of green direct payments in the CAP reform negotiations', in J. Swinnen (ed.), *The Political Economy of the 2014–2020 Reforms of the Common Agricultural Policy: An Imperfect Storm*, Brussels: Centre for European Policy Studies/Rowman & Littlefield International, pp. 245–76.

House of Commons, Environment, Food and Rural Affairs Committee (2013) 'Implementation of the Common Agricultural Policy in England 2014–2020', *Seventh Report of Session 2013–14, vol. 1, HC 745-I*, London: The Stationery Office Limited.

Jordan, G., Maloney, W. A. and McLaughlin, A. M. (1994) 'Characterizing agricultural policy-making', *Public Administration* 72(4): 505–26.

Kay, A. (2003) 'Path dependency and the CAP', *Journal of European Public Policy* 10(3): 405–20.

Keeler, J. T. S. (1996) 'Agricultural power in the European Community: explaining the fate of CAP and GATT negotiations', *Comparative Politics* 28(2): 127–49.

Lynggaard, K. and Nedergaard, P. (2009) 'The logic of policy development: lessons learned from reform and routine within the CAP 1980–2003', *Journal of European Integration* 31(3): 291–309.

Marsh, D. and Smith, M. (2000) 'Understanding policy networks: towards a dialectical approach', *Political Studies* 48(4): 4–21.

Matthews, A. (2013) 'The Cioloş CAP reform', *CAP Reform.EU*, 17 December, available at http://capreform.eu/the-Cioloş-cap-reform/.

Matthews, A. (2015) 'The multi-annual financial framework and the 2013 CAP reform', in J. Swinnen (ed.), *The Political Economy of the 2014–2020 Reforms of the Common Agricultural Policy: An Imperfect Storm*, Brussels: Centre for European Policy Studies/Rowman & Littlefield International, pp. 169–91.

Richardson, J. (2000) 'Government, interest groups and policy change', *Political Studies* 48(5): 1006–25.

Rieger, E. (2000) 'The common agricultural policy: politics against markets', in H. Wallace and W. Wallace (eds.), *Policy-making in the European Union*, Oxford: Oxford University Press, pp. 180–210.

Roederer-Rynning, C. (2010) 'The common agricultural policy: the fortress challenged', in H. Wallace, M. Pollack and A. Young (eds.), *Policy-Making in the European Union* (6th ed.). Oxford: Oxford University Press, pp. 181–206.

Roederer-Rynning, C. (2015) 'COMAGRI and the "CAP after 2013" reform: in search of a collective sense of purpose', in J. Swinnen (ed.), *The Political Economy of the 2014–2020 Reforms of the Common Agricultural Policy: An Imperfect Storm*, Brussels: Centre for European Policy Studies/Rowman & Littlefield International, pp. 331–56.

Rutz, C., Dwyer, J. and Schramek, J. (2014) 'More new wine in the same old bottles? The evolving nature of the CAP reform debate in Europe, and prospects for the future', *Sociologia Ruralis* 54(3): 266–84.

Skogstad, G. (1998) 'Ideas, paradigms and institutions: agricultural exceptionalism in the European Union and the United States', *Governance* 11: 463–90.

Smith, M. (1991) 'From policy community to issue network: salmonella in eggs and the new politics of food', *Public Administration* 69: 235–55.

Smith, M. (1992) 'The agricultural policy network: maintaining a closed relationship', in R. Rhodes and D. Marsh (eds.), *Policy Networks in British Government*, Oxford: Clarendon Press, pp. 27–50.

Spence, T. (2013) 'CAP 2014–2020: a long road to reform', Euractiv.com, 4 July, available at http://www.euractiv.com/section/agriculture-food/linksdossier/cap-2014-2020-a-long-road-to-reform/.

Swinbank, A. (1999) 'EU agriculture: agenda 2000 and the WTO commitments', *The World Economy* 22(1): 41–54.

Swinbank, A. (2012) 'Another reform? proposals for the post-2013 common agricultural Policy', *World Agriculture: Problems and Potential* 3(1): 32–7.

Swinnen, J. (ed.) (2009) *The Perfect Storm: The Political Economy of the Fischler Reforms of the Common Agricultural Policy*, Brussels: Centre for European Policy Studies.

Swinnen, J. and Knops, L. (2014) 'The first cap reform under the ordinary legislative procedure: a political economy perspective', *Centre for European Policy Studies (CEPS)*, A study prepared for the European Parliament's Committee on Agriculture and Rural Development. IP/B/AGRI/IC/2013-156.

Wilkinson, K., Lowe, P. and Donaldson, A. (2010) 'Beyond policy networks: policy framing and the politics of expertise in the 2001 foot and mouth disease crisis', *Public Administration* 88(2): 331–45.

Winter, M. (2003) 'Responding to the crisis: the policy impact of the foot-and-mouth epidemic', *The Political Quarterly* 74(1): 47–56.

Woods, M. (2005) *Contesting Rurality: Politics in the British Countryside*, Aldershot: Ashgate.

Environmental policy integration in the EU's common agricultural policy: greening or greenwashing?

Gerry Alons ⓘ

ABSTRACT
The increasing multidimensionality of agriculture, linking the domain with environmental, trade and food safety concerns, has mobilized new policy actors bringing new preferences and ideas into the Common Agricultural Policy (CAP) debate. This article investigates the extent to which this has contributed to Environmental Policy Integration (EPI) in the CAP. It puts forward the claim that an incomplete transformation in European agricultural policy from exceptionalism to post-exceptionalism explains the limited extent of EPI in the CAP. This claim is substantiated by a longitudinal comparative analysis of the CAP reforms over the last two decades, applying a multidimensional concept of EPI as *process* (how the formal and informal procedures and institutions in place allow for the integration of environmental concerns in policy deliberation), *output* (the translation of such concerns in changes in policies) and *outcome* (the performance of the new policies in terms of environmental benefits).

1. Introduction

The European Union's (EU) Common Agricultural Policy (CAP) has undergone significant changes during the nearly 60 years of its existence. Although the sector is characterized by a relatively insulated policy network – bringing together agricultural policy experts, ministers and interest groups – the increasing multidimensionality of agriculture has resulted in new concerns entering the debate, ranging from development and trade to environment and food safety. This contribution will focus on the role of environmental concerns in processes of CAP reform, addressing the question of in what form and to what extent Environmental Policy Integration (EPI) has taken place in the CAP since the 1990s with respect to (a) the decision-making process; (b) the policy output in terms of both substance and underlying policy ideas; and (c) the policy outcome in terms of effectiveness.

Existing research on EPI in the agricultural sector often concludes that environmental discourse or rhetoric has certainly increased, but that it seems to be difficult to move from political commitment to genuine EPI (Buller 2002), due to low priority of environmental issues and a closed agricultural policy network (Lowe and Baldock 2000: 31–33). The dominance of economic and producer interests resulting from these institutional power relations, together with budgetary and trade concerns, are emphasized in rationalist International Political Economy accounts of CAP reform, explaining the watering down of environmental concerns on the basis of material factors (Ackrill 2000; Swinnen 2015). This contribution, instead, applies a more discursive take on the CAP (Feindt 2017) emphasizing the role of policy ideas in constraining and enabling EPI. The argument I will develop in this contribution is that the incomplete transformation from exceptionalism to post-exceptionalism in European agriculture has had a limiting effect on EPI in the CAP (Daugbjerg and Feindt 2017). While the increasing multidimensionality of agriculture and food policy have instigated a shift in the four dimensions of exceptionalism and post-exceptionalism as applied to the CAP – policy ideas, institutions, interests and policy instruments – this shift has not resulted in a full or stable 'reframing' (Persson 2007) of agricultural policy ideas in more environmentally oriented terms. The integration of environmental goals in agricultural policy and the policies' effectiveness remain limited as a result.

This paper will build on and contribute to existing research on EPI in general and EPI in the CAP in two ways. First, it will introduce a multidimensional conceptualization and measurement of EPI that includes the analysis of policy ideas and discourse. This conceptualization enables a more nuanced analysis of EPI. The importance of ideas cannot be overstated, for changes in policy process and instruments are unlikely to endure without changes in the underlying policy ideas (Nilsson and Persson 2003). Existing analyses of EPI in the CAP – with the notable exceptions of Feindt (2010) and Lynggaard (2007) – tend to underestimate how policy changes are shaped by transformations in ideas. Secondly, this contribution will present a longitudinal and up-to-date multi-dimensional analysis covering the EU-level CAP reforms since the 1990s. In doing so it seeks to remedy the shortcoming in the literature observed by Nilsson and Persson (2003) and Feindt (2010) that studies in EPI are often constrained to single-country studies focusing on one or two dimensions of EPI only.

In the remainder of this contribution I will first engage in the debate on the concept and dimensions of EPI and introduce the conceptualization applied here. In the second section, I will explain how exceptionalism and post-exceptionalism are expected to affect the different dimensions of EPI. After explaining the methods that will be applied in the empirical research in section three, the fourth section will present the outcome of the empirical analysis. Finally, in the conclusion I will reflect on the relation between the ongoing transition to post-exceptionalism in European agriculture and the shape and degree of EPI in the CAP, and discuss the limits of this study as well as avenues for further inquiry.

2. Environmental policy integration

2.1. Conceptual distinctions

In the environmental policy studies literature there is an ongoing debate on how EPI should be conceptualized and measured. In essence, EPI is about 'the incorporation of environmental concerns in sectoral policies outside the traditional environmental policy domain' (Runhaar *et al. 2014*: 233). The underlying rationale is that sustainable development can only be achieved if environmental perspectives 'become a natural part of the goals, strategies and decision-making procedures of all major parts of public policy' (Nilsson *et al.* 2009: 228). A number of conceptual distinctions are made with respect to EPI which are relevant in this research: (a) *horizontal* versus *vertical*; (b) *weak* versus *strong*; and (c) *process* versus *substance*.

Horizontal EPI focuses on environmental co-ordination across policy sectors, while *vertical* EPI is concerned with environmental co-ordination in one particular sector without cross-sectoral modes of interaction (Lafferty and Hovden 2003: 12–14). Although vertical integration is in part instigated by horizontal requirements (Feindt 2010), this paper will limit itself to vertical EPI within the agricultural sector.

The distinction between *weak* and *strong* EPI revolves around the degree to which EPI requires a revision in the traditional hierarchy of policy objectives. Weak EPI merely requires that environmental considerations are taken into account in sectoral policy-making. Strong EPI additionally requires that environmental considerations are given principled priority over other con- siderations (Lafferty and Hovden 2003: 9). This paper takes a pragmatic point of departure: that for EPI to have occurred some degree of revision in priorities needs to have taken place, increasing the role of environmental con- siderations, but not necessarily giving them principled priority.

Finally, EPI can simultaneously be considered a *process* 'leading to changes in policy-making and policy outputs' and a '*substantive* result of changes in policy decision-making, behaviour or ideas' (Kivimaa and Mickwitz 2006: 731, emphasis added). Those interested in the policy process focus on how environmental considerations are institutionalized into the policy process, while those focusing on the substantive result of that process investigate whether it led to more environmentally friendly policies (output) and environ- mental performance (outcome) (Persson 2007: 30–1). A sole focus on the process dimension would uncover the institutional strategies applied to enhance EPI but neglect the connection with the ends this process aims to achieve. This paper will therefore take both process and substance into account, differentiating between a process, output and outcome dimension of EPI.

2.2. The CAP and dimensions of EPI

This section will present indicators for the three dimensions of EPI, inspired by the existing literature (Lafferty and Hovden 2003; Nilsson and Persson 2003; Nilsson *et al.* 2009), and adapted to the case where appropriate. Secondly, it will introduce ideational and discursive elements and connect these analytically to the process and output dimensions of EPI.

The measurement of **process** EPI focuses both on actors' structural power position (based in institutions) *and* their effect on policy formulation.[1] For the former, it analyses the procedures that are put in place to (a) co-ordinate decision-making; (b) enhance the comprehensiveness and inclusiveness of actor representation; and (c) institutionalize evaluation of and reporting on environmental impact. For the latter, it investigates whether these procedures contributed to the inclusion and relative weight attached to environmental concerns in the policy-formulation process. Although the first group of indicators may be considered institutional in nature (see Nilsson *et al.* 2009: 340), they are studied in and affect the policy-formulation *process* and are therefore included in the process dimension here.

The **output** dimension focuses on the policies introduced or adapted through the different CAP reforms. I distinguish between changes in policy settings, instruments and objectives, evaluating whether these have resulted in (potentially) greener policies. Whether these policy changes signify successful EPI, however, still depends on their environmental effects.

This is the focus of the analysis of EPI as **outcome** where first of all, the implementation of the policies will be analyzed, checking whether the policies are applied with the actual environmental aim of the policy in mind or if they are watered down during implementation. Secondly, the environmental performance of the policies is analyzed: do the policies have positive environmental effects?

The significance of a change in underlying policy ideas to achieve EPI is highlighted by the less commonly used 'reframing approach', emphasizing that EPI requires the reframing of 'fundamental problem perceptions, causal narratives and overall policy goals into more environmental terms' (Persson 2007: 43).[2] This resonates with the discursive approach taken in this contribution, allowing for the incorporation of ideational and discursive dimensions in the analysis (Feindt 2017). In the field of agricultural policy studies, the role of ideational factors is usually the subject of the debate on rival *policy paradigms* and their supporting discourses. Policy paradigms contain ideas with respect to the understanding of the policy problem, appropriate policy goals, and the proper instruments to achieve them (Hall 1993). Policy actors apply a certain justificatory discourse in the policy-making *process* legitimating the policy objectives and instruments associated with the policy paradigm they prefer to be 'institutionalized' in the policy *output* (Feindt 2017; Skogstad 1998; see also Weber and Driessen 2010). In this paper the ideational aspects of EPI are therefore conceptualized in the dimensions of EPI as *output* and *process* (see Table 1).

Three paradigms are usually distinguished in the agricultural domain: the 'dependent' or 'assisted agriculture' paradigm; the 'multifunctionality' or 'public goods' paradigm; and the 'competitive' or 'liberal agriculture' paradigm (Coleman 1998; Daugbjerg 2003; Skogstad 1998).

First, the state-assisted agriculture paradigm has a productivist focus, emphasizing that the farm sector contributes to a secure and safe food supply. Due to unstable natural conditions and the sub-optimality of the price mechanism to secure income stability and productivity, adherents to this paradigm argue that the farm sector is exceptional and warrants special treatment (i.e., public intervention) (Daugbjerg 2003; Skogstad 1998). Secondly, the multifunctionality paradigm emphasizes the environmental and social services of farming. Farmers are not sufficiently rewarded by the market for these public goods and should therefore legitimately receive public money (Coleman 1998, Daugbjerg 2003). Finally, the competitive paradigm argues that agriculture is an economic sector like any other in which the farmer should be treated as an entrepreneur and market forces should take precedence over state intervention (Coleman 1998; Skogstad 1998). The ideas contained in the multifunctionality paradigm resonate with the ideas underlying EPI, attaching importance to environmental concerns, whereas the other paradigms tend to prioritize economic concerns. A shift towards the multifunctionality paradigm should therefore be conducive to EPI (see also Feindt 2010: 296).

3. EPI and (post-)exceptionalism

Agricultural exceptionalism is about treating the agricultural sector differently from other economic sectors and includes a 'belief system that provides cognitive justification and political legitimation' for this special treatment (Daugbjerg and Feindt 2017). The idea of agricultural exceptionalism was part of the state-assisted policy paradigm both in European and US agriculture after the Second World War (Skogstad 1998) and became the dominant ideational framework (Feindt 2017). It became challenged since the 1980s, however, due to a mix of budgetary, trade-related and environmental considerations, and a transformation to a post-exceptionalist agriculture set in.[3] In this paper I take

Table 1. The effects of (post-)exceptionalism on EPI in agriculture.

	Exceptionalism	Post-Exceptionalism
Process	*Procedures/institutions:* • Very limited co-ordination between agricultural and non-agricultural departments • Environmental actors lack access to the agricultural policy network • Very limited attention to environmental considerations in evaluations	*Procedures/institutions:* • More comprehensive co-ordination between agricultural and non-agricultural departments • Environmental actors gain marginal ('tense' PE)/genuine ('complementary' PE) access to the policy network • Structural attention to environmental considerations in evaluations
	Discourse: • Zero-sum representation of economic (farm) and environmental interests • Legitimating discourse based on economic (producers') interests • Emphasis on agriculture's contribution to food supply	*Discourse:* • Positive-sum (interdependence) representation of economic (farm) interests and environmental interests • Legitimating discourse also based on environmental interests (but potentially strategically) • Emphasis on agriculture's provision of environmental public goods
Output	• Policies do not have environmental objectives • If policies contain environmental aspects, they will be voluntary	• Policies have (partly) environmental objectives • More mandatory environmental policies
Outcome	• Very limited positive environmental effects (unintended side-effects)	• More positive environmental effects • Policies watered-down during implementation if environmental discourse was 'strategic'

exceptionalism and post-exceptionalism as ideal-types, each characterized by a specific combination of ideas, institutions, interests and policies (see Daugbjerg and Feindt 2017). I hypothesize that each of these two specific combinations of variables has different effects on the likely forms and degrees of EPI in agriculture, affecting EPI as process, output and outcome (see Table 1).

During the *process* of policy formation the institutional and ideational aspects of exceptionalism and post-exceptionalism are likely to affect EPI. Institutionally, post-exceptionalism is likely to be more conducive to EPI than exceptionalism, because it is characterized by a more open policy network. Ideationally, agricultural exceptionalism fits with the state-assisted policy paradigm, while post-exceptionalism resonates with the multifunctionality paradigm (Daugbjerg and Feindt 2017). In the case of exceptionalist agriculture, I therefore expect a productivist discourse and a representation of interests in which farmers' economic interests are pitted against environmental interests while the former carry the day. In the case of post-exceptionalist agriculture, I expect the legitimating discourse also to be based on environmental considerations and a positive-sum (Persson 2007: 27) representation of economic and environmental interests.

The policy aspect of exceptionalism and post-exceptionalism – connected to the state-assisted and multifunctionality paradigms respectively – links up with the *output* dimension of EPI. Exceptionalism will result in policies aimed at production and farm-income related objectives. If environmental side effects occur, these are unintended (Lenschow 1999). To the extent that policies are considered (partly) 'environmental' in nature – they are likely to be voluntary. Post-exceptionalism is likely to result in the introduction of relatively more demanding and mandatory environmental policy objectives and instruments.

With respect to the *outcome* dimension of EPI, more positive environmental results are likely in a post-exceptionalist agriculture than in an exceptionalist agriculture, as the former will have more (partially) environmentally instigated policies. Environmental policies may be watered down during the implementation process, however, particularly when an environmental discourse was applied strategically during the policy-making process. I consider the use of environmental ideas strategic when actors apply them instrumentally in a discourse 'manipulating public images and ideas in order to build support for their policies' (Legro 2000: 423), not reflecting genuine motivation for action based on the internalization of environmental ideas. When environmental arguments are strategic justifications rather than genuine motivations for action, then environmental aspects of the CAP reform are more likely to be sacrificed in the negotiating compromise allowing for flexibility, and hence further watering-down, in the implementation process. Neither exceptionalism nor post-exceptionalism are thus likely to result in a high degree of outcome EPI as long as underlying policy ideas have not genuinely become more environmentally oriented.

4. Methods and sources

This contribution applies a qualitative research design. The sources used to conduct the empirical analysis include: (a) all official Commission proposals and communications to the Council and European Parliament (EP) with respect to the different CAP reforms as well as the relevant impact assessments; (b) 10 speeches for each Commissioner of Agriculture and Rural Development; (c) opinion papers of agricultural and environmental organizations; (d) four interviews; and (e) secondary literature. The policy documents enable measuring the policy *output* of the different reforms and the legitimating discourse applied to justify these reforms in the policy *process*. The speeches are selected on the basis of the variation in the audiences they address (EP, Council, interest groups) as well as their timing (public consultation/preparatory phase, decision-making, communicating the policy outcome). This enables verifying whether environmental discourse is strategically applied to certain audiences or over time, during policy preparation and communication of the results rather than during the actual decision-making. Together with the official EU documents, opinion papers and secondary literature analyzing previous CAP-reform processes, interviews provide additional insights in the policy-making *process* and the degree to which the mobilization of environmental actors was effective. The interviews were conducted with officials of COPA-COGECA (as representative of farm interests), Birdlife (as representative of environmental organizations) and representatives of two different DGs. Both of the latter had been involved in CAP reforms and related environmental measures since the 1990s, covering the whole of the period analyzed in this paper. With respect to EPI as *outcome*, it should be noted that the scope of this contribution and limited access to primary data do not allow for an independent assessment. The analysis will be based on existing evaluations and secondary sources. Many of these sources contain 'discourse on' or 'interpretation of' policy effectiveness rather than presenting verifiable primary data. Although this impedes drawing strong and objective conclusions, source triangulation was applied – using not only Commission evaluations, but also European Court of Auditors (ECOA) reports and publications of Environmental Research institutes – in an attempt to arrive at as reliable an assessment as possible.

A qualitative content analysis program (NVIVO) was used to code the policy documents and speeches on problem definitions and appropriate policy objectives and instruments (indicators of underlying policy paradigms). This enabled a structured analysis of the discourse in the *process* dimension of EPI.

5. The CAP 1993–2013: environment as genuine objective or justification strategy?

5.1. EPI as output

Over the last decades, the CAP has witnessed a shift from emphasis on price and market intervention to direct income payments – partly conditional on environmental requirements – and rural development. A number of the policy changes introduced by the five CAP reforms in this period – the 1992 MacSharry, 1999 Agenda 2000, 2003 Fischler, 2008 Health Check and 2013 CAP reforms – may be considered 'environmental' in nature in the sense that they either have environmental objectives, or could have positive environmental side effects (for more elaborate analyses see Buller 2002; Feindt 2010; Lowe and Baldock 2000; Mathews 2013). The first policy is the *set-aside* introduced in the 1992 MacSharry reform. In order to be eligible for the direct income payments, (larger) farms had to take land out of production. Combined with the 29 per cent reduction in intervention prices, this measure was expected to make farming more extensive. Secondly, the 1992 reform also included *agri-environment measures* as an accompanying measure.[4] These obliged member-states to develop schemes providing payments to farmers for voluntarily implementing specific environmentally friendly farming practices. Thirdly, the 1999 reform introduced voluntary *cross compliance*, which, if introduced by member-states, made the direct income payments conditional on meeting a number of basic environmental and animal husbandry conditions. The same reform also merged agri-environment measures together with other (non-environmental) measures in the so-called 'pillar II', introducing a Rural Development policy next to the existing market and price policy of 'pillar I'. The 1999 reform also introduced the instrument of *modulation*, which allowed member-states to reduce the direct payments in pillar I by a small percentage and shift these funds to pillar II. The subsequent 2003 reform made cross compliance and modulation compulsory, while the CAP Health Check in 2008 raised the modulation percentage, expanding the amount of money shifting towards rural development. The latter only increases potential spending on agri-environment measures, however, as pillar II also contains many non-environmental policies. Finally, the 2013 reform introduced the *greening* criteria, which made the payment of 30 per cent of the direct income payments dependent on compliance with three environmental requirements (maintaining permanent grassland,[5] 5 per cent environmental focus area and crop diversification). The same reform also introduced a change affecting the settings of the policy instruments in pillars I and II by enabling (but not requiring) member-states to decrease direct income payments (pillar I) above a certain level (*degressivity*) and inject the 'capped' funds into pillar II.

These measures could potentially have positive environmental effects, but these were not necessarily their main *objective* (Feindt 2010). Commission documents show that in 1992, set-aside was mainly instigated by economic considerations, such as over-production, farm income and budgetary constraints (Lenschow 1999: 101; MacSharry 1991a, 1991b; and Buller 2002 reach a similar conclusion). That environmental objectives were never a key objective (Lowe and Baldock 2000: 42) is evidenced by the fact that – when set-aside was no longer necessary or even undesirable in the light of changing market conditions and increased anxieties for food security – compulsory set-aside was first set at zero in the 2008 reform (with Fischer-Boel [2007] arguing that 'set aside is a support management tool, not an environmental tool') and phased out in 2013. Contrary to set-aside, the agri-environment measures in the 1992 reform were genuinely focused on alleviating environmental pressures, marking a start of more integrated policies (Buller 2002; Mathews 2013). They were, however, only an 'accompanying' measure, signifying merely a small part of total CAP spending. The cross compliance and greening criteria served environmental objectives – ranging from preventing soil erosion and water pollution to securing a minimum level of maintenance of the land and biodiversity. They introduced only limited additional environmental objectives, however, as part of the cross compliance criteria linked existing legislation to direct payments. The slow development in policies serving environmental purposes in the CAP (but their increasing compulsoriness) is in accordance with the fact that in 1992 the transformation from exceptionalism to post-exceptionalism was only in its early stages, while it had progressed but was still not complete by 2013. Although an increasing number of policy objectives and instruments in accordance with both the multifunctionality (e.g., agri-environment measures and cross compliance) and competitive paradigm (e.g., guarantee price reductions) became institutionalized in the CAP over time, this never fully eclipsed the existing institutionalization of the dependent agriculture paradigm (e.g., income support measures) that had resulted from the longstanding discursive hegemony of a productivist discourse rooted in agricultural exceptionalism (cf. Feindt 2017).

5.2. EPI as process

5.2.1. Procedures and institutions

Environmental considerations are brought into the CAP debate by environmentally oriented services and staff within DG AGRI, interlocutors of DG ENVI, environmental groups and by the EP's COMENVI. The formal institutional rules on co-ordination are that with respect to Commission proposals all DGs are consulted. Apart from that many informal contacts between the DGs exist. It is particularly through these informal contacts and consultations that DG ENVI influences the CAP (interviews with Commission officials, 1 April 2016; 28 April 2016).

Turning to access and influence, both farm interest groups and environmental groups have formal access through the Advisory Groups (Civil Dialogue Groups since 2014) of DG AGRI. The number and composition of these groups have changed over the years, improving the representation of environmental interests (Feindt 2010; interview with Birdlife official 19 May 2016).[6] Nevertheless, agricultural producers and traders still make up the vast majority of representatives in Civil Dialogue Groups and farm interest representatives have extensive informal access to decision-makers (interview with COPA-COGECA official 10 May 2016).

In the decision-making process on CAP reform, the Council of Agriculture Ministers plays a dominant role, and agriculture ministers tend to be more open to lobbying efforts of farm interest groups than those of environmental groups (Greer and Hind 2012). This is therefore a likely venue for the watering-down of environmental elements in reform proposals. Originally, the EP could only give its opinion on CAP reforms, but since the Lisbon Treaty, it acquired co-decision. The post-2013 reform is therefore the only reform until now in which we can see how this enhanced role of the EP played out (see Greer 2017).

Finally, when it comes to evaluation and reporting on environmental objectives a procedure of *ex ante* impact assessments and *ex post* evaluations is institutionalized. The degree to which environmental objectives are part of the impact assessments and evaluations compared to other criteria evolved over time. In the impact assessment for the 1999 and 2003 CAP reforms, the emphasis was on the expected consequences of the proposed policy for farm income and market stability mainly, while only a few pages of the extensive reports were devoted to the environment and rural development (Commission 1998, 2003). This conclusion is supported by existing research on EU *ex ante* impact assessments, indicating the narrow focus of such assessments and bias towards economic impacts (Hertin *et al.* 2009). From the 2008 Health Check onwards, estimated environmental consequences of different policy options are more consistently and substantially discussed in the impact assessments (Commission 2008, 2011).

5.2.2. The CAP reform negotiating process and legitimating discourse

With respect to the 1992 reform, the Commission champions a productivist discourse, but new discursive elements are introduced, including the 'dual role of the farmer as a producer of our food supplies and as a guardian of the countryside' (MacSharry 1991a). The latter 'multifunctional' environment-related consideration, however, surfaces in the policy preparation and result communication phases rather than in the decision-making arena, pointing at potentially strategic usage of the argument. Daugbjerg (2003) and Feindt (2017) reach similar conclusions, claiming that the Commission's recourse to a multifunctionality discourse appears to be its response to the neoliberal challenge in the early 1990s, enabling a reframing of the CAP in order to preserve agricultural exceptionalism, albeit based on a different rationale.

The role of DG ENVI and environmental groups was limited in the 1992 reform. Even the agri-environment measures were fully instigated and developed by DG AGRI (interviews with Commission officials, 1 April 2016; 28 April 2016). The demands of environmental groups had instead focused on environmental conditionality. When such conditionality through cross compliance rules was introduced on a voluntary basis in 1999 and made mandatory in the 2003 reform, it was genuinely co-developed by DG AGRI and DG ENVI (interviews with Commission officials, 1 April 2016; 28 April 2016). This was possible partly because within DG AGRI only a small number of reform-minded people, with close contacts to environmentalists, were instructed by Commissioner Fischler to prepare the reforms (interview with Commission official 28 April 2016). Member-state opposition to cross compliance and modulation, however, caused the Commission to leave the usage of these instruments up to member-states' discretion in the 1999 reform (Schwaag Serger 2001: 103–4).

Analysis of the discourse applied during the decision-making process on the two reforms allows for a good illustration of what can be expected (Table 1) under the circumstances of an incomplete shift towards post-exceptionalism. On the one hand, the Commission presents a consistent discourse (no significant variation in terms of audience or timing): (a) assuming potential harmony between economic and environmental objectives, combining producer interests and environmental concerns (Fischler 2003); and (b) justifying direct income payments on the basis of a multifunctionality discourse as 'payment for the delivery of public goods' (Commission 1998: 103; Fischler 2002). On the other hand, the Commission's arguments in favor of cross compliance emphasize political considerations – that consumers and society at large demanded more environmentally friendly production – rather than independent environmental goals (Fischler 1997). Environmental discourse appears strategically applied instead of indicating a 'reframing' of agricultural policy ideas in more environmental terms. Despite the application of productivist and multifunctionality discourses during the policy-making process, the CAP's policy heritage emphasizing income policy as the overarching goal remained intact (Daugbjerg and Swinbank 2016; Feindt 2017).

Together with DG ENVI, environmental groups such as Birdlife and the European Environment Bureau instigated the greening component in the 2013 CAP reform debate (Roederer-Rynning 2015: 346; interview Birdlife official 19 May 2016), which became a justification for continued direct payments. A stronger focus on pillar II policies could have been an alternative, but the Commission preferred measures that would be applied universally in the different member-states (Mathews 2013). Environmental organizations judged the eventual Commission proposals on greening insufficiently ambitious and feared the policy's fate once the Council and EP had their say (EEB and others 2010, 2012).

Both the Council of Ministers and the EP contributed to watering down the environmental aspects in the 2013 CAP reform.[7] The European Parliament's COMAGRI – whose members tend to be biased in favor of farm interests – had acquired the formal lead position in the deliberation, and demanded relaxation of the greening requirements (Roederer-Rynning 2015; interview with Commission official 1 April 2016; interview with Birdlife official 19 May 2016). The final agreement reduced the greening requirements in terms of crop rotation and ecological focus area and allowed them to be fulfilled by 'equivalent' (among others, agri-environment) measures.

The justificatory discourse applied in the 2013 reform process shows important commonalities with Fischler's discourse a decade earlier. Commissioner Cioloş assumed that the CAP could reconcile economic competitiveness and environmental sustainability (2010b), argued that the greening criteria would establish a closer link between the direct payments and public environmental services (2011), but also repeatedly emphasized that the underlying need of greening was to make the payments more acceptable to society (2010a, 2011). Environmental considerations therefore seem particularly important as a political legitimation of existing policies, rather than as an objective in itself (for a similar conclusion see Daugbjerg and Swinbank 2016: 275). What is different and striking with respect to the latest reform, however, is that – notwithstanding the application of a mix of discourses (Alons and Zwaan 2016) – the post-2013 CAP reform debate shows the most 'productivist' focus compared to the other four reform debates, supporting the assisted agriculture paradigm (see also Erjavec and Erjavec 2015). This renewed emphasis can be explained by the experience of food shortages after several price-hikes during the previous decade. It had a decisive impact on the Council and EP during the 2013 reform (Swinnen 2015), supporting Feindt's (2017) claim that in the decisive policy arenas, agricultural exceptionalism remains dominant.

5.3. EPI as outcome

In the 1992 reform, the compulsory set-aside and agri-environment measures could be expected to have positive environmental (side-)effects. The way set-aside was implemented in most member-states did not contribute to realizing this potential, however, both because non-productive land was taken out of production instead of environmentally vulnerable land, and because the land often was not fallowed, but original crops were replaced with allowed non-food crops (ECOA 2000; IEEP 2008: 16).

Existing evaluations of agri-environment measures tend to emphasize their effect on agricultural practices, rather than their actual effects on the environment, assuming that the agricultural practices supported by agri-environment measures will consecutively have positive environmental effects (Primdahl *et al.* 2003). Such analyses find that the uptake in terms of the percentage of utilizable agricultural area (UAA) enrolled in the programme has increased from 16 per cent in 1997 to 21 per cent in 2009, while the spending on agri-environment measures as a percentage of total expenditure has increased from 0.6 per cent in 1993 to 4.5 per cent in 1997 (Buller 2000), which many still consider limited (Lowe and Baldock 2000). This upward trend was not continuous either, and the 2013 reform even brought a decrease in agri-environment spending in real terms.

More importantly, though, the *design* and *monitoring* of agri-environment measures often undermine their assumed environmental effects as well as their assessability. First of all – notwithstanding good exceptions – the member-states' implementation of the measures overall seems to be geared towards maintaining existing practices and supporting farm income rather than ameliorating environmentally damaging practices (ECOA 2000, 2011; Hart 2015), impeding the policy's potential positive environmental effects. Next to this targeting problem, the objectives of the measures tend to be imprecise, lacking baseline levels and time frames for measurable achievements, which impedes monitoring and makes it difficult to judge whether or not objectives in terms of environmental effects are achieved (ECOA 2011; EEA 2006). The Commission, nevertheless, claims that the measures have prevented further intensification and resulted in a decreased usage of chemical fertilizers (Commission 1997). Whether this claim can be substantiated is questionable, as 'still very little information [is] available on the environmental benefits of agri-environment payments' (ECOA 2011).

For the 1999 reform, the ex-post evaluation shows that positive environmental externalities were limited. The implementation of voluntary cross compliance was lacking in many member-states and 'national envelopes' were used for income support rather than agri-environment measures (IEEP 2002). The fact that the more innovative and radical elements of the reform were optional, combined with the limited budget for pillar II, constrained the reform's impact (Buller 2002). After cross compliance became compulsory, research commissioned by DG AGRI found that, despite a wide variation in implementation between member-states, the policy had improved compliance with environmental obligations (Alliance Environment 2007). Reports of the ECOA countered these claims, lamenting the merely partial implementation of the requirements by member-states, their unreliable reporting on compliance and the weak sanctions (ECOA 2008), noting an increase in infringements from 21 per cent in 2011 to 27 per cent in 2014 (ECOA 2016). The Court furthermore argued that the indicators the Commission collected data on (percentage of CAP payments and acres covered by cross compliance) did not measure the effectiveness of cross compliance. Although, at the overall level of CAP, data is also collected on farmland bird indexes, water quality and soil erosion, the specific impact of cross compliance on these indicators remains unknown (ECOA 2016). As was the case with agri-environment measures, the (additional) environmental effects of cross compliance appear limited.

The positive estimates of the Commission's impact assessment of the 2013 reform were called into question by research institutes like the Institute for European Environmental Policy (IEEP) (2013). It is argued that farmers would hardly have to change their policies to be eligible for the greening payments and that, therefore, the overall environmental benefits would be limited (Bureau and Mahé 2015: 107–8). Moreover, the greening measures were watered down further in the implementation phase (Hart 2015). Commission officials also doubt that greening will have more positive environmental effects than the previously existing policies (interview with Commission officials 1 April 2016; 28 April 2016). While a recent Commission working document draws positive conclusions on the amount of ecological focus area, it emphasizes that farmers have 'optimized their EFA choices on economic grounds' rather than environmental ones (Commission 2016: 19). Although it is too early to draw robust conclusions, the greening requirements are unlikely to have significant environmental effects.

6. Conclusion

This paper developed the argument that the incomplete transformation from an exceptionalist agriculture to a post-exceptionalist agriculture policy in Europe – both in terms of the associated institutional power structures and dominant ideas – has brought only limited EPI in the CAP. While changes in policy-making procedures and institutions have provided environmental actors with enhanced access to the policy-making process, their impact on this process did not significantly increase. Although the legitimating discourse has increasingly emphasized environmental concerns, this discourse seems to be particularly applied strategically as a vehicle to legitimate existing practices (as is also claimed by Daugbjerg and Swinbank 2016). Environmental objectives have become a variable in the agricultural policy-making equation, but its coefficient remains small. This explains why dissatisfying effectiveness of environmental measures has not instigated more far-reaching policy adaptations.

The conclusions of this study are limited to agriculture policy in the European Union. Further research in the agricultural sector could investigate how EPI may have been shaped differently in countries where exceptionalism has given way to more market liberal perspectives on agriculture, such as in the United States. This study is furthermore limited in depth, as longitudinal comparison and development was prioritized over presenting the full intricacies of the reform process. Finally, the exclusion of horizontal EPI from the analysis may have resulted in insufficient appreciation of the indirect effects on the CAP of environmental obligations based on horizontal European regulations and agreements.

What does the analysis of EPI in the specific case of the CAP add to the broader EPI literature? First of all, the three-dimensional conceptualization developed in this paper can also be applied to EPI in other fields. Though exact measurements may need to be adapted, it is a rather general conceptualization that allows for a relatively comprehensive analysis of EPI and nuanced conclusions based on clear distinctions between the different dimensions of EPI. The importance of such a multi-dimensional approach is underlined by the findings in this paper that increased access of environmental actors to the decision-making *process* does not necessarily give them much influence, and that more mandatory policy instruments (*output*) do not guarantee more effective *outcomes*. This brings me to the second contribution of this paper, which is the focus on the crucial role of ideas in shaping EPI. The case study has shown that as long as institutional changes are not accompanied by a change in policy ideas, environmentally oriented policies will remain unstable and their effectiveness limited. While a shift from exceptionalism to post-exceptionalism may not be applicable to other domains (or may differ in similar domains in other countries), these domains will have their own policy paradigms affecting EPI trajectories. In the case of market-oriented agriculture, for example, environmental concerns would have to be connected to considerations of competitiveness and a level playing field, while a public goods justification would only be acceptable to the extent that these 'goods' are quantifiable to some degree in order for the idea of supply and demand to apply. This has important implications for both policy-makers and researchers. The former would have to apply domain-specific justificatory discourses to accomplish a durable 'reframing' of different sectors in more environmental terms, while the latter have to adapt their analytical lenses to a domain's ideational peculiarities.

Notes

1. Constraining and enabling factors for EPI (for an overview see Runhaar *et al.* 2014) are often located at the 'governance' level and overlap with the procedural and institutional factors I included in the process dimension.
2. Cashmore and Wejs (2014) develop a similar argument with respect to climate change planning, emphasizing that legitimacy is a prerequisite both for policy prioritization and effective outcomes.
3. See Feindt (2017) for an elaborate analysis of the relative importance of competing agricultural policy discourses in influencing the CAP policy paradigm over time.
4. Article 19 of regulation 797/85 that introduced special schemes for 'Sensitive Areas' may be considered a frontrunner of the agri-environment measures introduced in 1992.
5. Which had already been a cross compliance requirement since 2005.
6. Commission Decisions 87/70/EEC to 87/93/EEC (OJ L 45, 14.2.1978, pp. 1–68); 98/235/EC (OJ L88, 24.3.1998, pp. 59–71); 2004/391/EC (OJ L120, 24.4.2004, pp 50–60).
7. For a debate on the relative role of both institutions, see Swinnen (2015).

Acknowledgements

I would like to thank three anonymous reviewers for their helpful input. Many thanks go to Peter H. Feindt and Carsten Daugbjerg for their extensive feedback on earlier drafts of the article, which resulted in a significantly improved manuscript.

Disclosure statement

No potential conflict of interest was reported by the author(s).

Funding

This project has received funding from the European Union's Horizon 2020 research and innovation programme under the Marie Skłodowska-Curie grant agreement number 659838.

ORCID

Gerry Alons ⓘ http://orcid.org/0000-0003-2169-5510

References

Ackrill, R. (2000) *The Common Agricultural Policy*, Sheffield, UK: Sheffield Academic Press.

Alliance Environment (2007) 'Evaluation of the application of cross-compliance as foreseen under regulation 1782/2003', July 2007, available at http://ec.europa.eu/agriculture/eval/reports/cross_compliance/part2.pdf (accessed May 2016).

Alons, G. and Zwaan, P. (2016) 'New wine in different bottles: negotiating and selling the CAP post-2013 reform', *Sociologia Ruralis* 56(3): 349–370.

Buller, H. (2000) 'Agri-environment measures', in F. Brouwer and P. Lowe (eds), *CAP Regimes and the European Countryside*, Wallingford: CAB International, pp. 199–220.

Buller, H. (2002) 'Integrating European Union environmental and agricultural policy', in A. Lenschow (ed.), *Environmental Policy Integration. Greening Sectoral Policies in Europe*, London: Earthscan Publications, pp. 103–126.

Bureau, J.C. and Mahé, L.P. (2015) 'Was the CAP reform a success?', in J. Swinnen (ed.), *The Political Economy of the 2014–2020 Common Agricultural Policy*, London: Rowman and Littlefield, pp. 331–356.

Cashmore, M. and Wejs, A. (2014) 'Constructing legitimacy for climate change planning: a study of local government in Denmark', *Global Environmental Change* 24: 203–212.

Cioloş, D. (2010a) Speech to the European Parliament's agriculture committee, 12.4.2010, SPEECH/10/150.

Cioloş, D. (2010b) Speech for council of agriculture ministers, 1.6.2010, SPEECH/10/285.

Cioloş, D. (2011) Speech at the Oxford farming conference, 6.1.2001, SPEECH/11/13.

Coleman, W.D. (1998) 'From protected development to market liberalism: paradigm change in agriculture', *Journal of European Public Policy* 5(4): 632–651.

Commission (1997) 'Agriculture and the environment', *CAP Working Notes*, 15 January.

Commission (1998) 'CAP reports. CAP reform proposals. Impact analyses', October.

Commission (2003) 'Mid-term review of the common agricultural policy. July 2002 Proposal. Impact Analyses', February.

Commission (2008) 'Commission staff working paper. Impact assessment', SEC (2008)1885, 20 May.

Commission (2011) 'Impact assessment common agricultural policy towards 2020', SEC (2011)1153final/2, 20 October.

Commission (2016) 'Commission staff working document. Review of greening after one year', SWD(2016)218final, 22 June.

Daugbjerg, C. (2003) 'Policy feedback and paradigm shift in EU agricultural policy: the effects of the MacSharry reform on ruture reform', *Journal of European Public Policy* 10(3): 421–437.

Daugbjerg, C. and Feindt, P.H. (2017) 'Post-exceptionalism in public policy: transforming food and agricultural policy', *Journal of European Public Policy*. doi:10.1080/13501763.2017.1334081

Daugbjerg, C. and Swinbank, A. (2016) 'Three decades of policy layering and politically sustainable reform in the European Union's agricultural Policy', *Governance* 29(2): 265–280.

Erjavec, K. and Erjavec, E. (2015) '"Greening the CAP"- just a fashionable justification? A discourse analysis of the 2014–2020 CAP reform documents', *Food Policy* 51: 53–62.

European Court of Auditors (2000) 'Greening the CAP', Special Report No 14, 2000.

European Court of Auditors (2008) 'Is cross compliance an effective policy', Special Report No 8, 2008.

European Court of Auditors (2011) 'Is Agri-environment support well designed and managed?', Special Report No 7, 2011.

European Court of Auditors (2016) 'Making cross compliance more effective and achieving simplification remains challenging', Special Report No 26, 2016.

European Environmental Agency (2006) 'Assessing environmental integration in EU agriculture policy', *EEA Briefing*, 2006/01. Available at http://www.eea.europa.eu/publications/briefing_2006_1 (consulted May 2016).

European Environmental Bureau (2012) 'Briefing: reform proposals for the common agricultural policy', June, available at www.eeb.org (consulted October 2016).

European Environmental Bureau and others (2010) 'Environmental and farming NGO's response to CAP reform communication: rising to environmental challenges?', 18 November, available at www.eeb.org (consulted October 2016).

Feindt, P.H. (2010) 'Policy-learning and environmental policy integration in the common agricultural policy 1973–2003', *Public Administration* 88(2): 296–314.

Feindt, P.H. (2017) 'Agricultural policy', in H. Heinelt and S. Münch (eds), *Handbook of European Policy: Formulation, Development and Evaluation*, London: Edward Elgar.

Fischer-Boel, M. (2007) Speech at Birdlife conference, 3.10.2007, SPEECH/07/593.

Fischler, F. (1997) Speech at land use and food policy intergroup, 2.6.1997, SPEECH/97/126.

Fischler, F. (2002) Presentation of the CAP mid-term review at the Agriculture Council. 17.5.2002, SPEECH/02/342.

Fischler, F. (2003) Speech for COMAGRI, Committee for Agriculture, 22.1.2003, SPEECH/03/20.

Greer, A. (2017) 'Moving beyond de-compartmentalisation? Inter-institutional policy making in agriculture: an examination of the 2013 CAP Reform', *Journal of European Public Policy*. doi:10.1080/13501763.2017.1334080

Greer, A. and Hind, T. (2012) 'Inter-institutional decision-making: the case of the common agricultural policy', *Policy and Society* 31(4): 331–341.

Hall, P.A. (1993) 'Policy paradigms, social learning, and the state: the case of economic policymaking in Britain', *Comparative Politics*, 25(3): 275–296.

Hart, K. (2015) 'Green direct payments: implementation choices of nine Member State and their environmental implications', IEEP, London, available at http://www.eeb.org/index.cfm?LinkServID=0DFEF8B2-5056-B741-DB05EBEF517EDCCB (consulted June 2016).

Hertin, J., et al. (2009) 'Rationalising the policy mess? Ex ante policy assessment and the utilisation of knowledge in the policy process', *Environment and Planning A* 41(5): 1185–1200.

IEEP (2002) 'Environmental integration and the CAP', 9 October, available at http://www.ieep.eu/assets/139/EnvironmentalintegrationandCAP.pdf (consulted May 2016).

IEEP (2008) 'The environmental beneftis of set-aside in the EU. A summary of evidence', available at http://webarchive.nationalarchives.gov.uk/20130123162956/http:/www.defra.gov.uk/statistics/files/defra-stats-foodfarm-environ-obs-research-setaside-ieeprep ort-feb08.pdf (consulted October 2016).

IEEP (2013) 'Disappointing outcome for the environment from COMAGRI CAP Reform vote', 29 January, available at http://cap2020.ieep.eu/2013/1/29/disappointing-outco me-for-the-environment-from-comagri-cap-reform-vote (consulted June 2016).

Kivimaa, P. and Mickwitz, P. (2006) 'The challenge of greening technologies—environ- mental policy integration in Finnish technology policies', *Research Policy* 35: 729–744.

Lafferty, W. and Hovden, E. (2003) 'Environmental policy integration: towards an analytical framework', *Environmental Politics* 12(3): 1–22.

Legro, J.W. (2000) 'The transformation of policy ideas', *American Journal of Political Science* 44(3): 419–432.

Lenschow, A. (1999) 'The greening of the EU: the common agricultural policy and the structural funds', *Environment and Planning C: Government and Policy* 17: 91–108.

Lowe, P. and Baldock, D. (2000) 'Integration of environmental objectives into agricul- tural policy making', in F. Brouwer and P. Lowe (eds), *CAP Regimes and the European Countryside*, Wallingford: CAB International, pp. 31–52.

Lynggaard, K. (2007) 'The institutional construction of a policy field: a discursive insti- tutional perspective on change within the common agricultural policy', *Journal of European Public Policy* 14(2): 293–312.

MacSharry, R. (1991a) Statement to the European Parliament, 11.3.1991, SPEECH/91/24.

MacSharry, R. (1991b) Address to the conference on the future of agriculture and the rural areas, 21.6.1992, SPEECH/91/79.

Mathews A. (2013) 'Greening agricultural payments in the EU's common agricultural policy', *Bio-Based and Applied Economics* 2(1): 1–27.

Nilsson, M. and Persson, A. (2003) 'Framework for analysing environmental policy inte- gration', *Journal of Environmental Policy and Planning* 5(4): 333–359.

Nilsson, M., Pallemaerts, M. and von Homeyer, I. (2009) 'International regimes and environmental policy integration: introducing the special issue', *International Environmental Agreements: Politics, Law and Economics* 9: 337–350.

Persson, A. (2007) 'Different perspectives on EPI', in M. Nilsson and K. Eckerberg (eds), *Environmental Policy Integration in Practice: Shaping Institutions for Learning*, London: Earthscan Publications, pp. 25–47.

Primdahl, J., Peco, B., Schramek, J. Andersen, E. and Oñate, J.J. (2003) 'Environmental effects of agri-environmental schemes in Western Europe', *Journal of Environmental Management* 67: 129–138.

Roederer-Rynning, C. (2015) 'COMAGRI and the "CAP after 2013" reform', in J. Swinnen (ed.), *The Political Economy of the 2014–2020 Common Agricultural Policy*, London: Rowman and Littlefield, pp. 331–356.

Runhaar, H., Driessen P. and Uittenbroek, C. (2014) 'Towards a systematic framework for the analysis of environmental policy Integration', *Environmental Policy and Governance* 24(4): 233–246.

Schwaag Serger, S. (2001) 'Negotiating CAP reform in the European Union – Agenda 2000', Report 2001: 4, Swedish Institute for Food and Agriculture Economics.

Skogstad, G. (1998) 'Ideas, paradigms and institutions: agricultural exceptionalism in the European Union and the United States', *Governance* 11(4): 463–490.

Swinnen, J. (ed.) (2015) *The Political Economy of the 2014–2020 Common Agricultural Policy. An Imperfect Storm*, London: Rowman and Littlefield.

Weber, M. and Driessen, P.P.J. (2010) 'Environmental policy integration: the role of policy windows in the integration of noise in spatial planning', *Environment and Planning C: Government and Policy* 28: 1120–1134.

Party support for post-exceptionalism in agri-food politics and policy: Germany and the United Kingdom compared

Jale Tosun

ABSTRACT
The past few years have witnessed the emergence of new actors and ideas in agri-food politics discussed under the heading 'post-exceptionalism'. Yet our knowledge about which political actors promote a shift from exceptionalism toward post-exceptionalism is limited. How supportive are political parties of post-exceptionalism? Which political parties support a strong form for post-exceptionalism and which a weak one? To examine these research questions, the study concentrates on Germany and the United Kingdom. It shows that the green parties in Germany and the United Kingdom are the strongest advocates of opening up policy-making in the agri-food sector to new actors and of proposing policies that span across the boundaries of this policy sector. Parties that are more closely aligned with farmers' interests tend to support weaker forms of post-exceptionalism. What also matters for explaining the parties' positions on post-exceptionalism is how strongly they support state intervention in the economy.

1. Introduction

Agri-food politics and policy have moved up on the research agenda in the last few years as this policy sector has been strongly affected by Europeanization and globalization (e.g., Burch *et al.* 2013; Daugbjerg and Botterill 2012; Feindt 2017; Jensen and Ronit 2015; Lowe *et al.* 2010). The traditional approach to agri-food policy was characterized by adopting policy instruments that concentrated exclusively or predominantly on the interests and needs of farmers (Daugbjerg and Feindt 2017). Participation in policy-making was constrained to actors based in this specific policy sector (foremost among them agriculture ministries and farmers' associations), resulting in corporatist structures of interest intermediation (Skogstad 1998). Institutional

ⓘ Supplemental data for this article can be accessed at https://figshare.com/articles/ANNEX_03_06_2017_docx/5071699

arrangements that assign agricultural producers a special role, give priority to their interests, establish specific institutions and formulate policies that serve exclusively or predominantly the needs and interests of famers are considered to characterize 'exceptionalism' (Daugbjerg and Swinbank 2008; Daugbjerg and Feindt 2017).

Observers agree that nowadays, agri-food politics and policy in most countries have shifted towards new institutional arrangements, which Daugbjerg and Feindt (2017) label 'post-exceptionalism'. Post-exceptionalism recognizes that agricultural producers do not represent the sole focus of policy-making, and therefore treats them as one actor group among many. Yet this perspective still maintains the policy heritage that agricultural producers are special, but now for non-agricultural reasons. The hitherto marginalized actors in agri-food politics who are now explicitly acknowledged by this perspective include processors, suppliers, wholesalers, retailers and non-governmental organizations (NGOs) as well as consumers and consumer associations. Post-exceptionalism thus entails the participation of a greater number of actors and pluralist interest intermediation, which can lead to conflicts among the actors involved (Daugbjerg and Swinbank 2012; Ménard and Valceschini 2005).

The opening-up of agri-food politics to hitherto marginalized – also referred to as 'new' – actors is also discussed under the term 'de-compartmentalization' (Greer 2017) , which constitutes an integrative component of post-exceptionalism (Daugbjerg and Feindt 2017). De-compartmentalization refers to these actors bringing new ideas into agri-food politics, thereby increasing the policies' cross-sectoral character and aligning the policies with, for example, climate change, ethical, health and/or sustainability considerations (e.g., Feindt 2010, 2017). Furthermore, de-compartmentalization means that the discussion of agri-food issues is not limited to its traditional and specific political arena anymore, but is also introduced into new arenas (e.g., Botterill and Daugbjerg 2015; Farsund 2014; Ponte and Cheyns 2013). Thus, post-exceptionalism describes institutional arrangements in which the special role assigned to agricultural producers is reduced. This allows different interest groups like NGOs or retailers to influence policy-making, which can take place in several political arenas, and may lead to the adoption and implementation of policy instruments that serve the interests of actors other than farmers. From this, it follows that under post-exceptionalism, the policies adopted will depend on how the individual actor groups perform when competing against each other (Daugbjerg and Swinbank 2012).

Despite evident changes in agri-food politics and policy, the concept of post-exceptionalism also recognizes continuities and gradual changes in the policy sector (Daugbjerg and Feindt 2017). In other words, post-exceptionalism manifests itself in different degrees: in the most extreme case, it can either be characterized by ideas, interests, institutions and policy instruments that correspond to 'strong' post-exceptionalism, i.e., a radical re-orientation in politics and policy design, or be distinguished by 'weak' post-exceptionalism, i.e., a minor shift away from politics and policy design under exceptionalism. This differentiation in the empirical manifestation of post-exceptionalism is straightforward, as any policy change attempted will produce both losers and winners and therefore, the representatives of each group will strive to influence the policy decision in their favor (e.g., Jordan *et al.* 2013).

Previous research on agri-food politics has addressed the role of organized interests in facilitating or impeding policy change (see Steen 1985). While interest groups certainly represent influential actors in agri-food politics (see Sheingate et al. 2017), this study adopts a different analytical perspective. Its starting point is the classic cleavage theory put forward by Lipset and Rokkan (1967), which argues that historically evolved social cleavages are important for structuring political conflict. It is along these persistent cleavage lines that national party systems have developed. One of the numerous core functions of political parties is to supply different policy options and compete against each other in realizing them (Müller and Strøm 1999). Drawing on cleavage theory, this article presumes that some political parties are still likely to defend farmers' interests *vis-à-vis* the interests of other actors participating in agri-food politics, such as consumers. By concentrating on political parties, this article seeks to reduce the research gap identified by Grant (2012) concerning the factors shaping agricultural and food policy.

How supportive are political parties of post-exceptionalism in agri-food politics and policy? Which political parties support a strong form of post-exceptionalism and which a weak one? To examine these research questions empirically, this study concentrates on two European Union (EU) member-states: Germany and the United Kingdom (UK), where in 2014 agriculture accounted for 0.8 and 0.7 per cent of the Gross Domestic Product (World Bank 2017), respectively, and in which the production of agricultural products is mostly for domestic consumption and not exports. There are three theoretical motivations that make this comparison instructive. As the debate on exceptionalism vs. post-exceptionalism shares similarities with that of corporatism vs. pluralism, a comparison of these two countries promises valuable insights, as Germany is considered more corporatist than the UK (Siaroff 1999).

Second, Hall and Soskice (2001) classify Germany and the UK as contrasting cases: the first represents a so-called coordinated market economy while the latter constitutes a liberal market economy. Similar to the reasoning regarding styles of interest intermediation, one can expect that the involvement of state actors in the economy may be reflected in the political parties' support for post-exceptionalism.

Finally, and most importantly, Germany and the UK are worth comparing because of the different levels of electoral support for their respective green parties. These parties are likely to be the strongest supporters of post-exceptionalism, as they generally favor cross-sectoral policy approaches that aim to promote sustainable development. Yet having an electorally successful green party in a country is likely to have implications for how the other political parties position themselves on 'green' issues (Carter 2006). Therefore, comparing Germany (with its electorally successful green party) with the UK (with its electorally much weaker green party) promises an improved understanding of the effects of national party competition on how parties position themselves with regard to agri-food issues. Moreover, this comparison supports the main ambition of this article, which is to contribute to the literature on the relationship between public policy and political parties and party systems.

2. Theoretical considerations

The primary ambition of this study is to understand political parties' support for weak or strong forms of post-exceptionalism in agri-food politics and policy. Therefore, the relationship between political parties and policy ideas lies at the heart of this section. The support of political parties for specific policy ideas and instruments can be determined by both stable and flexible parameters.

The cleavage theory by Lipset and Rokkan (1967) suggests that individual political parties have stable policy ideas that are geared towards the preferences of the societal groups the parties consider themselves to represent (Müller 2009: 365–6). According to this approach, the policy ideas supported by the individual political parties are not only relatively stable over time, but should also lead to similarities regarding the policy ideas supported by political parties across countries that belong to the same party family. About 10 party families have been identified for Western Europe (see Mair and Mudde 1998), and there is a prolific scientific debate on how to apply the party-family approach to other world regions (e.g., Batory and Sitter 2004).

The four classic cleavages along which party families can be positioned are the following (Lipset and Rokkan 1967): center vs. periphery; state vs. church; rural vs. urban; and worker vs. employer. Furthermore, the work of Inglehart (1990) and others puts forth a 'new politics' cleavage that cuts across the traditional cleavages and includes an environmental issue dimension (Carter 2006: 748). Agrarian parties are rooted in the center–periphery and rural-urban cleavages (Batory and Sitter 2004: 524). In the past, agrarian parties were particularly common in the Nordic countries and proposed policies that would protect farmers from adverse effects (e.g., Farslund 2014; Steen 1985). In the meantime, however, differences between agrarian parties in Europe have arisen, as some of them decided to maintain close links to agrarian interests, while others have opened up their policy portfolios to include broader interests (Batory and Sitter 2004: 524). Some agrarian parties have developed an ecological dimension in line with the 'new politics' cleavage (e.g., the Swedish Centre Party; *Centerpartiet*), and again others have started to target white-collar workers in the urban private sector (e.g., Denmark's Liberal Party; *Venstre*).

Likewise, it is not only classic agrarian political parties that seek to protect the welfare of farmers. For example, it was a group within the Norwegian Labour Party (*Det Norske Arbeiderparti*) representing smallholders that opposed the country's accession to the EU as it was 'concerned with state protection of agriculture and other primary sectors' (Geyer and Swank 1997: 559). Since agrarian parties do not exist in all European countries, agrarian interests are also represented by political parties belonging to different party groups. Following these developments in the European party landscape, Grant (2012: 278) invites research to pay more attention to 'how competing narratives relating to agriculture and "the rural" are played out in a whole range of political parties'.

More broadly, we can expect all political parties to assert some agri-food policy ideas, as this policy sector represents a dimension of party competition in virtually all advanced democracies. However, the policy ideas the individual parties hold will vary according to their perception of which societal segments they represent. As political parties strive for maximizing their votes, they are also likely to change their positions on public policy – within certain boundaries that are given by their alignment with the social cleavages – if this yields the prospect of more votes (Müller and Strøm 1999).

The reasoning presented above suggests variation across the political parties *within* Germany and the UK. Political parties closely linked with agrarian interests will at best support a minor shift away from exceptionalism, whereas political parties that align themselves with the interests of other social groups will mostly advocate a major shift in the agri-food sector, either as a post-exceptional or as a neo-liberal transformation.

In Germany, the Christian Democratic Union (*Christlich Demokratische Union*, CDU) and its Bavarian sister party Christian Social Union (*Christlich-Soziale Union*, CSU) have traditionally supported the interests of farmers, which is also reflected in the fact that these two parties typically control the ministry of agriculture in coalition governments (Pappi *et al.* 2008: 278). On the other end of the continuum is Alliance'90/Greens (*Bündnis'90/Die Grünen*, B'90/Grüne), which maintains only weak ties with conventional farmers but has roots in alternative agriculture and advocates 'a "turnaround in agriculture policy" away from the traditional focus on competitiveness, efficiency and productivity towards priority for consumer protection' (Feindt and Kleinschmit 2011: 184). In the UK, the Party of Wales (*Plaid Cymru*) in particular has aligned itself with agrarian producers (McAngus 2014: 220). This also holds true – albeit to a more limited degree – for the Scottish National Party (SNP), which appeals to a mixed clientele, including both voters from rural and semi-rural areas (Mitchell *et al.* 2012: 67) and traditional working-class voters based in the larger cities (Bennie 2016: 37). The British Green Party has strong ties with the urban population and supports this social group's post-material orientation, suggesting that it does not concur with the traditional values of farmers or defend their interests (Van Atta 2003: 43).

From this, it follows that CDU/CSU in Germany and Plaid Cymru and – to a lesser degree – SNP in the UK should support a weaker form of post-exceptionalism due to their electoral alignment with conventional farmers (*Hypothesis 1*). By the same token, B'90/Grüne in Germany and the Green Party in the UK are hypothesized to support a stronger form of post-exceptionalism as a result of their electoral alignment with urban, post-materialist voters and – in the German case – alternative agriculture (*Hypothesis 2*).

When reflecting on party support for post-exceptionalism it is not only the alignment with farmers that is likely to matter, but also how the individual political parties generally position themselves on state intervention in the economy (see Ménard and Valceschini 2005). After all, exceptionalism is about adopting policy measures that allow the state to protect farmers from income risks (Daugbjerg and Feindt 2017; Greer 2017). Therefore, we must also take into account which political parties want the state to retain an active role in the economy – this refers to the economic dimension of party competition. In general, regarding their placement on the economic dimension, right parties – referring here to both center-right and right-wing parties – typically demand a reduction of the government's role in the economy, whereas left parties – referring here to both center-left and left-wing parties – want the government to have an active role. Consequently, right parties can be expected to be less supportive of the idea that the state intervenes in order to protect the interests of special groups, whereas left parties should be more in favor of it (e.g., Batory and Sitter 2004; Geyer and Swank 1997).

In Germany, the mainstream political party positioned at the left end of the ideological spectrum on economic issues is The Left (*Die Linke*, LINKE), while the Free Democratic Party (*Freie Demokratische Partei*, FDP) occupies the right end (Volkens *et al.* 2013). In the UK, SNP represents the most left party in terms of the economic ideology (Mitchell *et al.* 2012), while the Conservative Party and the Liberal Democratic Party (LDP) are considered the most economically liberal parties (Taylor-Gooby and Stoker 2011).

Based on this reasoning, LINKE in Germany and SNP in the UK should support a weaker form of post-exceptionalism (*Hypothesis 3*). In a similar vein, the German FDP and the British Conservatives and/or LDP are likely to support stronger forms of post-exceptionalism (*Hypothesis 4*).

To sum up, there are theoretical reasons to expect differences across the political parties within Germany and the UK with regard to their support for strong or weak post-exceptionalism in agri-food politics and policy. These differences stem from how closely the individual parties are aligned with the interests of farmers and how strongly they support state intervention in the economy.

3. First assessment of the support for protecting farmers and state control of the economy

To empirically test the hypotheses presented above, this study proceeds in two analytical steps. In the first step, it takes a rather general look at how the political parties position themselves with regard to protecting farmers' interests using the dataset by the MARPOR project, which offers cross-country information on the policy ideas of political parties on a large number of issues (Volkens *et al.* 2013). The MARPOR data is based on the statements of political parties in their election manifestos, which are coded in a standardized way by means of identifying 'quasi-sentences' relevant for a given policy domain. Since the MARPOR data allow for drawing only limited conclusions with regard to post-exceptionalism, in the second step, the study employs a nuanced qualitative analysis of 13 election manifestos published by the German parties for the 2013 federal election and by the British parties for the 2015 general election. This section presents the findings of the first analytical step.

The assumption underlying this and the next analytical step is that political parties use words in their election manifestos in a purposeful manner to participate in party competition. Parties compete against each other by offering different policy positions and ways of framing them as well as by selectively emphasizing certain policy issues over others (Elias *et al.* 2015). An election manifesto can be regarded as a valid basis for learning about the policy ideas and instruments supported by political parties (Däubler 2012). When entering government, political parties propose policies that correspond to their statements in the election manifestos and voters evaluate their policy performance on the same basis (Thomson 2011). The signals election manifestos seek to send to the voters can also be conveyed through the assistance of the media (e.g., Feindt and Kleinschmit 2011); however, what exactly the media communicate is still determined by the content of the election manifestos. Of course, one could also analyze speeches delivered by the members of the parliamentary factions. However, this would require a methodologically more sophisticated approach, involving the analyses of all speeches delivered in Parliament (e.g., Bäck and Debus 2016).

The MARPOR dataset contains information about how strongly political parties support agricultural policy that aims specifically at benefiting farmers. The empirical information provided by the MARPOR data is the outcome of joint coding efforts by national experts (for details, see Volkens *et al.* 2013). The more statements a political party makes about defending the interests of farmers and envisaging corresponding policy measures, the higher the value assigned to that party by the coders of the MARPOR project; these are the scores presented in Table 1. In Germany, the political party that had the greatest number of statements calling for farmer protection

Table 1. Parties' statements on supporting farmers and controlling the economy.

Party name (abbreviated)	Party name translated	Support for farmers	Support for state control
Germany (federal elections 2013)			
Christlich Demokratische Union/ Christlich-Soziale Union (CDU/CSU)	Christian Democratic Union/Christian Social Union	**2.64**	0.23
Freie Demokratische Partei (FDP)	Free Democratic Party	0.70	0.04
Sozialdemokratische Partei Deutschlands (SPD)	Social Democratic Party of Germany	0.52	1.03
Die Linke (LINKE)	The Left	0.48	**2.22**
Bündnis'90/Die Grünen (B'90/Grüne)	Alliance'90/Greens	0.31	0.55
United Kingdom (general elections 2015)			
Party of Wales (Plaid Cymru)		**2.84**	1.16
Scottish National Party (SNP)		1.91	**1.91**
United Kingdom Independence Party (UKIP)		1.63	0.15
Liberal Democratic Party (LDP)		1.51	0.52
Conservative Party		1.32	0.57
Labour Party		0.50	1.19
Green Party		0.09	0.63

Source: MARPOR dataset (2016 release) available at: https://manifesto-project.wzb.eu/; MARPOR variables per702 and per412.
Note: Highest scores per country and area are shown in bold letters.

was CDU/CSU, while B'90/Grüne had the lowest number of such statements in its election manifesto. In the UK, Plaid Cymru made the greatest number of statements on protecting farmers, whereas the lowest number was observed for the Green Party. Consequently, the MARPOR data provides some initial support for the reasoning put forward by Hypotheses 1 and 2.

As the MARPOR dataset also offers information on the parties' support for state control of the economy, Table 1 also reports this information. However, the display of this information only seeks to substantiate the categorization of the political parties inferred from the literature. The MARPOR data confirm that in Germany, FDP is least favorable to government control of the economy, while LINKE had the greatest number of statements in its election manifesto supporting state control. The data for the UK indicates that UKIP is the party that is least favorable to government control of the economy, followed by LDP and the Conservative Party. By the same token, SNP is the strongest supporter of state control of the economy. The information presented in the fourth column of Table 1 will be used in the next section to examine empirically Hypotheses 3 and 4.

4. Political parties' positions towards agri-food politics and policies

We now turn to the second analysis, which is based on the empirical information supplied by the election manifestos. The statements made by the individual parties are assigned into three categories reflecting Daugbjerg and Feindt's (2017) conceptual understanding of post-exceptionalism in agri-food politics and policy.

The first category regards which *actors* the individual political parties conceive to be involved in agri-food politics. The recognition of a broader set of actors points to the direction of a stronger form of post-exceptionalism, whereas the identification of fewer actors is thought to be in line with the more closed form of policy-making associated with exceptionalism. In the prior section, we used MARPOR data to obtain a first impression of the frequency of statements from political parties in their election manifestos that explicitly demand policies to defend the interests of agrarian producers. The second coding category presented in this section is complementary to the MARPOR data as it offers more detailed insight into whether there is party support for the *specific interests of farmers*. The third category gauges whether political parties strive to incorporate *concerns from other policy areas* into agri-food policies, which corresponds to the concept of de-compartmentalization. The empirical findings for all three coding categories are summarized in Table 2.

4.1. Actors involved in agri-food politics

Among the German parties, CDU/CSU and FDP – the two parties with the most pro-farmer positions according to the MARPOR data – state the greatest number of actors involved in agri-food politics. Both parties explicitly mention the multitude of actors involved in agri-food politics, including consumers, consumer protection organizations and NGOs. B'90/Grüne is very similar to CDU/CSU and FDP in its understanding of the actors involved in agri-food politics, which is a quite surprising finding in light of the theoretical considerations underlying this study. SPD mentions fewer actors in its election manifesto and the party does not, for instance, directly refer to farmers – something it shares with LINKE, which mentions the fewest number of actors involved in agri-food politics. When inspecting this coding category, the empirical picture derived from the MARPOR data becomes qualified, as the most (CDU/CSU) and the least (B'90/Grüne) pro-farmer parties were found to have a remarkably similar notion of the multiple actors participating in agri-food politics, suggesting they advocate or at least acknowledge a pluralist form of interest intermediation.

The picture looks different for the British parties, in which the Green Party recognizes the greatest number of actors involved, followed by LDP, Plaid Cymru and the Conservative Party. UKIP mentions fewer actors and also refers to the EU, but in a markedly different way than Plaid Cymru, for instance. While UKIP expectedly assigns the EU a negative role in British agri-food politics, Plaid Cymru refers to the EU in a more positive way by

Table 2. Overview of the parties' positions on actors, farmer interests and needs, and concerns from other policy areas.

Party	Actors	Farmer interests	Other policy areas
Germany			
B'90/Grüne	Consumers; consumer organizations; experts and scientists; farmers; food industry; NGOs; processors; public sector; retailing [9]	–	Animal welfare; climate change; health; human rights; social affairs; sustainability [6]
FDP	Consumers; consumer organizations; distributors; education institutions; EU; families; food industry; media; processors; public sector [10]	–	Animal welfare [1]
LINKE	consumers; consumer organizations; EU; food industry; public sector [5]	–	Animal welfare; biodiversity; consumer protection; health; social affairs; sustainability [6]
CDU/CSU	Animal-welfare organizations; consumers; consumer organizations; education institutions; EU; experts and scientists; families; farmers; food industry; public sector [10]	Partnership, but calls for protection of animals and environment	Animal welfare; health; sustainability [3]
SPD	Animal-welfare organizations; consumers; consumer organizations; EU; food industry; Groceries Code Adjudicator; public sector [7]	Protection from the practices of supermarkets	Animal welfare; environment; labor standards [3]
United Kingdom			
Green Party	Catering; Commission on Animal Protection; consumers; EU; farmers; G8; Groceries Code Adjudicator; hospitals/schools; International Labour Organisation; producers from other (low-income) countries; retailers [11]	Protection from the practices of supermarkets; protection from low-welfare imports	Animal welfare; biodiversity; development; health; sustainability; trade [6]
Conservatives	Consumers; EU; farmers; farm inspection taskforce; retailers; Groceries Code Adjudicator; international markets [7]	Reduce bureaucracy and protection from the practices of supermarkets	Animal welfare; health [2]
LDP	Catering; farmers; EU; Food Standards Agency; Grocery Code Adjudicator; media; retailers; hospitals/schools [8]	Protection from the practices by supermarkets; all support they need, but asks for sustainable production	Animal welfare; climate change; health; social affairs; sustainability [5]
Plaid Cymru	EU; farmers; Groceries Code Adjudicator; manufacturers; retailers; USA; public sector [5]	Protection from the practices of supermarkets	Animal welfare; health; social affairs; sustainability [4]
UKIP	Competition Commission; Consumers; EU; farmers; Groceries Code Adjudicator; retailers [5]	Protection from the practices of supermarkets; provide farmers the support they need	–
Labour	Farmers; Groceries Code Adjudicator; retailers [3]	Protection from the practices of supermarkets	Health [1]
SNP	Farmers; public sector [2]	–	

Source: Own elaboration.
Note: Statements on fishing and foodbanks are excluded.

explaining that the EU stands for the precautionary principle (e.g., Tosun 2013), which the party wants to be applied to agri-food policy. Finally, Labour and SNP demonstrate a more classic notion of the actors involved in agri-food politics. To Labour, agri-food politics is predominantly composed of farmers, retailers and the Groceries Code Adjudicator. The last represents an oversight authority with the competence to set standards and apply sanctions, and to whom farmers can appeal in cases of perceived abuse (Burch *et al.* 2013: 259). SNP is the only party that does not make a statement on the Groceries Code Adjudicator, mentioning only farmers and the public sector as actors in agri-food politics.

The parties show a pattern in terms of the actors they refer to, which both confirms and challenges the theoretical considerations guiding this study. First, in both countries, the green parties mention the greatest number of actors involved in agri-food politics and pluralist policy-making. If we accept that mentioning a greater number of actors indicates support for stronger post-exceptionalism, this finding supports the reasoning of Hypothesis 2. However, in Germany, CDU/CSU recognizes the second greatest number of actors, which stands in contrast to the reasoning of Hypothesis 1. Likewise, in the UK, according to its election manifesto, Plaid Cymru supports more pluralist policy-making, which is also at odds with Hypothesis 1. Yet the fewest number of actors are mentioned by SNP. From this, it follows that when looking at the two countries jointly, Hypothesis 1 is falsified. Turning to Hypothesis 3, the relatively small number of actors mentioned by SNP and LINKE supports the reasoning that these parties back state intervention, the assertion underlying this hypothesis. Also, FDP as well as the Conservative Party and LDP, respectively, paid greater tribute to the multitude of actors involved in agri-food politics, which supports the logic underlying Hypothesis 4.

4.2. Specific interests of farmers

B'90/Grüne, FDP and LINKE do not make any statements in their election manifestos suggesting farmers have specific interests. This is markedly different in the case of the remaining two German parties. CDU/CSU underlines that it acts in partnership with farmers and is aware of their needs, but it also calls on the farmers to take into account consumers' calls for animal and environmental protection. SPD goes one step further than CDU/CSU since it demands the creation of a Groceries Code Adjudicator, thereby recognizing the need to protect farmers from the practices of supermarkets.

Quite the opposite can be observed for the British parties: with the exception of SNP, in the context of the 2015 general election all British parties agreed that farmers must be protected from the practices of supermarkets by means of the Groceries Code Adjudicator. This institution was created in 2012 by the Groceries Code Adjudicator Bill under the Conservative

Government, but the legislative process had already started in 2010 under the Labour Government (Burch *et al.* 2013: 264). The fact that SNP did not mention the Groceries Code Adjudicator, however, does not mean that the party opposes it; on the basis of the data source consulted, no assessment of the party's position towards this institution can be given. What is remarkable is that compared to the German parties, the British parties demonstrate a greater support for the need to protect farmers' interests, suggesting they are all – or virtually all – in favor of a weaker form of post-exceptionalism, regardless of their ideological orientation.

We can conclude that the reasoning underlying Hypotheses 1 and 2 is supported for the German parties, as the pro-farmer CDU/CSU mentions the specific needs of farmers and B'90/Grüne does not. For the British parties, by marked contrast, the reasoning of these two hypotheses cannot be confirmed: SNP as a more pro-farmer party – according to the MARPOR data – did not mention the Groceries Code Adjudicator, whereas the Green Party did. Even weaker is the empirical support for the next set of hypotheses. The logic on which Hypothesis 4 rests is only supported in the case of the German FDP, which abstained from recognizing the specific interests and needs of agrarian producers. However, it is disconfirmed for the British parties. Hypothesis 3 must be rejected on the basis of the empirical findings for both countries.

4.3. Concerns from other policy areas

In Germany, B'90/Grüne calls for the broadening of agri-food policy to include considerations about animal welfare, climate change, health, human rights, social affairs and sustainability. In so doing, it is similar to LINKE, which mentions almost the same policy sectors agri-food policy should take into account. Both CDU/CSU and SPD mention three policy sectors that should be integrated into agri-food policy. CDU/CSU mentions animal welfare, health and sustainability, whereas SPD states animal welfare, environmental protection and labor standards. FDP only mentions one additional policy sector: animal welfare. In fact, all German parties mention animal welfare in their election manifestos, which corresponds to broader patterns of public concern over farm-animal welfare observed in various EU member-states (e.g., Vanhonacker and Verbeke 2014).

The growing concern over farm-animal welfare is also discernible with regard to the British parties – four out of seven refer to it in their election manifestos. Yet the concern is less widespread among them. Generally, and in line with our theoretical reasoning, the Green Party mentions the greatest number of concerns from other policy sectors that should be integrated into agri-food policy. Besides animal welfare, the policy concerns stated in the election manifesto include biodiversity, development, public health, sustainability and trade. LDP is quite similar to the Green Party in its calls to couple agri-food policy with animal welfare, climate change, public health, social affairs and sustainability. Plaid Cymru makes statements in line with those by LDP, but abstains from referring to climate change. The Conservative Party highlights farm-animal welfare and public health, and the Labour Party public health. Finally, UKIP and SNP make no relevant statements.

CDU/CSU mentions comparatively few other policy sectors, which supports the reasoning that the party is relatively more in favor of treating agri-food policy as exceptional, supporting Hypothesis 1. SNP mentioned no other policy concern, which corresponds to the causal relationship postulated by Hypothesis 1; but the empirical picture for Plaid Cymru looks quite different, thereby rendering mixed findings for this hypothesis. When looking at Germany and the UK jointly, however, the logic of Hypothesis 1 is confirmed rather than disconfirmed. The finding for B'90/Grüne and the Green Party is very clear: in both countries, this party family mentions several concerns from other policy areas, supporting Hypothesis 2.

There is no empirical support for the logic underlying Hypothesis 3 that LINKE supports an approach to agri-food policy that is concentrated on the sector, whereas this expectation is supported by the data for SNP. Conse-quently, the findings for this hypothesis are truly mixed. FDP mentions few concerns from other policy areas, whereas the findings for the Conservative Party and LDP are mixed, rendering no clear support for the reasoning of Hypothesis 4. In fact, when looking at the findings for the two countries, this hypothesis is disconfirmed. More generally, however, the set of hypoth-eses regarding how much a party supports state control of the economy is less compelling for this third category, while it works fine – as we have seen above – for the other two dimensions that concentrate on the actors and the specific interests of farmers.

4.4. Summary of findings

The qualitative assessment of the election manifestos has provided several interesting insights. Most importantly perhaps, if we had just relied on the MARPOR data (see Table 1), we would have found that CDU/CSU and Plaid Cymru are the parties that support a weak form of post-exceptionalism. Moreover, we would have expected the green parties in both countries to be the most likely supporters of a strong form of post-exceptionalism. To be sure, the complementary inductive analysis supports this picture for the green parties. Therefore, we can confidently state that strong post-excep-tionalism as conceptualized here is predominantly supported by green parties. For the other political parties, however, the empirical picture is more nuanced.

Both CDU/CSU and Plaid Cymru recognize a broader set of state and private actors participating in agri-food politics, which we could not have anticipated on theoretical grounds, since both parties are associated with the protection of agrarian interests.

Another merit that emerges from the comparison of the two countries is the empirical assessment of the theoretical reasoning that guided this study. The findings above show that concerning the second coding category, the specific interests of farmers, the theoretical reasoning was somewhat supported for Germany, but not for the UK. Almost all British political parties support the Groceries Code Adjudicator as an institution to defend the specific interests of farmers, whereas in Germany, only SPD does so. This finding indicates that despite the commonalities between the two countries, there are still country-specific dynamics in party competition that are worth addressing in greater detail.

Finally, the analysis for the third category, concerns from other policy areas, has shown that the hypotheses on the role of parties' alignment with farmer interests work well for both countries. In marked contrast, the hypotheses on the role of parties' support for state control over the economy were not confirmed for either country. The in-depth analysis of the third coding category corroborated the impression that it is useful to study post-exceptionalism along multiple dimensions, as this allows for a better understanding of Daugbjerg and Feindt's argument that post-exceptionalism is about both change and continuity in policy ideas.

This point can be illustrated by the example of Plaid Cymru: it supports policies protecting farmers from pressure, but at the same time acknowledges that agri-food politics involves new actors and that adopted policies need to pay attention to concerns from other policy areas. While the party's demand for defending the interests of farmers still corresponds to the logic of classic exceptionalism, its notions of agri-food politics and policy include new elements and indicate support for a stronger form of post-exceptionalism. From this perspective, Plaid Cymru appeared to be more adaptive to pluralist agri-food politics than SNP. The reason for this is probably that Plaid Cymru's voters are based in rural areas and so the party must make sure to appeal to this clientele by taking into account their needs and interests, whereas SNP strives to appeal to a mixed clientele (Bennie 2016: 37) and thereby pays less attention to adapting to new developments in agriculture and food politics. To be sure, these two parties were found to hold quite different positions on post-exceptionalism, despite being categorized by the MARPOR data as the two most pro-farmer parties in the UK.

For a more straightforward presentation of the findings, Table 3 summarizes which hypotheses were and were not supported on the basis of the empirical analysis.

Table 3. Summary of the findings.

Hypotheses	Actors	Farmer interests	Other policy areas
Alignment with farmers' interests			
1 CDU/CSU supports weak post-exceptionalism	-	+	+
Plaid Cymru/ SNP supports weak post-exceptionalism	0	0	0
2 B'90/Grüne supports strong post-exceptionalism	+	+	+
Green Party supports strong post-exceptionalism	+	-	+
State control of the economy			
3 LINKE supports weak post-exceptionalism	+	-	-
SNP supports weak post-exceptionalism	+	-	+
4 FDP supports strong post-exceptionalism	+	+	-
Conservatives/LDP support strong post-exceptionalism	+	-	0

Note: + = confirmed; - = disconfirmed; 0 = mixed findings.

5. Conclusion

This study has paid attention to an actor group in agri-food politics that has received only scant attention so far: political parties (see Grant 2012). In so doing, it has shown that the fundamental ideas of post-exceptionalism in agri-food politics and policies have been embraced by all parties in Germany and the UK, albeit to different degrees. Virtually all political parties analyzed here have demonstrated the understanding that agri-food politics is characterized by the involvement of a broad set of actors and interests. In other words, the great majority of political parties indicated their commitment to more pluralist agri-food politics.

A surprising observation was indeed that the British parties nearly unanimously supported the institution of the Groceries Code Adjudicator, whereas in Germany, only SPD – which is generally not closely aligned with farmers – formulated such a demand in its election manifesto. This observation is noteworthy since in liberal market economies, like the one in the UK, Hall and Soskice (2001) anticipate the state to be the primary adjudicator of conflict among market participants. From this perspective, this finding is in line with the thrust of the argument made by the literature on varieties of capitalism.

As shifts in the positions of political parties on agri-food politics and policies manifest, interesting repercussions on the electoral behavior of farmers are revealed. Scholars in electoral studies have shown that alliances between parties and specific societal groups have become increasingly fragile, thereby opening up the possibility for new alignments (Mair *et al.* 2004). This is currently happening in Germany, where B'90/Grüne is becoming increasingly popular among farmers – especially in rural areas with small production units, which are more suitable for extensive rather than intensive agriculture. The approximation of farmers and B'90/Grüne may, in principle, result in this party eventually abandoning its preference for strong post-exceptionalism in order to increase its vote share.

How would other groups like NGOs or consumers react to changes in a party's new strategic positioning? This example suggests that the analysis of party support for post-exceptionalism in agri-food politics and policy must take into account developments that affect both the parties' electoral competitiveness and the policy offers they make. When doing so, the study of party support for post-exceptionalism offers an insightful complement to the other analytical perspectives on this topic, as it enables insights into which actors political parties recognize as important, and which institutions and policy instruments political parties support.

Despite the insights gained, this study must be seen as a starting point rather than a conclusive piece of evidence. As explained earlier, the design of this study cannot claim to offer a hard empirical test of the hypotheses. For a genuine empirical test of the hypotheses guiding this analysis, the number of countries observed would need to be expanded. Moreover, to strengthen the methodological approach, longitudinal data would need to be used. Finally, for an even more robust empirical test of the hypotheses, it would be worthwhile to systematically contrast the agri-food sector with another policy domain. A policy domain that may be particularly suitable for such a research design is environmental protection, since policy-making in this area brings together a wide range of actors and consists of policy measures spanning across sectoral boundaries. Taken together, there are many insights to be gained by systematically comparing the political parties' positions on agri-food politics with their positions on other issues.

Acknowledgements

Previous versions of this paper benefitted from valuable comments by Carsten Daugbjerg and Peter Feindt as well as Rebecca Abu Sharkh, Marc Debus, Lena Partzsch, Jennifer Shore, and helpful suggestions by two anonymous reviewers.

Disclosure statement

No potential conflict of interest was reported by the author.

References

Bäck, H. and Debus, M. (2016) *Political Parties, Parliaments and Legislative Speechmaking*, London: Palgrave Macmillian.

Batory, A. and Sitter, N. (2004) 'Cleavages, competition and coalition-building: agrarian parties and the European question in Western and East Central Europe', *European Journal of Political Research* 43(4): 523–46.

Bennie, L. (2016) 'The Scottish Nationalist Party: nationalism for the many', in O. Mazzoleni and S. Mueller (eds), *Regionalist Parties in Western Europe: Dimensions of Success*. London: Routledge, pp. 22–41.

Botterill, L.C. and Daugbjerg, C. (2015) 'Commensalistic institutions and value conflicts: the World Trade Organization and global private food standards', *European Political Science Review* 7(1): 23–42.

Burch, D., Lawrence, G. and Hattersley, L. (2013) 'Watchdogs and ombudsmen: monitoring the abuse of supermarket power', *Agriculture and Human Values* 30(2): 259–70.

Carter, N. (2006) 'Party politicization of the environment in Britain', *Party Politics* 12(6): 747–67.

Däubler, T. (2012) 'The preparation and use of election manifestos: learning from the Irish case', *Irish Political Studies* 27(1): 51–70.

Daugbjerg, C. and Botterill, L.C. (2012) 'Ethical food standard schemes and global trade: paralleling the WTO?' *Policy and Society* 31(4): 307–17.

Daugbjerg, C. and Feindt, P.H. (2017) 'Post-exceptionalism in public policy: transforming food and agricultural Policy', *Journal of European Public Policy*, doi:10.1080/13501763.2017.1334081.

Daugbjerg, C. and Swinbank, A. (2008) 'Curbing agricultural exceptionalism: the EU's response to external challenge', *The World Economy* 31(5): 631–52.

Daugbjerg, C. and Swinbank, A. (2012) 'An introduction to the 'new' politics of agriculture and food', *Policy and Society* 31(4): 259–70.

Elias, A., Szöcsik, E. and Zuber, C.I. (2015) 'Position, selective emphasis and framing How parties deal with a second dimension in competition', *Party Politics* 21(6): 839–50.

Farsund, A.A. (2014) 'Norway: agricultural exceptionalism and the quest for free trade', in O. Langhelle (ed.), *International Trade Negotiations and Domestic Politics: The Intermestic Politics of Trade Liberalization*, London: Routledge, pp. 148–73.

Feindt, P.H. (2010) 'Policy-learning and environmental policy integration in the common agricultural policy, 1973–2003', *Public Administration* 88(2): 296–314.

Feindt, P.H. (2017). 'Agricultural policy', in H. Heinelt and S. Münch (eds), *Handbook of European Policy: Formulation, Development and Evaluation*. Cheltenham: Edward Elgar, forthcoming.

Feindt, P.H. and Kleinschmit, D. (2011) 'The BSE crisis in German newspapers: reframing responsibility', *Science as Culture* 20(2): 183–208.

Geyer, R. and Swank, D. (1997) 'Rejecting the European Union Norwegian social democratic opposition to the EU in the 1990s', *Party Politics* 3(4): 549–62.

Grant, W. P. (2012) 'Can political science contribute to agricultural policy?' *Policy and Society* 31(4): 271–79.

Greer, A. (2017) 'Post-exceptional politics in agriculture: an examination of the 2013 CAP reform', *Journal of European Public Policy*, doi:10.1080/13501763.2017.1334080

Hall, P.A. and Soskice, D. (2001) *Varieties of Capitalism: The Institutional Foundations of Comparative Advantage*, New York: Oxford University Press.

Inglehart, R. (1990) *Culture Shift*, Princeton: Princeton University Press.

Jensen, J.D. and Ronit, K. (2015) 'Obesity, international food and beverage industries, and self-regulation: the fragmentation of information strategies', *World Medical & Health Policy* 7(3): 278–97.

Jordan, A., Bauer, M. W. and Green-Pedersen, C. (2013) 'Policy dismantling', *Journal of European Public Policy* 20(5): 795–805.

Lipset, S. M. and Rokkan, S. (1967) *Party Systems and Voter Alignments: Cross-National Perspectives*, New York: Free Press.

Lowe, P., Feindt, P.H. and Vihinen, H. (2010) 'Introduction: greening the countryside? changing frameworks of EU agricultural policy', *Public Administration* 88(2): 287–95.

Mair, P. and Mudde, C. (1998) 'The party family and its study', *Annual Review of Political Science* 1(1): 211–29.

Mair, P., Müller, W. C. and Plasser, F. (eds) (2004) Political Parties and Electoral Change: Party Responses to Electoral Markets, Thousand Oaks: Sage.

McAngus, C. (2014) 'Office and policy at the expense of votes: plaid Cymru and the One Wales Government', *Regional & Federal Studies* 24(2): 209–27.

Ménard, C. and Valceschini, E. (2005) 'New institutions for governing the agri-food industry', *European Review of Agricultural Economics* 32(3): 421–40.

Mitchell, J., Bennie, L. and Johns, R. (2012) *The Scottish National Party: Transition to Power*, Oxford: Oxford University Press.

Müller, J. (2009) 'The impact of the socio-economic context on the Länder parties' policy positions', *German Politics* 18(3): 365–84.

Müller, W.C. and Strøm, K. (1999) *Policy, Office or Votes? How Political Parties in Western Europe Make Hard Decisions*, Cambridge: Cambridge University Press.

Pappi, F.U., Schmitt, R. and Linhart, E. (2008) 'Die Ministeriumsverteilung in den deutschen Landesregierungen seit dem Zweiten Weltkrieg', *Zeitschrift für Parlamentsfragen* 39(2): 323–42.

Ponte, S. and Cheyns, E. (2013) 'Voluntary standards, expert knowledge and the governance of sustainability networks', *Global Networks* 13(4): 459–77.

Sheingate, A., Scatterday, A., Martin, B. and Nachman, K. (2017) 'Post-exceptionalism and corporate interests in U.S. agricultural policy', *Journal of European Public Policy*, doi:10.1080/13501763.2017.1334082.

Siaroff, A. (1999) 'Corporatism in 24 industrial democracies: meaning and measurement', *European Journal of Political Research* 36(2): 175–205.

Skogstad, G. (1998) 'Ideas, paradigms and institutions: agricultural exceptionalism in the European Union and the United States', *Governance* 11(4): 463–90.

Steen, A. (1985) 'The farmers, the state and the social democrats', *Scandinavian Political Studies* 8(1–2): 45–63.

Taylor-Gooby, P. and Stoker, G. (2011) 'The coalition programme: a new vision for Britain or politics as usual?' *The Political Quarterly* 82(1): 4–15.

Thomson, R. (2011) 'Citizens' evaluations of the fulfillment of election pledges: evidence from Ireland', *The Journal of Politics* 73(1): 187–201.

Tosun, J. (2013) 'How the EU handles uncertain risks: understanding the role of the precautionary principle', *Journal of European Public Policy* 20(10): 1517–28.

Van Atta, S.A. (2003) 'Regional nationalist parties and 'new polities': the Bloque Nacionalista Galego and Plaid Cymru', *Regional & Federal Studies* 13(2): 30–56.

Vanhonacker, F. and Verbeke, W. (2014) 'Public and consumer policies for higher welfare food products: challenges and opportunities', *Journal of Agricultural and Environmental Ethics* 27(1): 153–171.

Volkens, A., Bara, J., Budge, I., McDonald, M.D. and Klingemann, H.D. (eds) (2013) *Mapping Policy Preferences From Texts: Statistical Solutions for Manifesto Analysts*, Oxford: Oxford University Press.

World Bank (2017). World development indicators: agriculture, value added (% of GDP). Online version: http://data.worldbank.org/indicator/NV.AGR.TOTL.ZS.

Post-exceptionalism and corporate interests in US agricultural policy

Adam Sheingate, Allysan Scatterday, Bob Martin and Keeve Nachman

ABSTRACT
This paper examines post-exceptionalism in US food and agriculture policy. Using data on lobbying activity and campaign contributions, we find that corporations and organizations representing the banking industry, manufacturers of agricultural inputs, food processors, and the retail food sector allocate significant financial resources trying to influence food and agriculture policy. Although traditional peak associations of farmers and organizations representing the growers of specific commodities remain an important constituency in policy debates, agriculture is no longer a compartmentalized policy domain dominated by producer interests. Instead, food and agriculture resemble other domains of US policy in which corporations and trade associations leverage advantages in money and personnel to protect their bottom line.

Introduction

Political scientists have long used agriculture to study interest group politics. For pluralists like Truman (1955), farmers were typical of 'pressure groups' that formed and pursued their interests through politics. For critics of pluralism, such as Theodore Lowi and Grant McConnell, agriculture illustrated the tendency for narrow interests to capture the policy process and exert control over federal programs that benefit them directly (Lowi 1969; McConnell 1966). Through the 1960s, in fact, agriculture stood out as an archetypal iron triangle: a highly compartmentalized policy domain jointly managed by a peak association of farmers, agriculture committees in Congress, and the US Department of Agriculture (Maass 1951).

As scholars refined their understanding of interest group politics, agriculture remained a popular case study. In an important comparative analysis,

---

ⓘ Online Supplement available at https://figshare.com/account/home#/projects/22387

Wilson (1977), examined how variation in national institutions and partisan dynamics shaped interest group politics and agricultural policy in the United States and Britain. Hansen (1991), also using agriculture as a case study, found that interest group access to Congress depended on the capacity of farm organizations to provide elected officials with information about recurring, politically salient issues. Hansen's work demonstrated how interest group access could wax and wane: during the 1970s, commodity organizations from the maize, cotton, and dairy sectors supplanted peak associations like the American Farm Bureau Federation in policy debates because they provided more specialized information about the concerns of producers. Another example of interest group research is the work of William Browne who documented an explosion of advocacy groups active in agricultural policy during the 1980s as an array of producer, consumer, industry, and environmental groups carved out narrow issue niches in the congressional policy process (Browne 1990). For Browne, agricultural policy illustrated a broader shift in American politics from iron triangles to issue networks, or from a highly structured form of interest intermediation to a kind of hyper-pluralism characterized by a 'hollow core' (Heclo 1978; Heinz *et al.* 1997).

This article similarly uses agriculture as a window into US interest group politics. Building on earlier work, we find that food and farming issues are a highly pluralistic policy domain in which a wide range of organized interests engage with Congress. Moreover, and like many other policy issues in the contemporary United States, we also find that corporations and business associations devote significant financial resources to agricultural issues that potentially impact their bottom line (Drutman 2015). Using data on lobbying and campaign contributions, we find that the financial sector, the food industry, and manufacturers of agricultural inputs, among other corporate interests, are actively involved in major food and agriculture-related legislation before Congress. These same corporations and trade associations are also central to a system of campaign finance in which political contributions fund the re-election campaigns of elected officials who bear primary responsibility for food and agriculture policy. In general, we find that the financial resources allocated by these business groups to food and agriculture issues exceed those of peak associations of farmers or producer organizations representing the growers of specific commodities.

Our findings speak directly to the central theme of this special issue. Across industrialized countries, farming is highly integrated into an industrial food production process heavily reliant on upstream inputs such as machinery, chemicals and seeds as well as downstream processors of agricultural commodities and distributors of fabricated foods. In the United States, industrialization has meant that agricultural organizations are one among many interests with a stake in a diverse food and agricultural policy domain that includes commodity supports, food safety regulations, biofuels, and environmental measures, among others. Farmers remain an important and powerful group in US agricultural policy because of the positive image of 'the family farm' among the wider American public (Strach 2007) and because of the electoral incentives of politicians who represent farming constituencies (Bellemare and Carnes 2015). However, the advantages farmers enjoy in the policy process are now rivalled by corporations and trade associations that can deploy significant resources to monitor and possibly influence policy decisions on food and agriculture.

The next section describes recent developments in US food and agriculture, including the recent passage of the Agricultural Act of 2014 (also known as the Farm Bill). This background helps situate a quantitative analysis of lobbying and campaign contributions by various groups involved in agricultural policy debates. The conclusion reflects on the importance of comparative research for understanding the relationship between interests and institutions and considers why, despite significant changes in the politics of food and agriculture, a move toward agricultural post-exceptionalism displays a great deal of continuity in policy (Daugbjerg and Feindt 2017).

The politics of food and agriculture in the United States

The contemporary politics of food and agriculture is shaped by the legacy of government farm programs, the rise of industrial food production, and the operation of US political institutions. Beginning in the 1930s, the United States instituted a system of price supports and production controls designed to raise prices and boost farm incomes. With the economic stability afforded by government supports, farmers invested in technologies that increased productivity, contributing to a glut of government-held commodities that raised the cost of agricultural programs. In the 1970s, the United States moved away from this system, relaxing supply controls and allowing prices to fluctuate so that excess production could move to global markets and domestic consumers could enjoy lower prices at home. Over the next forty years, Congress eliminated the remaining vestiges of supply controls while supporting farm incomes with direct payments that paid farmers the difference between market prices and support prices set by Congress (Sheingate 2003). These direct payments have come under scrutiny for supporting relatively affluent farmers, prompting a 'risk management' approach that provides subsidized crop insurance to cover crop losses or declines in revenues (Chite 2014).

This shift from price supports to direct payments to risk management contributed to the transformation of agriculture from a sector once characterized by small-scale, diversified crop and animal farming into one dominated by large-scale, concentrated commodity production. Freed from supply controls, farmers increased production, leading to a steady decline in the price of basic commodities. Between the 1970s and 2000s, for example, the price of maize dropped by more than 50 per cent in real terms (USDA 2016a). Whereas large farms could respond to lower prices by investing in mechanization and industrial inputs that increased output, smaller farms could not, contributing to an exodus of farm labor and a consolidation of land. Over a fifty-year period, in fact, the number of US farms declined by around 60 per cent while the average farm size doubled (Dimitri 2005). Those farms that remained continued to benefit from a system of government supports skewed toward large-scale producers of commodities like maize, cotton, soy, and wheat. In 2013, for example, farms with more than $1M in sales received 35 per cent of government supports even though they constitute just 4 per cent of all farms (USDA 2016c). Meanwhile, increases in productivity and falling prices fueled a growing food industry that transformed cheap raw commodities into industrial, processed foods. Production of high fructose corn syrup (an artificial sweetener) increased from 0.5 pounds per person in 1970 to more than 60 pounds per person in 2000, constituting around 40 per cent of the sweeteners used in domestic food and beverage production (USDA 2016b).

These developments occurred within an institutional context that grants the legislative branch primary responsibility for policy formation. Every five years or so, the US Congress must reauthorize the basic law governing food and agriculture. Known as the Farm Bill, the scope of this omnibus legislation extends well beyond government subsidies for farmers to include food assistance for the poor, land use and conservation programs, biofuels policy, agricultural research, and a host of miscellaneous programs and policies. In the most recent Farm Bill passed in 2014, 80 per cent of the projected $956 billion in spending over ten years will go toward food assistance programs (Chite 2014).

Within Congress, chief responsibility for drafting the Farm Bill falls to the agriculture committees of the House of Representatives and Senate. Because individual Members of Congress seek appointments on committees that provide policy benefits to their constituents, the House and Senate agriculture committees typically draw the vast majority of members from congressional districts and states where farming remains economically important (Hurwitz *et al.* 2001). These institutional features of the agricultural policy process – congressional authority and the committee system – historically provided farmers and their representatives with a great deal of influence over the Farm Bill. Although farm organizations continue to play an important role today, several factors have diminished their once-dominant position.

In particular, periodic redistricting in the lower chamber as required by the US Constitution has meant that the transformation and consolidation of the farm sector also diminishes the number of lawmakers with a sizable agricultural constituency. As late as 1970, over 50 districts in the House of Representatives had at least 10 per cent of the labor force in agriculture. By 1990, that number dwindled to just 15 (Adler 2016). Although the Senate moderates this effect by over-representing rural areas, the economic importance of agriculture is declining in these states. In North Dakota, for example, the contribution of farming to the state's Gross Domestic Product dropped from 15 per cent in 1970 to just over 5 per cent in 2015. Over the same period, the number employed in agriculture dropped from 20 per cent to 5 per cent of the state's labor force (US Bureau of Economic Analysis 2016). One can no longer equate rural with agricultural in US politics.

These demographic and economic changes have altered the politics of food and agriculture as more elaborate bargains are required to build a coalition to support each new Farm Bill. The most important of these bargains concerns food assistance programs. In 2015, the Supplemental Nutrition Assistance Program, previously known as the Food Stamp Program, provided government assistance to more than 45 million Americans at a cost of $74B (USDA 2016d). Because nutrition programs are administered by the US Department of Agriculture and re-authorized as part of each Farm Bill, the agriculture committees use their power over this part of the social safety net in order to secure urban support for agricultural programs that benefit rural constituencies.

In fact, the Farm Bill contains multiple elements that broaden its appeal. The 2014 legislation included twelve separate titles: farm subsidies, food assistance programs, conservation, export policy and food aid, agricultural credit, rural development, research, forestry, energy, organics, crop insurance, and miscellaneous programs (Chite 2014). This range of policies in the Farm Bill allowed many groups to focus on a narrow set of programs or issue niches of particular concern to their members (Browne 1990). For instance, environmental groups focused on conservation while universities concentrated on agricultural research.

In other words, post-exceptionalism in US agricultural policy is characterized by an increase in the number of issues and interests. Producer organizations like the Farm Bureau or specialized commodity groups remain important actors in the process, but they now encounter a wide array of interests with a stake in food and agriculture policy. The concentration of agriculture into a smaller number of larger farms coupled with a Congress-centred policy process that requires broad coalitions to pass legislation means that farming is but a single stage in a complex chain of industrial food production and farm organizations are one among many voices in an increasingly pluralistic policy domain.

There is another aspect of food and agriculture policy that deserves note: the financial rewards of agricultural subsidies extend beyond just farmers. According to the OECD, more than half of the benefits of agricultural supports go toward input suppliers and non-farming landowners (OECD 2003). In the United States, insurance companies benefit from government subsidized crop insurance programs that cover potential crop losses. Food and beverage companies, retail chain stores, and even large banks benefit from nutrition programs that subsidize the consumption of processed foods and pay processing fees on almost $70 billion of electronic debit transactions (USDA 2016d). Government programs also impose costs. Sugar and dairy price supports, for example, raise production costs on food manufacturers who rely on these commodities as inputs. In sum, several large industrial sectors have a financial stake in food and agriculture policy. Given this financial stake, many corporations and trade associations lobby Congress and contribute to the re-election campaigns of elected officials involved in food and agriculture legislation.

Farm bill politics: lobbying and campaign contributions

The contentious two-year period prior to passage of the Agricultural Act of 2014 illustrates another feature of post-exceptionalism. Once firmly controlled by leaders of the House and Senate agriculture committees, the most recent Farm Bill was buffeted by larger political forces, especially the wide partisan gulf that has made the conduct of once-routine business in Congress increasingly difficult (Mann and Orenstein 2016). In 2013, a coalition of Democrats and conservative Republicans defeated a version of the Farm Bill on the floor of the House of Representatives. At issue was the traditional bargain between rural and urban lawmakers to support legislation authorizing farm subsidies and food assistance programs for the poor. Undermining the coalition, the right wing of the Republican Party insisted on deep cuts in spending on food assistance and stricter limits on program eligibility. Democrats opposed the cuts and withheld their support unless funding was restored. In a surprise to the Republican leadership, however, more than sixty conservative members of their own majority party broke ranks and voted against the bill because in their view the proposed reductions in nutrition spending did not go far enough. In response, and in a departure from traditional Farm Bill politics, the House went on to pass two separate bills: one reauthorizing commodity programs and the other dealing with food assistance. Meanwhile, the Senate passed a version of the Farm Bill with smaller cuts to nutrition programs and modest changes to commodity programs. The more moderate Senate version became the basis for a bill that eventually passed both chambers and became the Agricultural Act of 2014 (Nixon 2014).

This protracted conflict provides a context to studying contemporary interest group politics in US agriculture. The traditional urban-rural coalition – farm subsidies in exchange for food assistance – has weakened, yet the core elements of policy remain intact. One explanation for this continuity is the significant number of interests with a financial stake in the Farm Bill. This includes organizations of farmers who represent large-scale commodity producers, receive the bulk of government subsidies, and remain a powerful voice on the Farm Bill. It also includes corporate interests that sell industrial inputs like machinery and chemicals to farmers, rely on cheap raw commodities to produce processed foods, and benefit from nutrition programs that subsidize the purchase of their finished products.

It is important to remember that interest group influence is less about buying votes or changing minds than it is about providing allies in Congress with information that will guide policy decisions (Hall and Deardorff 2006). Furthermore, recent scholarship suggests that lobbying and campaign contributions function as a kind of political risk reduction in which groups allocate resources to gathering political intelligence and shaping the content of legislation in order to reduce the likelihood that government action (or inaction) will impose significant financial costs (LaPira and Thomas 2017). This view is consistent with previous interest group research that finds no consistent link between lobbying or campaign contributions and policy outcomes (Baumgartner *et al.* 2009). In other words, groups spend money to keep their allies in office and prevent bad things from happening to them or their clients.

Our data on lobbying and campaign contributions support a similar conclusion about interest group politics and the resources available to various groups involved in the Farm Bill. Although traditional farm organizations remain important players because of constituency pressure in particular regions of the United States along with the positive image of farming more broadly in American culture, corporations and trade associations representing the food industry, manufacturers of agricultural inputs, food retailers, and the financial sector devote significant resources to the Farm Bill. Although we cannot extrapolate from our data exactly how these resources are deployed, the money and personnel allocated to the Farm Bill may contribute to the resilience of food and agriculture programs in an otherwise challenging political environment. In short, with the industrialization of food production, corporate interests have colonized various aspects of the agriculture policy domain and, consequently, leverage their considerable resources to maintain a status quo that benefits their bottom line.

Lobbying

To study lobbying on the 2014 Farm Bill, we analysed reports filed in accordance with the Lobbying Disclosure Act of 1995 (LDA). This law requires lobbying firms and organizations that hire lobbyists to file quarterly reports with the US Senate. Lobbying is defined as any activity relating to the planning or carrying out of contact with government officials (executive or legislative) on behalf of a client.[1] Reports include the revenue generated from (or an estimate of the cost of) lobbying, the specific issues or legislation lobbied, the names of individuals engaged in these activities, and if they previously held a position in government either as staff or as an elected official. A non-profit organization, the Center for Responsive Politics (CRP), has compiled these reports and made them available for bulk data download.[2]

Using the CRP data, we created a unique dataset of all lobbying reports for the House of Representatives and the Senate for the years 2012–2014. Each observation included an identifier for the original report, the name of the organization lobbying (either directly or through a contract lobbyist), their quarterly expenses, a brief description of the issue, the number of lobbyists engaged in the issue, and how many of them previously worked in government or held elective office in the federal legislative or executive branch.[3] We then coded each report according to whether it mentioned the Farm Bill and related legislation.[4] Out of more than 125,000 observations, we identified 2,118 unique reports from 574 organizations that lobbied Congress on the Farm Bill during the three-year period.

Of the 574 entities that filed reports, around 35 per cent were classified as belonging to the agribusiness sector, a broad category that includes farm organizations, commodity groups, as well as input manufacturers, food processors, and retailers. Miscellaneous business organizations, financial firms, energy, and transportation made up another 26 per cent. Universities, state governments, and other non-profit institutions were around 15 per cent of the total, while environmental, animal welfare, and other single-issue groups comprised around 10 per cent of groups. This distribution is similar to studies of the broader interest group universe that found businesses and trade associations constitute the majority of organizations in Washington (Baumgartner *et al.* 2009: 11).

There are two important caveats about our data. First, each observation lists the total amount an organization spent on all lobbying during a reporting period. Consequently, it is impossible to determine precisely how much an entity spent on the Farm Bill versus other issues. Second, lobbyists listed on a given report are not unique: the same lobbyists may be working on multiple issues for an organization and can be listed on various quarterly reports.

Despite these limitations, the data reveal important information about the quantity of lobbying resources available to different organizations active on the Farm Bill. The data also reveal something about the quality of these resources by reporting the number of lobbyists who previously worked in government. Research on 'revolving door' lobbying suggests that 'who you know' is valuable for securing access to policy makers and acquiring political intelligence (Blanes i Vidal *et al.* 2012; LaPira and Thomas 2017). Finally, the number of reports filed by each organization differentiates organizations consistently involved with the Farm Bill over a three-year period from those that lobbied on the bill intermittently.

Together, these measures of total spending on lobbying, the frequency of reports, the number of lobbyists employed, and whether they held previous positions in government allow us to assess the resource capacities of groups active in the 2014 Farm Bill. Using Principal Components Analysis (PCA), we created a single measure for each organization based on the four variables of interest: the total of expenses, the average number of lobbyists, the average of lobbyists with previous government experience, and the total reports for each organization.[5] Although this measure does not reveal which groups had the most influence over the Farm Bill, it does provide a means to compare the lobbying capabilities of different groups active in the Farm Bill. Table 1 lists the top 10 organizations ranked according to the composite measure and their corresponding industries based on a coding scheme created by the CRP.[6]

As indicated, commercial firms or trade associations representing the food industry, financial sector, transportation, and producers of agricultural inputs lead the list of well-resourced groups. Only one organization in the top ten, the American Sugar Alliance, represents producers of agricultural commodities along with cane and beet sugar refiners. The American Farm Bureau Federation, the largest farm organization, ranks 21st overall in resources. Among specialized commodity groups, the National Cotton Council ranked 41st and the National Corn Growers' Association ranked 51st out of more than 500 entities.

A similar pattern emerges when we look at specific issues in the Farm Bill.[7] Contrary to the notion that different groups occupy specific issue niches in agriculture (Browne 1990), corporations and trade associations are active across a range of programs and policies. On the issue of subsidies (e.g. commodity supports and crop insurance), for example, there were 109 reports from 49 different organizations. Calculating a PCA score for just this subset of reports reveals that the top three organizations in terms of resources were from the financial sector: the American Bankers Association, Wells Fargo, and Zurich Financial Services. Similarly, looking at the 262 reports from 81 organizations that lobbied food assistance programs, the top three organizations were from the food industry: the American Beverage Association, Coca-Cola Co., and the Grocery Manufacturers of America.[8]

It is important to emphasize that our data only reveal which groups allocated resources in terms of staff and expenditures to lobbying the Farm Bill. The data do not reveal the kind of direct constituency pressure on lawmakers

Table 1. Top ten Farm Bill organizations ranked in terms of lobbying resources.

Rank	Organization name	Industry
1.	National Association of Manufacturers	Misc. Manufacturing & Distributing
2.	American Bankers Association	Commercial Banks
3.	Coca-Cola Co	Food & Beverage
4.	American Sugar Alliance	Crop Production & Basic Processing
5.	Eli Lilly & Co	Pharmaceuticals/Health Products
6.	American Beverage Association	Food & Beverage
7.	Grocery Manufacturers Association	Food Processing & Sales
8.	Independent Community Bankers of America	Commercial Banks
9.	Berkshire Hathaway	Railroads
10.	Association of American Railroads	Railroads

that producer groups such as the American Farm Bureau Federation can leverage on issues of concern to its members. Despite this limitation, the data show that corporations and trade associations devote significant resources to lobbying the Farm Bill. Moreover, this activity is not restricted to narrow issue niches but involves central aspects of the bill such as subsidies and nutrition. This activity reflects the fact that crop insurance or food assistance programs potentially have great consequence for the profitability of the financial sector and food industry, respectively. As a result, corporations and trade associations representing these businesses allocate significant resources to monitoring the Farm Bill.

Campaign contributions

Another limitation of the lobbying data is that it does not reveal whether organizations target specific legislators. Nor does the lobbying data capture when groups work together in concert on legislation, which has been found to be an important source of influence (Heaney and Lorenz 2013; Mahoney and Baumgartner 2015). In an attempt to capture these aspects of interest group politics, we examine campaign contributions to Members of Congress, especially members of the House and Senate agriculture committees. Of the 574 organizations that reported lobbying on the Farm Bill, we found 368 that contributed to members of the 113th Congress. This includes contributions from an organization's political action committee (PAC) as well as non-PAC contributions from employees or individuals associated with the organization. For members of the House of Representatives, this included contributions during the 2012 election cycle. For Senators, we included donations from 2008, 2010, or 2012 depending on their most recent election.[9]

Together, these 368 organizations contributed $52.3 million to the campaigns of 520 Members of the House and Senate. Around 18 per cent of this money went to members of the two agriculture committees that have principal jurisdiction over the Farm Bill. These committee members received an average of $53,955 more in contributions from lobbying groups active on the Farm Bill compared to other Members of Congress. There was no statistically significant difference in contributions to Republicans and Democrats.[10]

Research on lobbying has examined campaign contributions as a means of building relationships between lobbyists and likeminded Members of Congress. Conceived as a social network, contributions may be considered a 'concrete manifestation' of these relationships, connecting multiple lobbyists and legislators in a dense web of political 'friends' (Victor and Koger 2015: 4). These relationships are useful for exchanging information, forging alliances, and exerting influence in the policy process.

In a similar fashion, campaign contributions reveal a network of shared ties among organizations involved in the 2014 Farm Bill. Using the tools of social network analysis (SNA), we find that certain groups are especially well placed in this network by virtue of their connections to other organizations that contributed to the same Members of Congress. Specifically, we use data on campaign contributions to calculate the 'degree centrality' for each group active on the 2014 Farm Bill.[11] Degree centrality is simply the number of ties an actor has within the network and is frequently used to assess a given actor's 'power potential' (Hanneman and Riddle 2005). That is, actors with more connections occupy a more advantageous position within a network because they can serve as brokers of information and enjoy access to multiple channels of communication. In the case of the Farm Bill, organizations that enjoy multiple connections (and higher degree centrality) through their contributions to Members of Congress might enjoy better access to political intelligence about the progress of legislation as well as greater capacity to build coalitions around issues of mutual concern.

Table 2 lists the top ten organizations (arranged alphabetically) and their corresponding industries in terms of degree centrality based on contributions to shared Members of Congress. As with the data on lobbying resources, firms and trade associations that represent the financial and telecommunications industries appear to have the highest number of shared connections in the donor network.

A similar pattern emerges among organizations that contributed to members of the House and Senate agriculture committees. Figure 1 visualizes a network of the top 50 organizations ranked according to degree centrality based on contributions to common legislators on the two committees; thicker lines indicate a larger number of shared recipients. The figure reveals a very dense network of connections, meaning that the top fifty groups gave money to many of the same legislators on the House and Senate agriculture committees. For ease of presentation, Figure 1 clusters groups according to industry. In the lower left there is a cluster of entities representing sugar,

Table 2. Top ten contributors to Members of Congress (in alphabetical order) by degree centrality.

Organization name	Industry
American Bankers Association	Commercial Banks
American Dental Association	Health Professionals
AT&T Inc.	Telephone Utilities
Comcast Corp	Telecom Services
Independent Community Bankers of America	Commercial Banks
Lockheed Martin	Defense Aerospace
National Cable & Telecommunications Association	Telecom Services
National Rural Electric Cooperative Association	Electric Utilities
Pfizer Inc.	Agricultural Services/Products
Wells Fargo	Commercial Banks

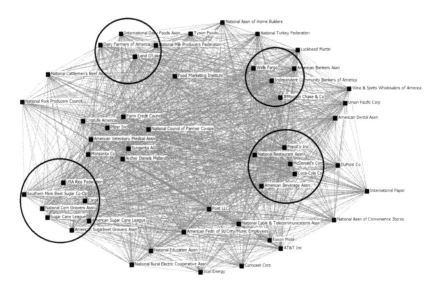

Figure 1. Network of top 50 Farm Bill lobbyists based on contributions to members of the House and Senate agriculture committees (grouped by common industry).

rice, and grain producers. In the lower right, there are food corporations such as McDonald's, PepsiCo, and Coca-Cola. In the upper left, there is a cluster of dairy producers such as the Dairy Farmers of America and Land O'Lakes. In the upper right, there are firms and trade associations from the financial sector such as J.P. Morgan Chase and Wells Fargo.

As with the lobbying data, the contribution data have both strengths and weaknesses as a measure of corporate political activity. Campaign contributions provide further evidence about the resource advantages of corporate actors. By helping to finance congressional campaigns, the financial sector and the food industry along with producers of crops and animal products comprise a network of contributors to the re-election campaigns of members responsible for crafting the Farm Bill. These contributions are a useful proxy for capturing the connections between lobbyists that afford certain organizations with access to information and the capacity to build coalitions in the agricultural policy process. However, the fact that an organization such as the American Farm Bureau Federation ranks low on our measure of degree centrality (337 out of 368) does not necessarily indicate a lack of capacity to gather information or broker coalitions. Using financial resources such as lobbying expenses and campaign contributions to measure activity may underestimate the role of organizations that rely on constituency pressure to gain access. Nevertheless, the resource advantages of corporate actors in lobbying and campaign contributions are an important feature of contemporary food and agriculture policy in the United States.

Conclusion

The industrialization of the food system is a global phenomenon that has introduced new issues to the agriculture policy domain and upset traditional policymaking arrangements. In the United States, this transformation occurred within an institutional context that enables corporations and trade associations to advance their interests through lobbying and campaign contributions. Declining rural representation in Congress coupled with an expanding array of issues and interests has produced a more pluralistic policy domain, but one where the food industry, financial sector, and input manufacturers devote considerable resources to shaping policy outcomes.

To better understand the consequences of corporate lobbying and campaign contributions on food and agriculture policies, continued comparative research on interest group politics is needed. There have been important advances in the study of EU lobbying, for example, thanks in part to the availability of data on interest group activity in the European policy process (Kluver *et al.* 2015; Mahoney 2008; Wonka *et al.* 2010). Unfortunately, a drawback of this data, such as the Transparency Register created by the European Parliament and European Commission, is that many of the registrants are public relations or professional lobbying firms that do not list the clients they represent when lobbying a particular issue like agriculture. Despite these hurdles, more comparative research on the United States and European Union would help scholars better understand how economic changes in the farm sector interact with political institutions to shape the interest group environment in agricultural policy. For instance, involvement by the food industry may be less extensive in European food and agriculture policy because there is no equivalent in the European Union to the 'pay-to-play' system of American campaign finance (Brown 2016).

As the editors of this special issue note in their introduction, agricultural post-exceptionalism displays elements of stability and change. Once highly compartmentalized in a narrow policy community dominated by farmers and their representatives, food and agriculture is today a hyper-pluralized policy domain characterized by a multitude of issues and interests. At the same time, changes in policy are incremental and many programs display a high degree of continuity with the past (Daugbjerg and Feindt 2017). In the case of the United States, it is important to note that the 2014 Farm Bill, as contentious as it was, eventually passed with only modest shifts in policy. Our research suggests that one explanation for this durability is that the food industry, financial sector, and manufacturers of agricultural inputs now serve as a critical bulwark helping to preserve the status quo. With policy authority centred in Congress and individual Members largely responsible for their own electoral fates, corporations have used their resource advantages to colonize various aspects of US food and agriculture policy, especially crop supports and nutrition programs that subsidize the production and consumption of manufactured foods. Although no longer insulated from broader political forces as was previously the case, the relative stability of policy in the United States reflects the important role powerful corporate actors have come to play in the post-exceptionalist world of food and agriculture.

Notes

1. For more details on LDA reports, see http://www.senate.gov/legislative/resources/pdf/S1guidance.pdf.
2. For more details on CRP data, see http://www.opensecrets.org/lobby/.
3. Each observation included codes for the category, industry, and sector of each organization. The data is organized by client, meaning that for-hire lobbyists and in-house lobbyists are listed according to the client name.
4. We identified reports using specific bill numbers (H.R. 1947, H.R. 2642, H.R. 6083, S. 10, S. 954, and S. 3240) as well as text searches with the words 'Farm Bill' or bill titles such as 'Agriculture, Reform, and Food.' We also include reports mentioning federal nutrition programs.
5. We standardized each variable to have a mean of 0 and a standard deviation of 1. Our measure of resources is based on the first component (of four) which explained 0.40 of the variance in the original data. For more information on PCA and an application, see Vyas and Kumaranayake (2006).
6. A full listing along with replication materials is available in an online appendix. and can be accessed at https://figshare.com/projects/Post-Exceptionalism_and_Corporate_Interests_in_US_Agricultural_Policy/22387.
7. We coded each of the 2,118 observations in the dataset by assigning a topic based on the brief description of each report and then consolidating topics into sixteen themes. Observations that did not mention a specific topic were coded as 'general/unknown' and made up around 44% of our reports.
8. As before, we used the standardized total spent on lobbying, total number of reports, average lobbyists, and average 'revolving door' lobbyists to measure resources and used the first component of the PCA to rank organizations.
9. Every two years, one third of Senate seats is up for election. Consequently, the period in which Congress debated the most recent Farm Bill included Senators elected in 2008, 2010, or 2012.
10. These differences were significant at $p < 0.01$ in a two-tailed t-test comparison of means with unequal variances.
11. We constructed an affiliations matrix (368×535) that captures whether or not an entity active on the Farm Bill contributed to a given Member of Congress. We then transformed this data into an adjacency matrix in which each node represents the number of common ties between entities (e.g. contributions to the same Member of Congress). All network analyses were done using UCINET 6 software (Borgatti et al. 2002).

Acknowledgements

The authors would like to thank the anonymous referees and editors of this special issue for their advice on earlier versions this paper.

Disclosure statement

No potential conflict of interest was reported by the authors.

References

Adler, E. S. (2016) 'Congressional District Data File, 92nd and 101st Congress', University of Colorado, Boulder.

Baumgartner, F.R., Berry, J., Hojnacki, M., Leech, B. and Kimball, D. (2009) *Lobbying and Policy Change: Who Wins, Who Loses, and Why*, Chicago, IL: University of Chicago Press.

Bellemare, M.F. and Carnes, N. (2015) 'Why do members of congress support agricultural protection', *Food Policy* 50: 20–34.

Blanes i Vidal, J., Draca, M. and Fons-Rosen, C. (2012) 'Revolving door lobbyists', *American Economic Review* 102(7): 3731–48.

Borgatti, S.P., Everett, M.G. and Freeman, L.C. (2002) *Ucinet for Windows: Software for Social Network Analysis*, Harvard, MA: Analytic Technologies.

Brown, Heath (2016) *Pay-To-Play Politics: How Money Defines American Democracy*, Santa Barbara, CA: Praeger.

Browne, William P. (1990) 'Organized interests and their issue niches: a search for pluralism in a policy domain', *The Journal of Politics* 52: 477–509.

Chite, R.M. (2014) 'The 2014 Farm Bill (P.L. 113-79): summary and side-by-side', *CRS Report R43076*, Washington, DC: Congressional Research Service.

Daugbjerg, C. and Feindt, P.H. (2017) 'Post-exceptionalism in public policy: transforming food and agricultural policy', *Journal of European Public Policy*. doi: 10.1080/13501763.2017.1334081

Dimitri, C. (2005) 'The 20th century transformation of U.S. agriculture and farm policy', *Economic Information Bulletin, Number 3*, Washington, DC: Economic Research Service, USDA.

Drutman, L. (2015) *The Business of America is Lobbying: How Corporations Became Politicized and Politics Became More Corporate*, Oxford, UK: Oxford University Press.

Hall, R.L. and Deardorff, A.V. (2006) 'Lobbying as legislative subsidy', *American Political Science Review* 100(1): 69–84.

Hanneman, R.A. and Riddle, M. (2005) *Introduction to Social Network Methods*, Riverside, CA: University of California, Riverside, available at http://faculty.ucr.edu/~hanneman/ (accessed April 2015).

Hansen, J.M. (1991) *Gaining Access: Congress and the Farm Lobby, 1919–1981*, Chicago, IL: University of Chicago Press.

Heaney, M.T. and Lorenz, G.M. (2013) 'Coalition portfolios and interest group influence over the policy process', *Interest Groups and Advocacy* 2(3): 251–77.

Heclo, H. (1978) 'Issue networks and the executive establishment', *Public Administration: Concepts and Cases* 413: 46–57.

Heinz, J.P., Laumann, E.O., Nelson, R.L. and Salisbury, R.H. (1997) *The Hollow Core: Private Interests in National Policy Making*, Cambridge, MA: Harvard University Press.

Hurwitz, M.S., Moiles, R.J. and Rohde, D.W. (2001) 'Distributive and partisan issues in agriculture policy in the 104th house', *American Political Science Review* 95(4): 911–22.

Klüver, H., Braun, C. and Beyers, J. (2015) 'Legislative lobbying in context: towards a conceptual framework of interest group lobbying in the European Union', *Journal of European Public Policy* 22(4): 447–61.

LaPira, T.M. and Thomas, H.F. (2017) *Revolving Door Lobbying: Public Service, Private Influence, and the Unequal Representation of Interests*, Lawrence, KS: University Press of Kansas.

Lowi, T.J. (1969) *The End of Liberalism: Ideology, Policy, and the Crisis of Public Authority*, New York, NY: W.W. Norton & Company.

Maass, A. (1951) *Muddy Waters: The Army Engineers and the Nation's Rivers*, Cambridge, MA: Harvard University Press.

Mahoney, C. (2008) *Brussels Versus the Beltway: Advocacy in the United States and the European Union*, Washington, DC: Georgetown University Press.

Mahoney, C. and Baumgartner, F.R. (2015) 'Partners in advocacy: lobbyists and government officials in Washington', *The Journal of Politics* 77: 202–15.

Mann, T. and Orenstein, N. (2016) *It's Even Worse than it Looks: How the American Constitutional System Collided with the New Politics of Extremism*, New York, NY: Basic Books.

McConnell, G. (1966) *Private Power & American Democracy*, New York, NY: Alfred A. Knopf.

Nixon, R. (2014) 'Farm bill compromise will change programs and reduce spending', *New York Times*, January 28: A13.

OECD (2003) *Farm Household Income: Issues and Policy Responses*, Paris: OECD Publications Service.

Sheingate, A.D. (2003) *The Rise of the Agricultural Welfare State: Institutions and Interest Group Power in the United States, France, and Japan*, Princeton, NJ: Princeton University Press.

Strach, P. (2007) *All in the Family: The Private Roots of American Public Policy*, Stanford, CA: Stanford University Press.

Truman, D.B. (1955) *The Governmental Process*, New York, NY: Alfred A. Knopf.

United States Bureau of Economic Analysis (2016) 'Regional data: GDP and personal income', available at http://www.bea.gov/iTable/iTableHtml.cfm?reqid=70&step=1&isuri=1 (accessed 10 October 2016).

United States Department of Agriculture (2016a) 'Feed grains: yearbook tables', available at http://www.ers.usda.gov/data-products/feed-grains-database/feed-grains-yearbook-tables.aspx (accessed 10 April 2016).

United States Department of Agriculture (2016b) 'Sugar and sweeteners: yearbook tables', available at http://www.ers.usda.gov/data-products/sugar-and-sweeteners-yearbook-tables.aspx (accessed 10 April 2016).

United States Department of Agriculture (2016c) 'ARMS farm financial and crop production practices', available at http://www.ers.usda.gov/data-products/arms-farm-financial-and-crop-production-practices.aspx (accessed 10 April 2016).

United States Department of Agriculture (2016d) 'Supplemental Nutrition Assistance Program (SNAP): participation and costs', available at http://www.fns.usda.gov/pd/supplemental-nutrition-assistance-program-snap (accessed 10 April 2016).

Victor, J.N. and Koger, G. (2015) 'Financing friends: how lobbyists create a web of relationships among members of Congress', Paper presented at the Political Networks Workshops & Conference, American Political Science Association, Portland, OR, 17, June.

Vyas, S. and Kumaranayake, L. (2006) 'Constructing socio-economic status indices: how to use principal components analysis', *Health Policy and Planning* 21(6): 459–68.

Wilson, G.K. (1977) *Special Interests and Policymaking: Agricultural Policies and Politics in Britain and the United States of America, 1956–1970*, New York: Wiley.

Wonka, A., Baumgartner, F., Mahoney, C. and Berkhout, J. (2010) 'Measuring the size and scope of the EU interest group population', *European Union Politics* 11(3): 463–76.

'Feeding 9 billion people': global food security debates and the productionist trap

Eve Fouilleux, Nicolas Bricas and Arlène Alpha

ABSTRACT

Food security, a long-established item on the international agenda, raises many issues including production, consumption, poverty, inequalities, healthcare and conflicts. However, in 2007/2008 the global food security debate was relaunched with a single dominant focus which continues to the present day: increasing agricultural production. This paper explains this productionist bias – which may translate into inadequate policies – by combining insights from institutionalist and cognitive analyses. We show that, despite recent reforms, the global food security field remains dominated by macro- and micro-institutions that put food availability and agricultural production at the heart of the problem and solutions. The political and discursive strategies developed by transnational corporations and private foundations to promote their productivist interests are also key, along with the demands of dominant farmers' unions in exporting countries. Although advocating opposite development patterns, civil society actors implicitly reinforce the productionist perspective through their focus on family agriculture.

Introduction

'Food security' is anything but a new issue on the international stage. It has been institutionalized since the post-1945 period through various international organizations. The term itself appeared during the 1970s and its conceptual content has evolved over time. The most commonly accepted definition was officially established by the 1996 World Food Summit: food security exists when 'all people, at all times, have physical and economic access to sufficient safe and nutritious food that meets their dietary needs and food preferences for an active and healthy life'. Food security/insecurity is a complex topic covering many dimensions, such as poverty, inequality, unemployment, prices, consumption habits and culture, gender and nutrition. Food insecurity causes can vary tremendously among areas, social groups or individuals.

Since global food prices soared in 2008, inducing 'food riots' around the world, 'food security' has regained priority on the global agenda and now appears as a buzzword in numerous public and privates initiatives, research programmes and policy debates. In contrast with previous crises, the 2008 crisis unfolded in a context, prevailing since the early 1980s, of a global surplus of food production over demand.[1] The 2007/2008 price spike had multiple causes, including increased demand for biofuels and declining stocks, which created market tension, while speculation on futures markets and export restrictions also contributed (Headey and Fan 2008; High Level Panel of Experts on Food Security and Nutrition [HLPE] 2011: 352). In brief, the problem did not result from a production crisis. However, the post-2008 crisis debate immediately focused on the balance between agricultural supply and demand and on production (Bricas and Daviron 2008; Tomlinson 2013). As Duncan's (2015: 34–6) framework analysis of key policy recommendations emerging from the 2007–2008 crisis shows, after 'immediate relief', 'increased production' was the main recommendation ahead of 'improved markets', 'financing and funding', 'country-led plans', 'policy cohesion', 'cooperation' and 'sustainability'. The discourse then turned towards the 2050 horizon, thrusting into the limelight the challenge of feeding the nine billion people expected to populate the planet by then. From 2008, calls multiplied for global food production to be doubled, and later on for a 70 per cent increase. The exhortation to produce more has become a leitmotif both nationally[2] (e.g., Rosin 2013) and internationally: the 2015 Milan Universal Exposition 'Feeding the Planet, Energy for Life' and the European Commission's[3] report *Global Food Security 2030* illustrate this trend. Discussions in scientific and expert forums evolved along similar lines (Godfray *et al.* 2010; Grafton *et al.* 2015).[4]

How can insistence on increasing production be so dominant when in most cases production has not been the most pressing problem? Why is the global food security debate so heavily biased towards productionist solutions? These are the questions we address in this paper. In the terms of that special issue (Daugbjerg and Feindt 2017), we want to understand how and why productionist ideas, which typically support exceptionalist privileges for agricultural producers, tend to colonize and shape the food security issue despite its post-exceptionalist (transversal and intersectoral) nature.

Thompson (2005) defines 'productionism' as a 'philosophy that emerges when production is taken to be the sole norm for ethically evaluating agriculture'. Productionism differs from productivism. The latter is a variant of the former, more directly tied to a specific socio-technical agriculture model that is input and technology oriented (see Wilson 2001). While productionism relates to a general discourse focused on the need to increase production without mentioning any technical or social specific agricultural pattern, productivism focuses on the need to increase productivity through increased use of chemical inputs (fertilizers, pesticides), hybrid seeds (possibly including genetically modified seeds), mechanization and larger-scale farms.

The first part of this paper presents a brief overview of the literature on global food security governance, followed by our analytical perspective and methods for collecting data (1). We then look at the main organizations in the global food security field (2) and analyse how food security/insecurity measurement tools have contributed to shaping the discussions (3). Finally, we analyse the visions of non-institutional actors (private sector, civil society, farmers' unions, etc.), and the resources, strategies, forums and arenas they use (4).

Beyond the fragmentation of global food-security governance: explaining discursive convergence

Complexity and fragmentation

The literature on the global governance of food security underlines its complexity and fragmentation. Food security falls within the remit of a decentralized patchwork of institutions, although none has the authority and legitimacy to take responsibility for all aspects or to coordinate the various institutions and manage potential conflicts (Margulis 2012; 2013). In addition to the increasing number and density of international institutions and private initiatives in the field since 2007/2008, Margulis (2012) notes a variation in institutional forms, from formal institutions to informal networks and voluntary guidelines, and the growing spread of food security as an objective in other sectors and organizations (World Health Organization [WHO], World Trade Organization [WTO], Sustainable Development Goals).

The literature also highlights the fragmentation of perspectives regarding the problem and its solutions. This is described through different concepts and approaches: complex international regimes in competition (Barling and Duncan 2015; Margulis 2013), different justification regimes (González 2010), consensus frames and contested claims (Maye and Kirwan 2013; Mooney and Hunt 2009). Other authors point to the divergences within dedicated institutions, such as the United Nations Food and Agriculture Organization (FAO) (Fouilleux 2009; González 2010). The plurality of ideas (resulting from the diversity of sectors, countries, governance levels, actors, interests, etc.) and ideational conflicts in the food security field are seen as a major challenge (Candel 2014). Most of these works show that fragmentation and competition eventually result in a failure of global governance and in a persistent food insecurity on the ground. A more integrated and inclusive system of governance, i.e., offering new ways of consensus-building while recognizing the existence of multiple and conflicting regulations and standards, is seen as essential for improving effectiveness (Candel 2014; Margulis 2013; McKeon 2015).

Analysing global food security debates

We assume that organizations and institutions have a primary role in framing the debate, which can be encapsulated through applying the concept of organizational field at the global level (Dingwerth and Pattberg 2009; Loconto and Fouilleux 2014).[5] This field is formed around a central issue (Hoffman 1999), namely food security. An organizational field includes 'two constitutive elements: a set of institutions, including practices, understandings and rules; and a network of organizations' (Lawrence and Phillips 2004: 692). Dynamics of change within a field imply processes combining institutionalization, deinstitutionalization, new practices, legitimation and specific balances of power (Hinings *et al.* 2004). To understand how ideas and meanings evolve in the field (Hoffman 1999: 352) and how they result in a specific problematization[6] of the global food security issue, one needs to analyse the interplay of existing organizations and institutions and the power balances within the network of actors involved.

As Carstensen and Schmidt (2016: 319) underline, one 'significant way ideas matter is through agents' promotion of certain ideas at the expense of the ideas of others'. Arenas (where policy negotiations take place) and forums (where policies are assessed and analysed and their impacts measured) (Fouilleux 2004, 2009) are key places where ideas are exchanged and ideational power[7] is exerted. Studying these is therefore crucial to understand policy debates. Firstly, macro-institutions influence the content of debates through the procedural rules they impose on stakeholders (deciding who is allowed to participate and talk and when, the way in which arguments are framed and decisions are taken, etc.). The different arenas do not have the same influence and ability to shape the debate, and their relative importance may vary across historical periods. Secondly, the content of debates is determined by the micro-institutions of the field, i.e., policy instruments, statistics, measurement and assessment tools, etc. These can directly influence the problematization of issues through the aspects of the situation that are highlighted or concealed (Desrosières 1998; Ilcan and Phillips 2003; Lascoumes and Le Gales 2007). Thirdly, the capability of actors (individuals or organizations) to influence the debate and affect the definition of the field's institutions – e.g., public policies – must be assessed. In addition to the arena chosen for the discussion (which can enable or impede participation), their potential influence depends upon actors' available resources (financial, discursive, political, etc.). Scholars have identified an increasing transnationalization of social movements and their will to participate in policy debates, notably in the global food security field (Brem-Wilson 2017; Thivet 2012). Others have emphasized the increasing weight of private actors in global governance and their ability to defend their interests (Djelic and Quack 2010; Stone 2013), in particular the discursive power of transnational corporations (TNCs). These actively 'participat[e] in public debates on the definition of political problems and solutions as well as offensively and defensively shap[e] their image as economic, political, and societal actors' (Fuchs 2005: 272; see also Clapp 2012; Clapp and Fuchs 2009).

Many studies emphasize the dominance of neoliberal ideas in the global food security field (Duncan and Barling 2012; González 2010; Jarosz 2011; McKeon 2015). Corresponding discourses consider increasing trade as the main avenue to achieve food security (Fouilleux 2009; Jarosz 2011). In this paper, we examine another dominant discourse in the field: productionism, i.e., the tendency to reduce the complex food security issue to a need to increase production. For this purpose, we develop two interlinked hypotheses. The first regards the institutions in the global food security field. At the macro-institutional level, we argue that the 2007/2008 crisis provided an opportunity for states and organizations advocating productionist stances to regain a central position. At the micro-institutional level, until very recently, food security/insecurity measurement tools were almost exclusively focused on food availability and therefore on production. Our second hypothesis points to the relative influence of civil society movements and large firms in the debate. Thanks to their abundant resources, TNCs are able to promote their productivist interests in the various influential forums and arenas of the global food security field, while civil society actors, whose interests, values and visions diverge dramatically from those of the firms, have fewer resources available to promote their positions.

Methodology and data collection

This paper is based on an explaining-outcome process-tracing methodology (Beach and Pedersen 2013), i.e., a case-centric method that attempts to craft a minimally sufficient explanation of an outcome (here, the productionist bias in global food security debates) using an eclectic combination of theoretical mechanisms and non-systematic, case-specific mechanisms.

Empirical data were collected via different channels. The authors have conducted applied research and obtained significant expertise in the field of food security/insecurity for more than 20 years. Their experience gives them a deep understanding of technical and institutional issues and access to a wide network of people in international organizations (e.g., FAO, International Fund for Agricultural Development [IFAD], World Food Programme [WFP], World Bank, Comité Inter-États de Lutte contre la Sécheresse au Sahel [CILSS], Sahel and West Africa Club Secretariat [SWAC]/Organization for Economic Co-operation and Development [OECD]), national/regional administrations (Mali, Burkina Faso, Senegal, Cameroon, Ethiopia, African Union, France, European Commission), non-governmental organizations (NGOs) (Oxfam, Institute for Agriculture and Trade Policy [IATP], Action Contre la Faim [ACF], Comité Catholique contre la Faim et pour le Développement [CCFD], Cenesta) and other actors in the field. Another source of evidence was participant observation. Among other events, we attended the nine annual sessions of the Committee on World Food Security (2008–2016); the International Conference on Nutrition (2014); and the monthly meetings of the French Groupe Interministériel sur la Sécurité Alimentaire (GISA) (2008–2015). During these events, we had privileged access to drafts, non-papers and other preparatory documents for negotiations and the opportunity for informal discussions with many actors. We have also analysed selected documents (HLPE and FAO reports), websites and exchanges on specialized online forums (e.g., Global Forum on Food Security and Nutrition [Forum FSN], HLPE e-consultations). Documents are the main source of direct evidence for this paper, but we have also conducted 15 explorative interviews on the issue of productionism with top-level managers and lower-level bureaucrats in various organizations (Committee on World Food Security [CFS], FAO, HLPE, GISA, World Bank [WB], Via Campesina, CCFD) to informally test and discuss our hypotheses.

We have processed the collected data through a classical case study approach with multiple data sources to allow triangulation, i.e., through a mixture of content analysis of policy documents and an iterative interpretation of field notes, refined and validated through discussions on preliminary interpretations among authors and actors.

Global food security organizations and institutions

From Rome to Washington, and back to Rome

Food security was discussed at the 1943 Hot Springs Conference, which examined ways to protect humanity from neediness and poverty (Jarosz 2011). It became truly institutionalized in the early 1970s. In the context of food crises, the World Food Council (WFC), created in Rome in 1974, was a coordinating body for national ministries of agriculture to address malnutrition and hunger, especially through the development of new agricultural techniques (Shaw 2010). A Committee on World Food Security (CFS) was created in the same year as a simple FAO Committee, bringing state representatives from ministries of agriculture together for regular meetings in Rome. At that time, the debate was focused mainly on ways to increase agricultural production as well as on food security stocks in countries suffering from droughts. Another focus was on food aid, as illustrated by the World Food Programme

(WFP), created in 1963 to provide emergency distribution. The International Fund for Agricultural Development (IFAD), created in 1977 and also headquartered in Rome, extended the discussion to rural development. But issues of income, markets, diets, etc. in rural and urban areas remained largely overlooked at that time.

During the 1980s, however, the WB emerged as a new actor in the field. With the fight against poverty as its new flagship priority and inspired by Amartya Sen's work, in its 1986 annual report the WB proposed a new vision of food security based on the notion of *access* to food, which notably includes the ability to pay in order to get food. This notion was formally taken up at the 1996 World Food Summit in Rome and gave rise to the consensual definition mentioned above (see introduction). In addition to promoting an individualized neoliberal approach to food security (Jarosz 2011), the report puts forward the idea that food security should not be considered solely as an agricultural and production-related issue but also as encompassing social, land tenure, infrastructural, gender and other related issues. The increasing influence of the WB meant that the Rome institutions suffered progressive delegitimization. The CFS's role has weakened year by year. The WFC's activities were even suspended – one of very few, if not the only, example of a discontinued United Nations (UN) organization (Shaw 2010). The 1990s and 2000s were marked by a decline in the importance of agriculture in official development assistance; the FAO was criticized from all sides and its political influence on the international arena declined (Fouilleux 2009). An independent external evaluation launched by the UN called for deep reform of the organization in 2007.

The same year, the WB released its annual report, entirely devoted to agriculture (the first time since 1986), acknowledging the mistake of having abandoned this key sector for poverty reduction (WB 2007). The report was crucial in reopening debates on the role of agriculture for development within the WB, and was well received by the international community. However, the report did neither anticipate the looming price crisis, although it was brewing at the time of writing, nor the urban riots that would spread across several countries in 2008. Meanwhile, the WB focused on promoting its report, although its content appeared at odds with reality. It thus missed the opportunity to coordinate a policy response to the crisis[8] and kept its focus on commodity markets and trade liberalization. Although no better prepared, the FAO was the first to react formally by transforming an international climate change and biofuels conference that was long planned for June 2008 into a high-level food crisis summit. The solutions proposed were immediately oriented towards food assistance, safety nets and 'immediate support for agricultural production and trade' (Duncan 2015: 34–6; McKeon 2015: 95–7). By using the crisis as an opportunity to regain legitimacy in the global arena, the FAO immediately took the lead and strongly advocated its productionist approach.

Since the 2008 crisis: an opening up of the global food security field

The 2008 crisis fuelled important changes within the global food security field, including institutional creations and reforms.

In 2008, the High Level Task Force on the Global Food Security Crisis (HLTF) was created by the Secretary General of the UN to coordinate a crisis response by international organizations. Using the 1996 consensual definition of food security, which had been reaffirmed at the 2002 World Food Summit, the HLTF recognized the multi-faceted nature of the crisis and advocated for an inter-sectoral approach.[9] Although criticized for being too technocratic and without any input from political or societal constituencies (Duncan 2015), the HLTF 'articulate[d] policy responses to the multiple and complex factors that cause food security instead of focusing on a single issue' (Margulis 2012: 242). It emphasized social assistance and protection, adjusting tax and trade policies affecting food consumers, and developing an international biofuels policy (to avoid food/fuel competition). The only mention of increasing/improving production related to smallholders. Since 2009, the HLTF's work has mainly shifted to ensuring operational coherence at the national level, with no follow-up on unresolved – and highly political – issues such as export bans and biofuels (Margulis 2012).

Another change within the field has been the affirmation of the G8 and G20 as a new arena for global food security policy. After various calls in 2008, G8 heads of state/government made food security a priority in L'Aquila in 2009 and formally committed to providing over US$20 billion over three years to this end (Margulis 2012: 246–7). The G8 initiative then shifted to the G20 and gave birth to the Global Agriculture and Food Security Programme (GAFSP), which involves public donors[10] and the Gates Foundation and is administered by the WB. Contrasting dramatically with the HLTF's inter-sectoral approach, but also with the historical focus on access from the WB, the GAFSP's first priority has been to boost agricultural productivity in developing countries. The G20 'has shied away from tackling the broader structural economic dimensions of the food crisis with bold regulatory reforms, and instead has pressed for initiatives that smooth markets by increasing food production and encouraging information flows' (Clapp and Murphy 2013: 130). In addition to the narrowing of its own food security agenda, the G20 has had a chilling effect on discussions in other arenas, putting productivity issues at the centre and impeding more in-depth debate on structural causes of food insecurity, i.e., commodity speculation, biofuels and unbalanced trade policies (Clapp and Murphy 2013: 134). Distancing itself from its former focus on access, the WB now advocates similar discourses, saying, 'Investment in agriculture and rural development to boost food production and nutrition is a priority.'[11]

A third change was the reform of the CFS in 2009. Converging with a long-standing demand of many civil society organizations (McKeon 2015), the idea was to reform a governance system that hitherto had been exclusively inter-state by opening the debate to other sections of society. Many actors also hoped to render food security issues less dependent on the FAO and its agri-culturally oriented perspective and to expand the CFS to include other sectors (health, trade, employment, etc.) to ensure broader political mobilization. The reform thus induced two main innovations aiming to make the global debate on food security more pluralistic. The Civil Society Mechanism (CSM) and the Private Sector Mechanism (PSM) allow non-state actors to take part in both plenary discussions and the advisory group to the CFS Secretariat (with – until 2016 at least – four seats for the CSM versus two for the PSM). The High Level Panel of Experts on Food Security and Nutrition (HLPE) is in charge of integrating inputs from independent experts into CFS debates (Duncan and Barling 2012).

Does the CFS truly change the global debate?

This reform, which was supposed to make the CFS 'the foremost inclusive international and intergovernmental platform … towards the elimination of hunger' (CFS 2009), was not achieved without resistance. The FAO was reluctant to accept any de-sectoralization and sought to maintain its hegemo-nic position. For example, the CFS Secretariat continued to be headed by a senior FAO officer until 2014. Similarly, the CFS website is hosted by the FAO, and CFS meetings continue to be held at the FAO headquarters. Further-more, some competition is visible in the publication of reports and the leading of debates. While HLPE reports are built on the basis of e-consultations that allow any individual to react and contribute, the FAO organizes online dialo-gues in parallel on similar topics through its Global Forum on Food Security and Nutrition (Forum FSN). When the first HLPE report on price volatility was released in 2011, the FAO published its annual 'State of Food Insecurity in the World' report on the same subject at the same time.[12] This parallel report clearly promoted more productionist arguments than the HLPE report (Clapp and Murphy 2013: 134) and, with the explicit aim of weakening the latter, the FAO ensured that it was submitted to the CFS plenary, in con-tradiction to the spirit of the CFS reform (Duncan 2015: 103).

Furthermore, despite a broadening of the issues under discussion, the CFS has remained very agriculture oriented, a majority of its 500 to 650 partici-pants being from this sector. Member states are mainly represented by their embassy staff in Rome, who are also their representatives at the FAO, the WFP and IFAD, and by their colleagues in ministries of agriculture and national agricultural institutions. Contrastingly, civil society actors have been more explicit supporters of cross-cutting objectives. During the four-year period from 2010 to 2013, agricultural representatives increased from 65 per cent to 74 per cent, self-acclaimed 'food security' actors represented less than 10 per cent, while the share of representatives from other sectors (health, nutrition, employment, poverty alleviation) decreased from 27 per cent to 17 per cent.[13] An analysis of the agendas of the CFS plenary sessions and side events shows the priority given to agriculture-related topics, i.e., land management, agricultural investment and farming systems, compared with intersectoral issues such as poverty, health and nutrition.

In addition, while many actors would like to see the CFS playing a cross-cutting role in the global debate, G20 governments refuse to allow the CFS to table cross-cutting issues like trade (the domain of the WTO) or climate change (the domain of the United Nations Framework Convention on Climate Change) (Clapp and Murphy 2013:135; Duncan 2015:118). Another example illustrating the difficulties of broadening the scope of debate within the CFS occurred in 2012 when the CFS plenary session proposed to debate the possible extension of the term 'food security' to 'food and nutrition security' in order to highlight the links between the two issues and to encourage collaboration between the related policy communities.[14] Due to strong opposition – especially from Russia, China and the Netherlands – a decision on the proposal was postponed and the debate has not been formally reopened since then. In 2014, the Second International Conference on Nutrition was held independently of the CFS. Since 2015, however, the decision to produce an HLPE report specifically on nutrition has reflected a political will for better collaboration.

Measuring food security

Food security/insecurity measurement tools are key micro-institutions of the global food security field. As constant and inescapable reference points for the discussions, they directly shape debates and negotiations.

For decades, the FAO has measured the number of food-insecure people by estimating the number of people falling below a critical level of food availability, based on two elements. First, the national average number of calories available per person is derived from the Food Balance Sheet by food type, i.e., quantities produced, subtracting non-food uses (field losses, animal feedstuff, industrial use) and adding the import–export and stock balances. Divided by the population, this measurement is then correlated with standards relating to individual energy nutritional needs (WHO standards in particular). The second element is based on budget and consumption survey data and refers to the population distribution around mean consumption: below a certain level of availability, the population is considered food insecure. This method favours a particular solution: increasing food availability (through production or importation) statistically moves people above the critical threshold out of food insecurity. Although criticized for decades (Maxwell 1996a; 1996b) and despite the emergence of many alternative indicators, these tools have remained dominant until very recently, due to their simplicity and economy (Barrett 2010).

In the 1990s, the World Bank developed a poverty indicator based on basic needs, which can be considered a food insecurity measure. It is based on household expenditure surveys that measure food acquired (including home-produced food, purchases and food gifts), which are then compared with the amount of goods considered essential for one to live. Still, this approach has its limits because it is based on data from cumbersome national surveys that are not repeated annually and therefore do not allow the tracking of annual changes.

The 2008 crisis, however, led experts to question classical food security measurement tools and especially FAO estimates (see Cafiero *et al.* 2014; Headey 2011). New indicators have been developed, notably by private actors,[15] and previously marginal alternative approaches have become more visible, such as International Food Policy Research Institute's annual Global Hunger Index, which is based on a combination of indicators of nutritional status and causes of food insecurity. Another example is the Household Food Security Survey Module, which has been promoted internationally by the United States Agency for International Development USAID since the 2000s. This method evaluates food insecurity through surveys asking people about their experiences over the last 12 months. It has inspired the FAO (Cafiero *et al.* 2014), which began collecting data for a Food Insecurity Experience Scale (FIES) in 2014, by leveraging private data (the Gallup World Poll, which surveys nationally representative samples of the adult population annually in 150 countries), and has set a Global FIES reference standard, against which all experience-based food security scales can be calibrated. While promising, this new generation of indicators are not yet widely used. Neither have they been extended to the calculation of projections of future food demand, including for the well-known 2050 target date.

New actors and new arenas in the global food security field

The increasing role of transnational corporations in global food security initiatives

TNCs, agricultural supply companies in particular, are increasingly active in the field, promoting both productionist and productivist visions of food security and related policies. They are organized globally and offer global technical solutions for a problem presented as a global one, using food security as a justification for their business by citing the need to increase productivity levels to feed nine billion people. For the multinational company Dupont, 'The growing global population – and the need for more and more nutritious food to feed us all – has particularly captured our attention as a company because of the sweeping challenges involved.'[16] With the support of USAID,[17] the International Fertilizer Development Center actively promotes mineral fertilizers as a way to 'address critical issues such as international food security, the alleviation of global hunger and poverty'.[18] Biotechnology companies are also involved: for example, the BIO International Convention (the main global event for biotechnology industries) annually awards a 'Feeding the World' prize, which was presented to the agrochemical firm Syngenta in 2010. The Prize for Innovation in Food Security (€45,000), initiated in 2014, is awarded by Olam International, a major global agribusiness and trader based in Singapore.

Other influential private sector actors include the philanthropic foundations, in particular the Bill and Melinda Gates Foundation, which has invested massively in agriculture since 2006.[19] Their discourse focuses on increasing agricultural productivity by increasing the use of inputs, i.e., hybrid seeds including genetically modified organisms (GMOs) and mineral fertilizers.[20] Such a productivist stance is reflected in the name of their oldest agri-food initiative, launched with the Rockefeller Foundation: the Alliance for a Green Revolution in Africa (AGRA).[21] Private foundations and TNCs also have objective interests in common, as the former are often shareholders of the latter. These common interests shape their common framing of food security strategies in terms of market-led approaches, new technologies, innovation and management techniques (Morvaridi 2012).

In the field of nutrition, firms and private foundations actively promote the idea of the 'fortification' of food products, thus directly reflecting the interests of agricultural and food businesses. Input companies promote varietal selection (biofortification, i.e., enriching crops with certain nutrients through genetic modification of seeds) or fertilizers (especially zinc in recent years) as providers of nutrients. Food industries propose to improve food by creating new processed products. These technicist discourses have become so dominant in international discussions and activities on nutrition (e.g., the research programme HarvestPlus of the Consultative Group on International Agricultural Research) that they overshadow those relating to food diversification, a highly valuable and much easier approach to implement on the ground according to many specialists (Fanzo et al. 2013; Kimura 2013; Villar 2015).

These private actors also act indirectly, through lobbying strategies aimed at governments (both donors and aid recipients). TNCs and philanthropic foundations are also present in the CFS through the PSM[22] and their participation in annual sessions is growing (46 participants in 2012 [Duncan 2015: 103], 170 in 2016). However, they do not consider the CFS the main decision arena (see Duncan 2015: 103–4) and privilege more powerful ones. We have already mentioned the G8/G20 GAFSP, which invites only a few developing countries to meetings – and only for certain stages – and allows no civil society involvement, but has strong connections to private actors (Clapp and Murphy 2013: 135–6). TNCs also actively engage in public–private partnerships. Formally established in 2012, the New Alliance for Food Security and Nutrition (NAFSN) brings together 10 African governments, the African Union, private sector actors and donors to encourage private foreign investment in agriculture. The NAFSN's official agenda is to improve the living conditions of rural inhabitants and fight against poverty. McKeon (2014) describes the tight links between the NAFSN and AGRA, Grow Africa (an agriculture-oriented initiative of the World Economic Forum in collaboration with the African Union), the Gates Foundation, the Rockefeller Foundation and specific multinationals (e.g., Yara, the Norwegian worldwide fertilizer supplier, Monsanto and Coca-Cola). The NAFSN has been denounced by civil society organizations as a means of opening new markets and a threat to the food security of communities through large-scale acquisitions of land for agribusinesses.[23] Even the European Parliament has recently highlighted its distortive approach.[24]

Unequal access to political arenas, unequal influence on the debate, but an implicitly converging discourse

The main approach of civil society groups in this context has been to re-politicize the debate by asking questions about how food is produced and by whom (McKeon 2015; Thivet 2012). Compared with businesses that have vast resources available to impose their productivist mantra on the various arenas and to shape policies accordingly, social movements and civil society organizations have far fewer resources. They cannot be present and active simultaneously in all global forums and arenas to defend their more complex and locally anchored visions of agriculture and food security. They regularly organize side events at G8 or G20 meetings, but must remain outside the formal negotiating room. The reformed CFS is the only arena where civil society groups can officially raise their dissonant voices within the formal debates and directly express their views to state representatives and exchange arguments on controversial topics.

Given that family farms account for around 70–80 per cent (FAO 2014; United Nations Environment Programme [UNEP] 2011) of global food production and 98 per cent of all farms (Graeub et al. 2016), and that smallholders are among the first victims of food insecurity, peasant movements consider 'family farming' as the essential lever to fight food insecurity. The international peasant's movement La Via Campesina and its global food sovereignty campaign and the Network of Farmers' and, at the regional level, Agricultural Producers' Organizations of West Africa (ROPPA) are very influential organizations that advocate this perspective. They strongly oppose productivism and agribusiness and do not explicitly support productionism. However, they do not fundamentally oppose the latter either; their core focus on peasants, smallholders and farm workers in some ways ensures convergence with productionist strategies that consider agriculture and production to be the main problem and the main solution. Alternative approaches exist, however, such as those that emphasize the right to food, or focus on the urban poor or non-farming rural populations (Maye and Kirwan 2013). These perspectives are mainly promoted by development NGOs.

Interlocked global and national debates

Like the global debate, national debates also put the emphasis on production and have similar underlying asymmetries of power. In agricultural exporting countries such as the European Union (EU) member states, US, Brazil, Argentina, Ukraine and New Zealand (Rosin 2013), debates on agriculture and farming often evoke food insecurity and hunger in Southern countries in a misleading way. Together with the national branches of TNCs, dominant agricultural actors argue for the need in order to produce more to feed the world to defend interests that are actually poorly linked to the issue. In France, the Fédération Nationale des Syndicats d'Exploitants Agricoles (FNSEA) – the main farmers' union – systematically uses this rhetoric to advocate for French and EU policies supporting its export-oriented vision, which is actively echoed by the government: 'Our agriculture has a major role to play in the supply of agricultural commodities and in the balance of world markets. This is the goal I set for it. France must help feed the population of the planet.'[25] In reality, French exports mainly go to European markets (cereals, mainly for animal feed) and wealthy consumers worldwide (wines and cheeses) rather than to food-insecure countries and people.[26] However, such viewpoints actively spread the productionist myth among politicians and the public.

Similarly, the 2008 price crisis reinvigorated productionist arguments in developing countries, especially in Africa, most often justified in terms of the risks of becoming excessively dependent on the international market. For example, various initiatives set ambitious goals for food self-sufficiency with public support reinforcement (mainly input subsidies), such as in the Rice Initiative in Mali and Guinea, or the regional offensive to boost rice production in West Africa. The regional agricultural policy of the Economic Community of West African States (ECOWAP), explicitly refers to food sovereignty among its objectives. India and China use similar arguments to justify their positions in international negotiations.

Conclusion

The logic of consumerism and production at any cost, a logic that, cloaked in good justifications, such as the increasing population, is in reality aimed solely at the increase of profit.[27]

This article seeks to understand why the simple and singular message of increasing production is so often repeated in current food security public debates – and even presented as a moral imperative – while other critical dimensions of food security tend to be overlooked (poverty, unemployment, prices, gender aspects, consumption patterns, nutrition, etc.).

To explain this we have focused on the role of the organizations and institutions. They provide reports and analyses and offer forums for policy discussions and arenas for negotiation. Despite institutional creations (HLTF) and reforms (CFS) that have opened the debate to new dimensions of food security via the entry of new actors, the 2008 crisis also served as an opportunity for agricultural institutions to re-legitimize their productionist approach on the international stage. In addition, new arenas with disproportional geopolitical and economic power (G8/G20) have entered the field with a clearly productivist agenda, backed by large TNCs and exporter interests. We have also underlined the crucial role of micro-institutions (instruments used to measure food security/insecurity) in shaping the field, through their historical focus on the availability of food. However, this dominance may now be changing through the integration of nutritional indicators and the recognition of actual experience.

In addition to these institutionalist explanations, we highlight the significant asymmetry of resources available to the various actors to promote their visions, and the political consequences in a multi-level and multi-arena globalized political system. While TNCs and private foundations are increasingly active in spreading their productivist approach to food security, civil society organizations have much less influence. TNCs use their considerable resources to enter new (CFS) or tailor-made (NAFSN) institutions while actively lobbying less open arenas (G8/G20). Although civil society organizations have gained increased visibility due to the reformed CFS, they still have limited resources and no direct access to the most powerful arenas in the field. In supporting family farming and food sovereignty, by focusing their attention on agriculture, farmers' organizations are not opposed to productionism. In contrast, productionist (and productivist) views are clearly promoted by the dominant agricultural actors in exporting countries, echoed by their governments with the justification of maintaining their trade balance. In developing countries, the productionist agenda is advocated by governments as a means to decrease dependency on food imports, especially in Africa.

In such an asymmetric political and institutional context, the simplicity and general nature of the productionist paradigm, combined with the ability of hegemonic actors to develop multilevel strategies for its promotion, explain its discursive power. With its focus on the global level, this mantra impedes the ability of actors to grasp the diversity of local situations. Planning for the future, it prevents actors from adequately orienting policy solutions for the present. Through its focus on technical fixes and its close relationship with the productivist discourse, it avoids considering both social and environmental impacts of increasing production, which affect vulnerable people disproportionately (Ericksen *et al.* 2009). Re-politicising the productionist mantra by more explicitly taking into account power balances within and among food systems (International Panel of Experts on Sustainable Food Systems food 2015) is clearly an urgent matter for the global food security debate. The recent opening of an international debate on agroecology, notably in the FAO, may be a first step in this direction.

Notes

1. The WHO requires 2,500 Kcal per day for a working adult to be in good health. Theoretically, the volumes of food produced on a global scale have met this target for the world population as a whole since 1981. Food production has been ever increasing since then, reaching 2,870 Kcal/capita/day in 2011 (authors' calculation based on FAOSTAT database: http://www.fao.org/faostat/en/#data).
2. In addition, only a few countries (e.g., Brazil, India) explicitly promote social policies as a key means for achieving their own food security.
3. http://publications.jrc.ec.europa.eu/repository/bitstream/JRC94867/lbna27252enn.pdf
4. Of 359 articles published in the journal *Food Security* between February 2009 and February 2015, 191 refer to 'agricultural production' or 'food availability' in their titles.
5. We encompass the literature on both institutional and organizational fields.
6. 'Problematization' is the way in which problems are conceived and enounced (Callon 1984), from which the solutions proposed directly derive.
7. 'Ideational power' is the capacity of actors to influence actors' normative and cognitive beliefs through the use of ideational elements (Carstensen and Schmidt 2016: 320).
8. Interview, former WB staff member, June 2015.
9. See the Comprehensive Framework for Action (HLTF 2008)
10. Australia, Canada, Japan, Korea, the Netherlands, Spain, USA, United Kingdom.
11. http://www.worldbank.org/en/topic/foodsecurity/overview (accessed November 2016).
12. FAO, IFAD, WFP (2011: 51).
13. Authors' calculations based on lists of participants at CFS plenaries.
14. CFS Secretariat's preparatory notes.
15. Dupont's Global Food Security Index, Maplecroft Food Security Index and Gallup World Poll.
16. http://foodsecurity.dupont.com/2015/05/15/eiu-special-report-the-role-of-innovation-in-meeting-food-security-challenges/
17. http://www.feedthefuture.gov/model/international-fertilizer-development-center
18. http://www.vfrc.org/Fertilizer_Needs/Chemical_Fertilizers_and_Food_Security
19. In 2006–2009, the foundation invested US$1.4billion, 40 per cent more than the FAO budget for 2010–2011 (US$1billion) (McKeon 2014).
20. http://www.gatesfoundation.org/What-We-Do/Global-Development/Agricultural-Development

21. See http://agra-alliance.org/
22. The participation of the private sector in the CFS has increased significantly in recent years.
23. Among others, see Hunger: just another business. How the G8's new alliance is threatening food security in Africa. Paris: Oxfam-France, ACF, CCFD-Terres-Solidaires. Available at http://www.actioncontrelafaim.org/fr/espace-jeunes-enseignants/content/hunger-just-another-business.
24. See European Parliament resolution of 7 June 2016 on the NAFSN (2015/2277 (INI)).
25. F. Hollande, speech at a national agriculture fair, 11 September 2012. Quote afterwards used as a slogan at the French pavilion of the Milan Universal Expo.
26. These discourses also meant to dissimulate specific conflicts of interests tightly related to globalization, as illustrated by the case of Xavier Beulin, both the FNSEA president and the CEO of Avril, a global agribusiness player.
27. Pope Francis, address to the FAO Director General, October 2016, available at http://press.vatican.va/content/salastampa/it/bollettino/pubblico/2016/10/14/0735/01640.html#eng

Acknowledgements

We thank colleagues and actors in the global food security field who have commented on earlier versions of this paper, as well as the three anonymous reviewers and the guest editors for their constructive comments

Disclosure statement

No potential conflict of interest was reported by the authors.

Funding

This work was supported by Agence Nationale de la Recherche: [grant number ANR-13-JSH1-0008].

References

Barling, D. and Duncan, J. (2015) 'The dynamics of the contemporary governance of the world's food supply and the challenges of policy redirection', *Food Security* 7(2): 415–424.

Barrett, C.B. (2010) 'Measuring food insecurity', *Science* 327(5967): 825–828.

Beach, D. and Pedersen, R.B. (2013) *Process-tracing Methods: Foundations and Guidelines*, Ann Arbor: University of Michigan Press.

Brem-Wilson, J. (2017) 'La Vía Campesina and the UN committee on world food security: affected publics and institutional dynamics in the nascent transnational public sphere', *Review of International Studies* 43(2), 302–329.

Bricas, N. and Daviron, B. (2008) 'De la hausse des prix au retour du «productionnisme» agricole: les enjeux du sommet sur la sécurité alimentaire de juin 2008 à Rome', *Hérodote* 131(4): 31–39.

Cafiero, C., Melgar-Quiñonez, H.R., Ballard, T.J. and Kepple, A.W. (2014) 'Validity and reliability of food security measures', *Annals of the New York Academy of Sciences* 1331(1), 230–248.

Callon, M. (1984) 'Some elements of a sociology of translation: domestication of the scallops and the fishermen of St Brieuc Bay', *The Sociological Review* 32(S1), 196–233.

Candel, J.L. (2014) 'Food security governance: a systematic literature review', *Food Security* 6(4): 585–601.

Carstensen, M.B. and Schmidt, V.A. (2016) 'Power through, over and in ideas: conceptualizing ideational power in discursive institutionalism', *Journal of European Public Policy* 23(3): 318–337.

CFS. (2009) *Reform of the Committee on World Food Security Final Version*, Rome: FAO.

Clapp, J. (2012) *Food*, Cambridge: Polity Press.

Clapp, J. and Fuchs, D.A. (2009) *Corporate Power in Global Agrifood Governance*, Cambridge: MIT Press.

Clapp, J. and Murphy, S. (2013) 'The G20 and food security: a mismatch in global governance?', *Global Policy* 4(2): 129–138.

Daugbjerg, C. and Feindt, P.H. (2017) 'Post-exceptionalism in public policy: transforming food and agricultural policy', *Journal of European Public Policy*. doi:10.1080/13501763.2017.1334081

Desrosières, A. (1998) *The Politics of Large Numbers: a History of Statistical Reasoning*, Cambridge and London: Harvard University Press.

Dingwerth, K. and Pattberg, P. (2009) 'World politics and organizational fields: the case of transnational sustainability Governance', *European Journal of International Relations* 15(4): 707–743.

Djelic, M.L. and Quack, S. (2010) *Transnational Communities. Shaping Global Economic Governance*, New York: Cambridge University Press.

Duncan, J. (2015) *Global Food Security Governance: Civil Society Engagement in the Reformed CFS*, Oxon and New York: Routledge.

Duncan, J. and Barling D. (2012) 'Renewal through participation in global food security governance: implementing the international food security and nutrition civil society mechanism to the committee on world food security', *International Journal of Sociology of Agriculture and Food* 19(2): 143–161.

Ericksen, P.J., Ingram, J.S.I. and Liverman, D.M. (2009) 'Food security and global environmental change: emerging challenges', *Environmental Science & Policy* 12 (4): 373–377.

Fanzo, J., Hunter, D., Borelli, T. et al. (2013) *Diversifying Food and Diets. Using Agricultural Biodiversity to Improve Nutrition and Health*, Oxon and New York: Routledge.

FAO. (2014) *The State of Food and Agriculture. Innovation in Family Farming*, Rome: FAO.

FAO, IFAD, WFP. (2011) *The State of Food Insecurity in the World: How does international price volatility affect domestic economies and food security?*, Rome: FAO.

Fouilleux, E. (2004) 'CAP reforms and multilateral trade negotiations: another view on discourse Efficiency', *West European Politics* 27(2): 235–255.

Fouilleux, E. (2009) 'À propos de crises mondiales … Quel rôle de la FAO dans les débats internationaux sur les politiques agricoles et alimentaires ?', *Revue française de science politique* 59(4): 757–782.

Fuchs, D. (2005) 'Commanding heights? The strength and fragility of business power in global politics', *Millennium-Journal of International Studies* 33(3): 771–801.

Godfray, H.C.J., Beddington J.R., Crute I.R., Haddad, L., Lawrence, D., Muir, J.F., Pretty, J., Robinson, S., Thomas, S.M. and Toulmin C. (2010) 'Food security: the challenge of feeding 9 billion people', *Science* 327(5967): 812–818.

González, H. (2010) 'Debates on food security and agrofood world governance', *International Journal of Food Science & Technology* 45: 1345–1352.

Graeub, B.E., Chappell M.J., Wittman H., Ledermann, S., Kerr, R.B. and Gemmill-Herren, B. (2016) 'The state of family farms in the world', *World Development* 87: 1–15.

Grafton, R.Q., Daugbjerg C. and Qureshi M.E. (2015) 'Towards food security by 2050', *Food Security* 7(2): 179–183.

Headey, D. (2011) 'Was the global food crisis really a crisis? Simulations versus self-reporting', *East Asia* 16: 18–15.

Headey, D. and Fan S. (2008) 'Anatomy of a crisis: the causes and consequences of surging food prices', *Agricultural Economics* 39(1): 375–391.

Hinings, C.R., Greenwood, R., Reay, T., et al. (2004) 'Dynamics of change in organizational fields', in M.S. Poole and A.H. Van de Ven (eds.), *Handbook of Organizational Change and Innovation*, New York: Oxford University Press, pp. 304–323.

HLPE. (2011) *Price Volatility and Food Security*, Rome: CFS.

Hoffman, A.J. (1999) 'Institutional evolution and change: environmentalism and the U.S. chemical Industry', *The Academy of Management Journal* 42(4): 351–371.

Ilcan, S. and Phillips, L. (2003) 'Making food count: expert knowledge and global technologies of Government', *Canadian Review of Sociology/Revue Canadienne de Sociologie* 40(4): 441–461.

International Panel of Experts on Sustainable Food Systems food. (2015) *The New Science of Sustainable Food Systems. Overcoming Barriers to Food System Reform*.

Jarosz, L. (2011) 'Defining world hunger: scale and neoliberal ideology in international food security policy discourse', *Food, Culture and Society* 14(1): 117–139.

Kimura, A.H. (2013) *Hidden Hunger: Gender and the Politics of Smarter Foods*, Cornell: Cornell University Press.

Lascoumes, P. and Le Gales, P. (2007) 'Introduction: understanding public policy through its instruments? From the nature of instruments to the sociology of public policy Instrumentation', *Governance* 20(1): 1–21.

Lawrence, T.B. and Phillips, N. (2004) 'From Moby dick to free willy: macro-cultural discourse and institutional entrepreneurship in emerging institutional fields', *Organization* 11(5): 689–711.

Loconto, A. and Fouilleux, E. (2014) 'Politics of private regulation: ISEAL and the shaping of transnational sustainability governance', *Regulation & Governance* 8 (2): 166–185.

Margulis, M. (2012) 'Global food security governance: the committee on world food security, comprehensive framework for action and the G8/G20', in R.R.N. Weisfelt (ed.), *The Challenge of Food Security: International Policy and Regulatory Frameworks*, Cheltenham: Edward Elgar, pp. 231–254.

Margulis, M. (2013) 'The regime complex for food security: implications for the global hunger challenge', *Global Governance* 19(1): 53–67.

Maxwell, D.G. (1996a) 'Measuring food insecurity: the frequency and severity of "coping strategies"', *Food Policy* 21(3): 291–303.

Maxwell, S.S. (1996b) 'Food security: a post-modern perspective', *Food Policy* 21(2): 155–170.

Maye, D. and Kirwan, J. (2013) 'Food security: a fractured consensus', *Journal of Rural Studies* 29: 1–6.

McKeon, N. (2014) 'The new alliance for food security and nutrition: a coup for corporate capital?', *TNI Agrarian Justice Programme Policy Paper*. Amsterdam: Transnational Institute, 19.

McKeon, N. (2015) *Food Security Governance. Empowering Communities, Regulation Corporations*, London: Routledge.

Mooney, P.H. and Hunt, S.A. (2009) 'Food security: the elaboration of contested claims to a consensus frame', *Rural Sociology* 74(4): 469–497.

Morvaridi, B. (2012) 'Capitalist philanthropy and the new green revolution for food security', *International Journal of Sociology Agriculture Food* 19(2): 243–256.

Rosin, C. (2013) 'Food security and the justification of productivism in New Zealand', *Journal of Rural Studies* 29: 50–58.

Shaw, D.J. (2010) 'The world food council: the rise and fall of a united nations body', *Canadian Journal of Development Studies* 30(3-4): 663–694.

Stone, D. (2013) *Knowledge Actors and Transnational Governance. The Public-Private Policy Nexus in the Global Agora*, Basingstock: Palgrave Macmilan.

Thivet, D. (2012) 'Des paysans contre la faim. La "souveraineté alimentaire", naissance d'une cause paysanne transnationale', *Terrains&Travaux* 20(1): 69–85.

Thompson, P.B. (2005) *The Spirit of the Soil: Agriculture and Environmental Ethics*, London: Routledge.

Tomlinson, I. (2013) 'Doubling food production to feed the 9 billion: A critical perspective on a key discourse of food security in the UK', *Journal of Rural Studies* 29: 81–90.

UNEP. (2011) *Towards a Green Economy: Pathways to Sustainable Development and Poverty Eradication*.

Villar, J.L. (2015) *Tackling Hidden Hunger: Putting Diet Diversification at the Centre*, Penang, Malaysia: Third World Network.

Wilson, G.A. (2001) 'From productivism to post-productivism … and back again? Exploring the (un)changed natural and mental landscapes of European agriculture', *Transactions of the Institute of British Geographers* 26: 77–102.

World Bank. (2007) *World Development Report 2008, Agriculture for Development*, Washington, DC: The World Bank.

Global organic agriculture policy-making through standards as an organizational field: when institutional dynamics meet entrepreneurs

Sandra Schwindenhammer

ABSTRACT
Scholars of public policy point to standards as a new form of food and agriculture policy-making. The contribution complements this literature applying analytical concepts from International Relations research and organizational theory. Taking into account the increasingly complex and fluid nature of global food politics, the study undertakes a critical re-evaluation of the organizational field approach. Considering the interconnectedness of structure and agency it adds the concepts of entrepreneurship and calibration to the analysis of global organizational fields. The empirical analysis conducts a qualitative historical examination of the construction of the organizational field of organic agriculture policy-making through standards. It traces three phases of institutional development, identifies areas of contestation and distinct paths of institutional change influenced by the interplay of entrepreneurship and the institutional dynamics of structuration, homogenization and calibration.

Introduction

There is a growing body of literature that points to standards as a popular form of global policy-making (Büthe and Mattli 2011; Mattli 2001; Mattli and Woods 2009), especially in the food and agriculture sector (Gibbon *et al.* 2010; Ponte *et al.* 2011). Food and agriculture standards are part and parcel of the fundamental changes in food policies that fuel theoretical and practical policy debates. The editors of this collection introduce 'post-exceptionalism' as a diagnostic concept to characterize the simultaneous continuity and change in the agricultural policy arena and convincingly argue that food and agriculture policy-making increasingly takes place in open, cross-sectoral internationalized and contested contexts (Daugbjerg and Feindt 2017).

This contribution analyses the historical development of the global field of organic agriculture policy-making through standards as an illustrative example of post-exceptionalism. Although organic agriculture receives broad academic attention (e.g., Freyer and Bingen 2015), research on the emergence and outcomes of organic agriculture standard-setting is just developing (Arcuri 2015; Schmid 2007; Schwindenhammer 2016). Organic agriculture governance is particularly attractive to scholars engaged in post-exceptionalist food policy studies for several reasons. From the very beginning, the organic policy agenda has been interlinked with several extra-sectoral policy issues. Organic entrepreneurs raised specific normative concerns, promoted organic agriculture 'as the best practical expression of the idea of sustainable farming', and created a very specific set of public and private standards (Daugbjerg and Feindt 2017). Organic agriculture policy-making through standards is cross-cutting environmental, health, social, developmental and trade policies. It serves as a good laboratory for analyzing the regulatory shift towards the new interplay between the state, business and civil society and an increased use of voluntary approaches to regulation (Flohr *et al.* 2010). It allows for research of a policy context characterized by various actors with different values and control over the setting and implementation of organic agriculture standards. Facilitated by globalized flows of trade, demand for healthy products, and growing consumer awareness, organic agriculture is rapidly internationalizing (Willer and Lernoud 2017). It constitutes a dynamic and fluid global policy field that, right from the outset, deviated from exclusive policy-making in the national domain. The field is characterized by several standard-setting schemes with a similar policy focus on different regulatory levels (Schwindenhammer 2016) that add 'a co-regulatory layer to an already complex set of public and private regulations' (Daugbjerg and Feindt 2017). Only a few studies deal with the construction of this policy field (Fouilleux and Loconto [2017]; Lynggaard [2007] with a special focus on the European Union (EU)).

The contribution conducts a qualitative historical examination and analyses how specific institutional and agency-related dynamics interact in field development. The framework for analysis links organizational field analysis (DiMaggio and Powell 1991a, 1991b; Scott 1995; Wooten and Hoffman 2008), research on entrepreneurialism (e.g., Greenwood and Suddaby 2006; Mintrom and Norman 2009), private authority (Cutler *et al.* 1999), and global governance through standards (e.g., Abbott and Snidal 2001; Büthe and Mattli 2011). The empirical analysis traces three phases of field development, reveals distinct paths of institutional change, and detects areas of cooperation and contestation. The analysis has three purposes in the light of the ongoing theoretical debates on food and agriculture policy-making.

The first purpose is to locate organic agriculture policy-making in the context of conceptual debates about organizational fields, entrepreneurialism, private authority and global governance through standards. The contribution shows that food policy studies can benefit from looking at institutional change through the lens of sociological neo-institutionalism.

With its focus on institutional interactions between public and private organizations, the organizational field approach well accounts for the new actor constellations and inter-institutional interactions in the post-exceptionalist food policy arena. While the classical organizational field approach assumes that field-level dynamics lead to similar structures over time (DiMaggio and Powell 1991a, 1991b), I argue that field development may involve processes of institutional homogenization and divergence. The conceptual framework extends the classical approach to show that *entrepreneurship* is of crucial importance in the formation and development of the organizational field. I add a new institutional dynamic – calibration – to account for the flexible adjustment of field institutions by means of inclusive and exclusive balancing activities of strategic entrepreneurs. Entrepreneurs likely pursue the adjustment of organizational structures to maintain or strengthen their social position in the field (Greenwood and Suddaby 2006). The opportunities for entrepreneurial activities grow with the increasing degree of field institutionalization (Dorado 2005). The resulting homogeneity or divergence of institutional structures is an empirical question that is analyzed in this contribution. The second purpose is to reveal how far organizational field development involves contestation. Organizational fields do not only emerge around organizations with similar orientations; they also constitute around agents with various and competing interests and normative understandings of policy issues (Wooten and Hoffman 2008). The third purpose is to discuss the implications of the results for future organic agriculture policy-making through standards and research.

Policy-making through standards and the organizational field approach

Sixteen years ago, Walter Mattli and colleagues published the special issue of the *Journal of European Public Policy* on the politics and economics of international institutional standard-setting. At that time, the literature on standards lacked a sustained theoretical argument to assess and explain standards schemes and none of the standards research had carefully considered the political and economic roles played by institutions in standard-setting (Mattli 2001). Today, scholars of public policy can build on extended inter-disciplinary knowledge on institutional and actor-related factors that influence the development and impact of standards (e.g., Abbott and Snidal 2001; Büthe and Mattli 2011). The theoretical framework combines these findings with organizational field analysis, research on entrepreneurialism and political authority to detect the institutional and agency-related dynamics of field development in organic agriculture policy-making through standards.

DiMaggio and Powell (1983: 48) define an organizational field as 'those organizations that, in the aggregate constitute a recognized area of institutional life'. Field entities pursue 'a common meaning system' and 'interact more frequently and fatefully with one another than with actors outside the field' (Scott 1995: 56). Early organizational field analysis was mainly about explaining the outcome of organizational fields in terms of common standards of behavior and similar structures (DiMaggio and Powell 1991a, 1991b). The behavior of field entities is motivated by forces in the institutional environment. Institutions constrain or enable action and elaborate the rules to which field entities must conform to receive support and legitimacy. Institutions consist of regulatory and legal frameworks, norms and value systems, and cultural elements and beliefs that create shared meanings (Scott 1995).

As Schmidt (2008: 313) rightly criticizes, the institutions classical organizational field analysis defines are 'overly sticky' with field entities largely fixated in terms of norms. The classical reading predicts a relative stability and fails to explain processes of institutional change. It leaves the question open why there is so much evidence of both processes of convergence and divergence within organizational fields (Beckert 2010). A new line of reasoning in organizational field analysis moves beyond stability and inertia to introduce notions of institutional change. Field-level interactions are regarded as being vital to 'develop collective understandings regarding matters that are consequential for organizational and field-level activities' (Wooten and Hoffman 2008: 138). Although field entities seek guidance from general standards of obligation they might have various and competing preferences that influence institutional change. Hence, the translation of actor capabilities into policy outcomes systematically depends on the power and preferences of other actors (Young 2014). Moreover, organizational fields are increasingly regarded as parts of a wider inter-institutional context of different societal sectors that mutually influence each other (Scott et al. 2000).

The new line of reasoning well corresponds to research on global governance through standards. Global standards likely emerge from the interplay of contestation and co-operation between public and private entrepreneurs (Büthe and Mattli 2011) and differ with regard to the type of policy problems, actor preferences and capabilities involved (Abbott and Snidal 2001). The institutional context is considered as significantly affecting whose policy interests prevail in standard-setting (Mattli and Woods 2009). Although classical organizational field analysis highlights the influence of field entities promoting certain scripts that are consistent with salient norms, it does not deal with the influence of entrepreneurs in *changing* the organizational field. The extended organizational field approach benefits from own findings on the crucial importance of entrepreneurship in the development of standards (Schwindenhammer 2016). I argue that field institutions may be the object of ongoing skirmishing as strategic entrepreneurs seek advantage through redirecting institutions in pursuit of their goals. Depending on different values, preferences and capabilities entrepreneurs collaborate or compete with each other in standard-setting (Abbott and Snidal 2001) and, thus, may establish, maintain or disrupt the organizational field (Beckert 2010).

Structuration, homogenization and calibration

Each organizational field has institutional *self-organizing dynamics* of its own (DiMaggio 1983) that differentiate the field from static concepts of institutional environments. While environments are given, organizational fields are made (Dingwerth and Pattberg 2009).

The first self-organizing dynamic, *structuration*, is especially important in the formation of organizational fields. Structuration involves the gradual specification of roles, behaviors and interactions, a low degree of institutionalization, and the co-existence of different normative understandings (Hinings *et al.* 2004: 305). It comprises four elements (DiMaggio 1983: 148): an increase in the extent of interaction among organizations; the emergence of sharply defined inter-organizational structures of domination and coalition patterns; an increase in the information load with which organizations must contend; and the development of mutual awareness among organizations that they are involved in a common enterprise.

The second self-organizing dynamic is *homogenization*. Once organizational models are institutionalized, they diffuse, cause organizational structures to grow more and more alike, and lead to a higher degree of field institutionalization. The mechanism through which field entities adopt similar procedures is institutional isomorphism. Coercive, mimetic or normative isomorphic pressures influence one unit in a population to resemble others (DiMaggio and Powell 1991a: 67). Coercive isomorphism involves one organization exerting power over another to force the adoption of preferred practices. Mimetic isomorphism rests on habitual taken-for-granted responses to circumstances of social disorientation. Organizations model themselves on others and copy what appears to be a desirable practice. Normative isomorphism works through professional training and educational programs that create a pool of almost interchangeable individuals who possess a similarity of orientation and over-ride organizational variations.

Following the new reasoning in organizational field analysis, I argue that field development may involve homogenization and divergence. Institutional change may emanate from interactions within the field as well as from the overarching inter-institutional policy context in which the field is located (Friedland and Alford 1991: 244). I add *calibration* as a third self-organizing dynamic to the analysis of organizational fields. Following Zito (2015), calibration involves the progressive adjustment of policy-instruments in specific contexts. Calibration is especially important in the development of organizational fields that are exposed to inter-institutional or inter-sectoral pressures.

It implies the flexible balancing of internal and external pressures. Applying findings from International Relations (IR) research, the mechanism through which calibration works is *institutional balancing* (He 2008). He (2008: 493) differentiates inclusive and exclusive balancing. In inclusive balancing, states build institutions to constrain other states' behavior or control and manipulate agendas to address issues related to their interests. In exclusive balancing, states consolidate their political and economic unity to resist pressures from outsiders. With regard to organizational field development, inclusive balancing involves strategic institution-building activities by entrepreneurs that adapt and include new policy issues, actors, coalitions and institutions outside the field. Exclusive balancing involves entrepreneurs strategically consolidating already existing organizational structures to resist external pressures without including them. It involves dealing with ambiguity and implies the future-oriented questioning, modification or even elimination of organizational structures and behaviors within the field.

The role of entrepreneurship

Applying constructivist IR literature, I argue that agency is of crucial importance in processes of institutional or normative change (Flohr *et al.* 2010). A broad range of individuals and institutional actors, such as non-governmental organizations (NGOs), activist networks, epistemic communities, international organizations (IOs), governments or business actors is regarded as norm- or policy-entrepreneurs (Schwindenhammer 2016). Entrepreneurs strategically create new cognitive frames, establishing 'new ways of talking about and understanding issues' (Finnemore and Sikkink 1998: 897). They reframe a formerly unproblematic phenomenon to become problematic or illegitimate and 'attempt to convince a critical mass' (Finnemore and Sikkink 1998: 895) to embrace newly established norms. When entrepreneurs are joined by like-minded actors who accept the new norm and socialize other actors to become norm-followers, the success or failure of a norm depends on whether it reaches wide acceptance and, thus, the 'tipping point' (Finnemore and Sikkink 1998: 895–896). In doing so, entrepreneurs can act as facilitators of organizational field development.

Entrepreneurs must establish *authority* to influence other actors (Boström and Tamm Hallström 2013). Political authority exists, 'when an individual or organization has decision-making power over a particular issue and is regarded as exercising that power legitimately' (Cutler *et al.* 1999: 5). Entrepreneurs strategically pool different authority sources (legal, moral and technical) (Boström and Tamm Hallström 2013; Schwindenhammer 2016) and use various policy tools, such as displaying social acuity, defining problems, network-building and leading by example (Mintrom and Norman 2009). The claim of entrepreneurs contributing to governance through standards is based on their commitment to universally accepted norms, knowledge-based professional expertise or problem-solving resources (Flohr *et al.* 2010).

Interlinking entrepreneurship and institutional dynamics

Since all institutional change processes in organizational fields depend on the influence of agency (Friedland and Alford 1991: 254), the term *self-organizing* institutional dynamics is misleading. Structuration, homogenization and calibration evolve with the engagement of entrepreneurs. However, the relationship between entrepreneurship and the three institutional dynamics needs clarification. I argue that the potential of entrepreneurs to facilitate institutional change cannot be sufficiently evaluated by only looking at the actors' sources of authority. The extent to which regulatory capacities of entrepreneurs are valuable in organic agriculture policy-making is a context-specific matter that varies across institutional contexts and through time (Boström and Klintman 2006: 175; Halpin *et al.* 2011: 148).

Following scholars who analyze institutional entrepreneurship in organizational fields, I argue that the position of entrepreneurs inside (Greenwood and Suddaby 2006) or outside (Maguire 2008) the field, as well as the degree of field institutionalization (Dorado 2005: 391) matter for entrepreneurship. While entrepreneurs that locate in the center of the organizational field promote change to preserve their influential social position, entrepreneurs at the periphery promote change to improve their position (Greenwood and Suddaby 2006: 29). The activities of entrepreneurs outside the field are sources of new ideas for change and may cause institutional contradictions in the field (Maguire 2008: 675). They may lead to the inclusion of new field entities and a change in ideas and institutional structures (inclusive balancing).

The institutional opportunities of entrepreneurs to pursue strategic goals grow with a higher level of field institutionalization (Dorado 2005). A high level of field institutionalization permits entrepreneurs to identify more institutional combinations and facilitates the mobilization of resources (Dorado 2005: 391). During the field structuration, entrepreneurs first locate outside and influence the pre-institutionalization of activities externally. In the course of structuration, field institutions incrementally develop. Flexible boundaries allow entrepreneurs to enter the field. In homogenization, entrepreneurs locate within the field. As field entities, entrepreneurs exert (cause) and are influenced by mimetic pressures, e.g., when they lead by example through putting an idea into action (Mintrom and Norman 2009). In calibration, entrepreneurs may locate within and outside the field. As members of the field they are influenced by and engage in inclusive and exclusive institutional balancing. Outsider entrepreneurs may challenge the field with new policy proposals from outside, bring along ambiguity and confusion in the field (Maguire 2008: 675), and may cause the institutional balancing dynamics.

A conceptualization that refers to the positioning of entrepreneurs inside or outside the field raises questions of defining field boundaries. Organizational fields are bounded by the presence of actors that share certain cultural, cognitive or normative frameworks (Scott 1995). In a fluid inter-institutional and inter-sectoral global context, field boundaries are continuously negotiated in struggles over hierarchies, legitimate actions and the characteristics of members considered being included in the field (Wedlin 2006: 26). Thus, the analysis applies a processual view of boundary-drawing and investigates the shaping of boundaries for each phase of field development.

The construction of the organizational field of organic agriculture policy-making through standards

The empirical analysis conducts a qualitative historical examination of the development of the organizational field of organic agriculture policy-making through standards (dependent variable). The analysis reveals significant variation on the dependent variable over time that allows for the division of three phases of institutional change: while organic agriculture policy-making through standards first was decentralized and fragmented (1920–1969); it became more and more harmonized on the global level (1970–2002); and finally oscillates between global harmonization and regional integration (2002–2016). Each phase of institutional development is analyzed inductively based on the empirical data under analysis and deductively upon the theoretical framework to explore the interplay of structuration, homogenization, calibration and entrepreneurship.[1] I received empirical data from IOs, NGOs and business actors (standards, reports and website material), and five semi-structured expert interviews conducted in 2012 as background information.

Initial structuration, individual entrepreneurship and decentralized standards (1920–1969)

The emergence of the 'biological systems-based paradigm of agricultural production' (Bowen 2013: 4) constitutes the normative basis for field development. In the 1920s, individual organic pioneers such as Rudolph Steiner, Ehrenfried Pfeiffer and Sir Albert Howard formed up a small but rapidly growing countermovement against the chemicalization of agriculture[2] (Paull 2011a). The pioneers practiced and promoted the holistic approach 'that the health of a nation built on agriculture is dependent on the long-term vitality of its soil' (Kuepper 2010: 2). They engaged in the provision of scientific knowledge and initiated small inter-personal networks in which they regularly discussed their ideas. Steiner emphasized the farmer's key role in guiding and balancing the interaction of animals, plants and soil and laid the intellectual foundation of the development of 'biodynamic agriculture' through a lecture series in 1924 (Paull 2011b). Biodynamic agriculture involved a holistic understanding aspired towards social and normative trans-formations. Lord Northbourne, Pfeiffer and other leading European biody-namics were the first to link biodynamic agriculture with organic farming at the 'Betteshanger summer school on biodynamic farming' in Kent in 1939 (Paull 2011c). The British botanist Howard (1940) analyzed traditional Indian farming practices and promoted organic techniques as superior to conven-tional agriculture in his 'agricultural testament'. Influenced by Howard's work, Jerome I. Rodale gave the impetus to the development of the organic farming movement in the United States (US) where he founded the 'organic farming and gardening magazine' in 1942.

In the emerging field, organic standards constituted more the exception than the rule. Individual farmers sold organic products directly to consumers and these personal relationships made standards, inspection and certification schemes superfluous (Schmid 2007: 152). Although one might arguably state that the primary objective of the pioneers was not to change policies, they *de facto* engaged in early entrepreneurship through defining organic agriculture and how it could be politically codified (Reed 2010). They formed a dominant discourse with which most actors agreed. Although different understandings of the nature of agriculture existed (biodynamic versus organic), the pioneers shared the notions of orienting agriculture toward local communities and of placing relationships ahead of profits (Haedicke 2016: 37).

After the interruption by the Second World War, the organic sector experienced the creation of the first broader associations, such as the Soil Association (United Kingdom) in 1945 or the Demeterbund (Germany) in 1955. In the 1960s, the organic sector was challenged by the success of the Green Revolution and an overall policy environment that intended the creation of stable markets with assured prices fixed by governments (Reed 2010: 60). The ideas of organic agriculture regained momentum in the 1970s when the Green Revolution's negative impacts became visible. Entrepreneurs successfully questioned the loss of agricultural biodiversity and the monopolization of seed and chemical inputs by northern compa-nies and, thus, established a new way of talking about and understanding global agriculture (Reed 2010: 89). In the 1970s organic food chains rapidly increased when consumer awareness of environmental, develop-mental and health issues grew in Europe, North America and Japan, leading to a willingness to pay premium prices for organic foods (Asche-mann et al. 2007: 124). With the organic market becoming more impersonal, the demand for standards to prevent fraud and unfair competition was growing. Whereas the demand for standards among producers was driven by the increasing industrialization of organic production, the demand among consumers was driven by anxiety about this very same phenomenon. This trend resembles the development of third-party certification of kosher food in the US (Lytton 2013: 4). Private organic associations were the first entrepreneurs to develop organic standards at the national or local level, e.g., the British Soil Association (1967), soon followed by the French Nature et Progrès (1974), the California Certified Organic Farmers (1974) and the Swedish KRAV Economisk Förening (1985). However, the first organic standards remained decentralized and fragmented.

All in all, organic pioneers first located outside and laid the intellectual foundation for the formation of the organizational field. They taught and promoted the organic philosophy through the provision of expert knowledge (lectures and publications), leading by example (practicing traditional farming techniques) and through networking-building (the founding of the first local and national organic farmers associations). In the course of structuration, field institutions incrementally developed with the entrepreneurs (newly established organic associations) locating inside the field setting the first standards. Although there was a remarkable increase in the extent of interaction among organic movement actors, the structuration of the global organizational field had not been fully completed. Sharply defined inter-organizational structures of domination and mutual awareness among organic organizations of being involved in a common enterprise were still some way off. The decentralized structure led to mutual tolerance and limited contestation over different visions of agriculture (Haedicke 2016: 37). With no overarching regulatory framework, field entities had no 'compelling reasons to interpret their peers' ideological and organizational differences as threatening' (Haedicke 2016: 49).

Homogenization, institutional entrepreneurship and global standard-setting frameworks (1970–2002)

This changed in 1972, when entrepreneurs engaged in the institutionalization of global structures and paved the way towards global standard-setting frameworks. Roland Chevriot, President of Nature et Progrès, organized an international conference with the support of US entrepreneur Rodale to work for the launch of an international organic federation (Bourgeois 1997). The five organizations that founded the International Federation of Organic Agriculture Movements (IFOAM) in 1972 were Nature et Progrès, Rodale Press, the Soil Association, the Swedish Biodynamic Association and the Soil Association of South Africa.

As the global umbrella organization of the major organic farming organizations IFOAM facilitated the final structuration of the field and the mutual awareness among field entities of being involved in a common enterprise. IFOAM contributed to institutional homogenization and soon became a central institutional entrepreneur with the legitimacy to prescribe how organic standard-setting ought to be designed (Paull 2010). In 1980, IFOAM adopted its 'recommendations for international standards of biological agriculture' as the first globally agreed-upon private organic standards. As a global reference framework the IFOAM standards exerted mimetic pressures with regard to content and procedure of organic standard-setting. IFOAM was (and still is) central in the definition of what can be called 'core organic values' (Arcuri 2015: 146). Most organic standards past and present refer to the IFOAM standards.

Until the 1980s only private organizations were considered to belong to the organizational field. The field boundaries significantly extended when public actors engaged in entrepreneurial activities on the national, regional and global levels. Several European countries, e.g., France and Denmark, had started developing national organic regulations even before the 1980s (Schmid 2007: 155).[3] The European Commission developed the first public organic standard on the regional level. It considered drafting a directive to define and control organic farming and turned to IFOAM 'as the primary source of organic expertise' (Schlüter and Blake 2009: 8). The willingness of governmental actors to enter the field posed external pressure on the newly established field institutions and led to early calibration. IFOAM engaged in inclusive balancing and formed the EC Delegation[4] in 1987 to co-operate with the EU. This step was highly disputed within IFOAM and led to contestation over standard ownership. There was 'considerable unease [...] about the attentions of the authorities. Recognition potentially could bring financial support, but control meant losing control. However, the die was already cast – it was an almost inevitable consequence of success' (Schlüter and Blake 2009: 8). In 1991, EU regulation (EEC)2092/91[5] on organic production of agricultural products and indications was published.

In the 1990s, the Codex Alimentarius Commission (CAC) of the Food and Agriculture Organization of the United Nations (FAO) and the World Health Organization (WHO) was the second international agency that placed organic standard-setting on the agenda of IOs. The CAC Committee for Food Labeling invited IFOAM as an observer organization, at that time an unusual step, since observers normally had been states that, while not members of FAO or WHO, had to be members of the United Nations. IFOAM influenced the work of the CAC working group on the draft guidelines through the provision of expert knowledge between 1997 and 1999. In 1999, WHO and FAO jointly released the CAC guidelines. They are the second global reference framework for organic agriculture standard-setting and 'a first step into official international harmonization of the requirements for organic products in terms of production and marketing standards, inspection arrangements and labelling requirements' (CAC 1999). The global regulatory efforts further facilitated national standard-setting initiatives, e.g., the US National Organic Program (2000) or the Japanese Agriculture Standard (2001).

All in all, the second phase is characterized by the final structuration of the organizational field, homogenization and early forms of calibration. At first, individual entrepreneurs engaged in the institutionalization of global structures by means of network-building (founding of IFOAM) and fostered early institutional harmonization in the private organizational field through the setting of the IFOAM standards. The field boundaries fundamentally extended when IFOAM engaged in inclusive balancing and co-operated with public entrepreneurs from outside the field (EU, FAO and WHO). These institutional changes represent a disruptive event in field development and a significant blurring of field boundaries. The previously private field evolved towards a public-private area of institutional life with the inclusion of public actors as new entrepreneurs. At the end of the second phase, two global standards reference frameworks (IFOAM standards and CAC guidelines) provided a point of orientation for the establishment of more specific organic standards at a regional, national or private level. These institutional developments provide empirical evidence of field homogenization. However, disputes in the field emerged with the inclusion of public actors and growing market orientation. IFOAM felt its central field position and influence diminished with the incursion of public entrepreneurs (contestation over ownership). Global organic market and profit orientation were antagonistic to the ambitions of those field entities that still promoted social and cultural change towards small-scale solutions (contestation over ideas) (Haedicke 2016: 38–39).

Calibration, institutional entrepreneurship and standard-setting between global and regional integration (2002–2016)

Institutional homogenization continued in the third phase but did not proceed automatically as classical organizational field analysis predicts. In the early 2000s, regulatory fragmentation became the opposing trend. Although the two global reference frameworks provided normative guidance, they are not legally binding and allow for variation (Daugbjerg 2012). A myriad of public and private organic standards and certification systems emerged on different regulatory levels.

Ideas about efficiency and growth filtered into the field from the business world (Haedicke 2016: 48) and facilitated mutual consent among central public and private entrepreneurs in the field about the benefits of market orientation and global trade. IFOAM, FAO and the United Nations Conference on Trade and Development (UNCTAD) engaged in exclusive balancing to minimize standard multiplicity and fragmentation and to consolidate their political influence. They strategically intensified their professional connections and established a global public–private partnership in 2002 to improve standard harmonization, recognition and equivalence (Bowen 2013). The International Task Force on Harmonization and Equivalence in Organic Agriculture (ITF) (2002–2008) and its follow-up Global Organic Market Access Project (GOMA) (2009–2012) defined their main objectives as facilitating regulatory harmonization, international organic trade and access of developing country producers to international markets. In 2008, ITF established a system of equivalence and mutual standard recognition including the two practical tools – Guide for Assessing Equivalence of Standards and Technical Regulations and International Requirements for Organic Certification Bodies.

By means of ITF and GOMA, IFOAM, UNCTAD and FAO also engaged in inclusive balancing to enhance global organic trade and market access for producers from developing countries. The entrepreneurs reached a common understanding of *regional* standard-setting as an appropriate strategy to adapt (and include) different cultural-normative contexts. They paved the way towards the 'new regionalism for organic agriculture' (UNCTAD et al. 2012: i) and promoted the multi-stakeholder approach 'as a successful and replicable model for developing regional standards worldwide' (UNEP and UNCTAD 2010: 37).

The trend of regional standard-setting reveals the overall transformation of private into public policy-making through standards in the organizational field, where the setting of minimum standards has become the monopoly of public actors ('publicization') (Arcuri 2015). Although the subsequent regional organic standard-setting processes in East Africa (2005–2007), the Pacific (2006–2008) and Asia[6] (2010–2012) applied the public–private partnership approach, each process resulted in an official legal document – the East African Organic Products Standard (EAOPS) (2007), the Pacific Organic Standard (POS) (2008) and the ASEAN Standard for Organic Agriculture (ASOA) (2014). Other regional standard-setting processes in Europe and Central America were dominated by public actors right from the outset. Although the IFOAM EU Group continuously influenced the review process of the European legal framework for organic agriculture (2005–2007), (EC)834/2007 was not designed as a public–private partnership. The Harmonized Organic Regulations for Central America, Panama and the Dominican Republic (HORCA) (2010–2012) were neither initiated by the entrepreneurs, nor did they participate in the standard-setting meetings. GOMA defined its role in Central America as to provide the necessary resources to finish a standard-setting process that the regional authorities had started in 2004, but stalled by 2007 (GOMA 2012).

On the one hand, central entrepreneurs in the field (IFOAM, UNCTAD and FAO) provided an overarching normative floor on which regional organic standard-setting today takes place. Although EAOPS, (EC)834/2007, POS, ASOA and HORCA are adaptations to context-specific characteristics of the different world regions, they directly or indirectly refer to the IFOAM standards, the CAC guidelines and the GOMA tools. On the other hand, the promotion of global organic trade and market development through regionalization fueled the contestation over ideas between central field entities and actors at the periphery (small-scale farmers) promoting the orthodox organic philosophy.

All in all, the third phase is characterized by calibration and the coexistence of global and regional standard-setting frameworks. Organic standard-setting oscillates between global harmonization and regional integration facilitated by exclusive and inclusive institutional balancing. IFOAM, UNCTAD and FAO simultaneously engaged in exclusive balancing by means of two global public–private partnerships (ITF and GOMA) to maintain their central position in the field and in inclusive balancing by means of regional standard-setting to adapt different cultural-normative contexts. The new regionalism for organic agriculture further extended the field boundaries through the inclusion of new policy actors. It also paved the way for the development of meta-policy frameworks that exceed several institutional and sectoral contexts. In 2013, FAO, UNCTAD, the United Nations Industrial Development Organization, the United Nations Environment Programme and the International Trade Centre initiated the United Nations Forum on Sustainability Standards (UNFSS) as a platform for international and cross-sectoral dialogue on voluntary sustainability standards, their inter-operability and potential as tools for developing countries to achieve the Sustainable Development Goals (UNFSS 2016). The future will show how the organizational field will take up these new policy ideas from outside. While public actors still stick to the governance through standards paradigm, IFOAM launched 'Organic 3.0' as an alternative, localized approach to mainstream organic agriculture and better position it in global sustainability policies. In the light of the empirical results, one might ask whether IFOAM's initiative is another strategy of a central field entrepreneur to regain control in a field where standard ownership shifted to public actors. To put it in a nutshell, whereas publicization exacerbated the contestation over ownership, the greater focus on global organic trade and market growth reinforced the contestation over ideas in the field.

Conclusion

The contribution has shown that the extended organizational field approach is valuable for analyzing the institutional and agency-related dynamics of the development of the global field of organic agriculture policy-making through standards. The combination of research on organizational fields, entrepreneurialism, private authority and global governance through standards avoids the pitfalls of generalized system-level explanations, broadens the perspective beyond single policy processes and, thus, allows for a more adequate analysis of inter-institutional and open networked post-exceptionalist food policies. Organic agriculture policy-making through standards constitutes a dynamic and fluid global organizational field that oscillates between global standard harmonization (including meta-policy arrangements) and regional integration.

The qualitative historical examination of field development reveals that the institutional dynamics of structuration, homogenization and calibration systematically inter-relate with entrepreneurship. While organic pioneers and national private organic associations engaged in entrepreneurship to promote structuration and homogenization in the first and early second phase of field development, global institutional entrepreneurs (IFOAM, FAO, WHO and UNCTAD) significantly influenced change processes towards homogenization and calibration in the late second and third phase. Although each institutional dynamic was analyzed separately, the empirical findings indicate that harmonization and calibration overlap, occur simultaneously and span across the second and third phase. Organizational field development is a dynamic process that involves homogenization and divergence. Any analysis of organic agriculture governance through standards should take into account the multifariousness and complex inter-dependency of institutional dynamics, flexible field boundaries and entrepreneurship. In the course of field development, central field entrepreneurs gained the legitimacy to prescribe how organic standard-setting ought to be designed. On the one hand, entrepreneurs brought broader concerns on sustainability issues and social justice into the internationalizing organic agricultural policy domain (Reed 2010), developed cultural meaning systems and criteria of social belonging and, thus, significantly shaped the incremental extension of the boundaries of the organizational field. These findings substantiate the claim that post-exceptional policy ideas can trigger policy innovations (Daugbjerg and Feindt 2017). On the other hand, field development involved ongoing claims and counterclaims. With new policy issues and actors arising, conflicts over ideas and ownership exacerbated. While in the first phase standards brought organic farmers together, later the standards divided them (Schmid 2007: 158). Whereas the opposite ideals of orthodox organic philosophy and global market growth resulted in a more adversarial policy discourse, publicization likely fuels struggles for influence among central field entrepreneurs.

Future organic agriculture policy-making has to grapple with the competing demands and contestation over ideas and ownership. There is an ongoing debate on the future role and impact of organic standards. Should organic policy-making still be focused on the standard paradigm, or should it be based on wider ideas, principles and goals of organic farming (Niggli *et al.* 2016: 77)? The detected disputes within IFOAM (phase two) point to the impact of inner-organizational processes and make contestation over values and policies within organizations a future research task. Another challenge relates to the legitimacy and effectiveness of organic agriculture policy-making through standards. In the absence of a central authority in global food politics in charge to safeguard the stringency of standards and the credibility and legitimacy of standard-setting (Derkx and Glasbergen 2014), policy-making through standards is limited by an 'orchestration deficit' (Abbott and Snidal 2009). Because of their legal authority sources, IOs seem to be particularly well equipped to overcome the orchestration deficit (Abbott *et al.* 2015) and to establish and protect the constitutional rules of the game for policy-making through standards. Meta-policy schemes, such as the UNFSS, seem at first sight to be a desirable policy solution. However, in how far the growing influence of public entrepreneurs leads to a process of organic standards' strengthening or weakening is a matter of ongoing debate. According to Schmid (2007), organic agriculture was originally understood as a natural form of farming characterized mainly by the non-use of chemicals and other synthetic inputs. This narrow understanding improved when organic agriculture was defined in private and later also public standards, e.g., by emphasizing a more preventive approach to crop and animal production. In contrast, Arcuri (2015) argues that, with state participation, the content of organic standards is increasingly watered down, e.g., by excluding social and normative issues. Further research is needed to reveal the actual role of public actors, and to assess – from a normative perspective – their appropriate role in the overall architecture of global organic agriculture policy-making through standards.

Notes

1. I do not conduct an overall historical assessment of organizational field development. The presented data reflect the specific focus of the dependent variable on policy-making through standards.
2. The discovery of the conversion of nitrogen and hydrogen to ammonia in 1909 and its commercialization by the chemical company BASF gave impetus to the chemicalization of agriculture (Paull 2009).
3. The 96-year observation period did not allow for further in-depth assessment of national standard-setting. For further analysis see e.g., Schmid (2007).
4. The IFOAM EC Delegation first transformed into the IFOAM EU Working Group (1990) followed by the IFOAM EU Group (2000).
5. (EEC)2092/91 was supplemented by regulation (EC)1804/1999 which regulated the raising, labelling and inspection of the most relevant animal species.
6. The regional organic standard of the GOMA ASIA-Working Group served as the basis for the setting of the public organic standard by the ASEAN member-states (2014).

Acknowledgements

I am grateful to the guest editors, the reviewers and Farhood Badri for insightful feedback.

Disclosure statement

No potential conflict of interest was reported by the author.

References

Abbott, K.W. and Snidal, D. (2001) 'International 'standards' and international governance', *Journal of European Public Policy* 8(3): 345–70.

Abbott, K.W. and Snidal, D. (2009) 'Strengthening international regulation through transnational new governance: overcoming the orchestration deficit', *Vanderbilt Journal of Transnational Law* 32(2): 501–78.

Abbott, K.W., Genschel, P., Snidal, D. and Zangl, B. (eds) (2015) *International Organizations as Orchestrators*, Cambridge: Cambridge University Press.

Arcuri, A. (2015) 'The transformation of organic regulation: the ambiguous effects of publicization', *Governance & Regulation* 9(2): 144–59.

Aschemann, J., Hamm, U., Naspetti, S. and Zanoli, R. (2007) 'The organic market', in W. Lockeretz (ed.), *Organic Farming. An international History*, Wallingford: CABI, pp. 123–52.

Beckert, J. (2010) 'Institutional isomorphism revisited: convergence and divergence in institutional change', *Sociological Theory* 28(2): 150–66.

Boström, M. and Klintman, M. (2006) 'State-centered versus nonstate-driven organic food standardization: a comparison of the US and Sweden', *Agriculture and Human Values* 23: 163–80.

Boström, M. and Tamm Hallström, K. (2013) 'Global multistakeholder standard setters: how fragile are they?', *Journal of Global Ethics* 9(1): 93–110.

Bourgeois, D. (1997) *How it all Began*, Bonn: IFOAM.

Bowen, D. (2013) 'Review of key systemic issues and findings resulting from activities of the international task force on harmonization and equivalence in organic agriculture (ITF) and the global organic market access (GOMA) project', *UNFSS Discussion Paper 2/2013*, New York: UNFSS.

Büthe, T. and Mattli, W. (2011) *The New Global Rulers: The Privatization of Regulation in the World Economy*, Princeton: Princeton University Press.

CAC (1999) 'Guidelines for the production, processing, labelling and marketing of organically produced foods', *CAC/GL32-1999*, Rome: FAO, available at http://www.fao.org/organicag/doc/glorganicfinal.pdf (accessed April 2017).

Cutler, A.C., Haufler, V. and Porter, T. (1999) 'Private authority and international affairs', in A.C. Cutler, V. Haufler and T. Porter (eds), *Private Authority and International Affairs*, Albany: State University of New York Press, pp. 3–28.

Daugbjerg, C. (2012) 'The world trade organization and organic food trade: potential for restricting protectionism?', *Organic Agriculture* 2(1): 55–66.

Daugbjerg, C. and Feindt, P.H. (2017) 'Post-exceptionalism in public policy: transforming food and agricultural policy', *Journal of European Public Policy*. doi:10.1080/13501763.2017.1334081

Derkx, B. and Glasbergen, P. (2014) 'Elaborating global private meta-governance: an inventory in the realm of private sustainability standards', *Global Environmental Change* 27: 41–50.

DiMaggio, P.J. (1983) 'State expansion and organization fields', in R.H. Hall and R.E. Quinn (eds), *Organization Theory and Public Policy*, Beverly Hills: Sage, pp. 147–61.

DiMaggio, P.J. and Powell, W.W. (1983) 'The iron cage revisited: institutional isomorphism and collective rationality in organizational fields', *American Sociological Review* 48(2): 147–60.

DiMaggio, P.J. and Powell, W.W. (1991a) 'The iron cage revisited: institutionalized isomorphism and collective rationality in organizational fields', in W.W. Powell and P.J. DiMaggio (eds), *The New Institutionalism in Organizational Analysis*, Chicago: University of Chicago Press, pp. 63–82.

DiMaggio, P.J. and Powell, W.W. (1991b) 'Introduction', in W.W. Powell and P.J. DiMaggio (eds), *The New Institutionalism in Organizational Analysis*, Chicago: University of Chicago Press, pp. 1–40.

Dingwerth, K. and Pattberg, P. (2009) 'World politics and organizational fields: the case of transnational sustainability governance', *European Journal of International Relations* 15(4): 707–43.

Dorado, S. (2005). 'Institutional entrepreneurship, partaking, and convening', *Organization Studies* 26(3): 385–414.

Finnemore, M. and Sikkink, K. (1998) 'International norm dynamics and political change', *International Organization* 52(4): 887–917.

Flohr, A., Rieth, L., Schwindenhammer, S. and Wolf, K.D. (2010) *The Role of Business in Global Governance. Corporations as Norm-Entrepreneurs*, Basingstoke: Palgrave Macmillan.

Fouilleux, E. and Loconto, A. (2017) 'Voluntary standards, certification, and accreditation in the global organic agriculture field: a tripartite model of techno-politics', *Agriculture and Human Values* 34(1): 1–14.

Freyer, B. and Bingen, J. (eds) (2015) *Re-thinking Organic Food and Farming in a Changing World*, Dordrecht: Springer.

Friedland, R. and Alford, R.R. (1991) 'Bringing society back in: symbols, practices, and institutional contradictions', in W.W. Powell and P.J. DiMaggio (eds), *The New Institutionalism in Organizational Analysis*, Chicago: University of Chicago Press, pp. 232–63.

Gibbon, P., Lazaro, E. and Ponte, S. (eds) (2010) *Global Agro-food Trade and Standards: Challenges for Africa*, Basingstoke: Palgrave Macmillan.

GOMA (2012) 'Harmonization & Equivalence', *The Newsletter of GOMA* 1(2): 1–19.

Greenwood, R. and Suddaby, R. (2006) 'Institutional entrepreneurship in mature fields: the big five accounting firms', *Academy of Management Journal* 49(1): 27–48.

Haedicke, M.A. (2016) *Organizing Organic. Conflict and Compromise in an Emerging Market*, Stanford: Stanford University Press.

Halpin, D., Daugbjerg, C. and Schvartzman Y. (2011) 'Interest-group capacities and infant industry development: state-sponsored growth in organic farming', *International Political Science Review* 32(2): 147–66.

He, K. (2008) 'Institutional balancing and international relations theory: economic interdependence and balance of power strategies in Southeast Asia', *European Journal of International Relations* 14(3): 489–518.

Hinings, C. R., Greenwood, R., Reay, T. and Suddaby, R. (2004) 'Dynamics of change in organizational fields', in M.S. Poole and A.H. Van de Ven (eds), *Handbook of Organizational Change and Innovation*, Oxford: Oxford University Press, pp. 304–23.

Howard, S.A. (1940) *An Agricultural Testament*, London: Oxford University Press.

Kuepper, G. (2010) *A Brief Overview of the History and Philosophy of Organic Agriculture*, Poteau: Kerr Center for Sustainable Agriculture.

Lynggaard, K. (2007) 'The institutional construction of a policy field: a discursive institutional perspective on change within the common agricultural policy', *Journal of European Public Policy* 14(2): 293–312.

Lytton, T.D. (2013) *Kosher. Private Regulation in the Age of Industrial Food*, Cambridge: Harvard University Press.

Maguire, S. (2008) 'Institutional entrepreneurship', in S. Glegg and J.R. Bailey (eds), *International Encyclopedia of Organization Studies*, London: Sage, pp. 674–78.

Mattli, W. (2001) 'The politics and economics of international institutional standards setting: an introduction', *Journal of European Public Policy* 8(3): 328–44.

Mattli, W. and Woods, N. (2009) 'In whose benefit? Explaining regulatory change in global politics', in W. Mattli and N. Woods (eds), *The Politics of Global Regulation*, Princeton: Princeton University Press, pp. 1–43.

Mintrom, M. and Norman, P. (2009) 'Policy entrepreneurship and policy change', *Policy Studies Journal* 37(4): 649–67.

Niggli, U., Willer, H. and Baker, B.P. (2016) *A Global Vision and Strategy for Organic Farming Research*, Frick: Technology Innovation Platform of IFOAM.

Paull, J. (2009) 'A century of synthetic fertilizer: 1909–2009', *Elementials – Journal of Bio-Dynamics Tasmania* 94: 16–21.

Paull, J. (2010) 'From France to the world: the international federation of organic agriculture movements (IFOAM)', *Journal of Social Research & Policy* 1(2): 93–102.

Paull, J. (2011a) 'The uptake of organic agriculture: a decade of worldwide development', *Journal of Social and Development Sciences* 2(3): 111–20.

Paull, J. (2011b) 'Attending the first organic agriculture course: Rudolf Steiner's agriculture course at Koberwitz, 1924', *European Journal of Social Sciences* 21(1): 64–70.

Paull, J. (2011c) 'The Betteshanger summer school: missing link between biodynamic agriculture and organic farming', *Journal of Organic Systems* 6(2): 13–26.

Ponte, S., Gibbon, P. and Vestergaard, J. (eds) (2011) *Governing Through Standards: Origins, Drivers and Limitations*, Basingstoke: Palgrave Macmillan.

Reed, M. (2010) *Rebels for the Soil. The Rise of the Global Organic Food and Farming Movement*, London: Earthscan.

Schlüter, M. and Blake, F. (2009) 'History of the EU organic regulation and its recent revision', in IFOAM EU Group (ed.), *The New EU Regulation for Organic Food and Farming: (EC) No 834/2007*, Brussels: IFOAM, pp. 8–13.

Schmid, O. (2007) 'Development of standards for organic farming', in W. Lockeretz (ed.), *Organic Farming. An International History*, Wallingford: CABI, pp. 152–74.

Schmidt, V.A. (2008) 'Discursive institutionalism: the explanatory power of ideas and discourse', *Annual Review of Political Science* 11: 303–26.

Schwindenhammer, S. (2016) 'Authority pooling and regional organic agriculture standard-setting: evidence from East Africa', *Journal of Environmental Policy & Planning* 18(1): 102–20.

Scott, W.R. (1995) *Institutions and Organizations*, Thousand Oaks: Sage.

Scott, W.R., Ruef, M., Mendel, P.J. and Caronna, C.A. (2000) *Institutional Change and Healthcare Organizations: From Professional Dominance to Managed Care*, Chicago: University of Chicago Press.

UNCTAD, FAO and IFOAM (2012) 'Let the good products flow! Global organic market access in 2012 and beyond', Conference Reader, GOMA, Nuremberg, 13–14 February, available at http://www.fao.org/docrep/015/an455e/an455e00.pdf (accessed April 2017).

UNEP and UNCTAD (2010) 'Organic agriculture: opportunities for promoting trade, protecting the environment and reducing poverty', *UNEP-UNCTAD Capacity Building Task Force Report*, Geneva: UNEP.

UNFSS (2016) *Working Group on Enhancing Interoperability of VSS*, New York: UNFSS, available at http://unfss.org/work-areas/working-groups/working-group-on-enhancing-interoperability-of-vss/ (accessed April 2017).

Wedlin, L. (2006) *Ranking Business Schools. Forming Fields, Identities and Boundaries in International Management Education*, Cheltenham: Edward Elgar.

Willer, H. and Lernoud, J. (eds) (2017) *The World of Organic Agriculture: Statistics and Emerging Trends 2017*, Frick: Research Institute of Organic Agriculture.

Wooten, M. and Hoffman, A.J. (2008) 'Organizational field: past, present and future', in R. Greenwood, C. Oliver, R. Suddaby and K. Sahlin (eds), *The Sage Handbook on Organizational Institutionalism*, London: Sage, pp. 130–47.

Young, A.R. (2014) 'Europe as a global regulator? The limits of EU influence in international food safety standards', *Journal of European Public Policy* 21(6): 904–22.

Zito, A.R. (2015). 'Environmental policy and governance: bringing the state back in (again)?', in G. Capano, M. Howlett and M. Ramesh (eds), *Varieties of Governance. Dynamics, Strategies, Capacities*, Basingstoke: Palgrave, pp. 74–100.

The resilience of paradigm mixes: food security in a post-exceptionalist trade regime

Carsten Daugbjerg, Arild Aurvåg Farsund and Oluf Langhelle

ABSTRACT
This paper argues that a policy regime based on a paradigm mix may be resilient when challenged by changing power balances and new agendas. Controversies between the actors can be contained within the paradigm mix as it enables them to legitimize different ideational positions. Rather than engaging in conflict over the foundation of the regime, they are more likely to rebalance the paradigm blend. We show that despite being a mixture of two contradictory paradigms, the World Trade Organization (WTO) Agreement on Agriculture has proven resilient when the power balance within the WTO and the policy context changed. The paradigm mix proved sufficiently flexible to accommodate food security concerns and at the same time continue to take steps toward further liberalization. Indeed, the main players have not challenged the paradigm mix.

Introduction

This paper addresses the issue of agricultural trade which has been considered 'one of the longest running paradigm contests in the history of public policy' (Princen and 't Hart [2014]: 472). The current international food trade regime is based on the Agreement on Agriculture (AoA) which was agreed in the Uruguay Round negotiations (1986–1994) under the GATT.[1] The agreement forms part of the World Trade Organization's (WTO) legal framework. It signified a break with the former GATT agricultural trade regime which treated agriculture as an exceptional economic sector exempted from trade disciplines which applied to other economic sectors. The AoA changed the ideational underpinning of the food trade regime by assuming that markets are basically stable and capable of providing society's desired outcomes and that agriculture operates in a way similar to other economic sectors (Coleman *et al.* [2004]: 106; Daugbjerg and Swinbank [2009]). Yet, it includes significant exceptionalist legacies of the old GATT regime. There-fore, the international food trade regime can be considered a post-exception-alist policy arrangement based on a combination of two contradictory paradigms. As explained in the introductory paper of this collection, in a post-exceptionalist policy regime, some exceptionalist features have been maintained while other parts of the regime have been, or are being, 'normal-ized' through a process of marketization. In other words, a post-exceptional regime is characterized by partial or incomplete transformation of a policy regime with the result that 'old and new ideas, institutions, interests and policy instruments coexist' (Daugbjerg and Feindt [2017]).

An international regime can be defined as 'the principles, norms, rules and decision-making procedures around which actors' expectations converge in a given area of international relations' (Krasner [1982]: 186). The food trade regime is defined by the AoA and more generally the WTO legal framework. Though it has been widely recognized that a mixture of ideas underpins many public policies, the existence of two contradictory ideas in the inter-national food trade regime raises the question of the resilience of paradigm mixes. A paradigm mix may reflect a delicate balance between actors subscrib-ing to different ideas, and when the power balance or the policy context changes, the policy regime could potentially collapse. However, in this paper we argue that a policy regime based on a paradigm mix may remain resilient when circumstances change. The current debate on the role of trade in provid-ing food security can serve as a useful case to substantiate this argument.

The AoA was a result of a cumbersome compromise between the European Union (EU) and the United States (US), the two key players in the Uruguay Round. Though most of the discussions on the AoA concerned technical issues, the policy positions of the EU and the US rested on two contradictory paradigms. While the US pursued market liberalism in world agricultural trade, the EU based its position on an exceptionalist view (Daugbjerg and Swinbank [2009]). Therefore, at first glance, one might expect the regime to be vulner-able to changes in the broader policy context or in power relations.

During the Doha Round (2001–) the negotiating context has changed sig-nificantly. Two years into the Round it became apparent that the balance of power had changed with the developing countries achieving veto power in the agricultural trade negotiations. The food price spikes in 2007/2008 and 2011 also affected the negotiating context. While surplus production and depressed world market prices had dominated the negotiating agenda in the Uruguay Round and in the Doha Round up until the food crisis in 2007, food security and the fear of under-supply and resulting price volatility is now a key concern for many developing countries. Though the Doha Round negotiations stalled in 2008 mainly as a result of the inability to agree on agricultural trade, the recent decisions on public stockholding and export subsidies have demonstrated that the regime is viable. Despite increased focus on agricultural policy and trade measures originating from exceptionalist ideas, such as public stockholding and special safeguard measures, negotiators have succeeded in balancing the mix between the two paradigms underpinning the regime. Given its foundation on two contradictory paradigms, it is indeed puzzling why the regime has proved resilient to the significant changes in the negotiation context. This raises the broader question of why a mixed paradigm regime may remain resilient.

Our analysis demonstrates that the controversies and negotiations have remained within the existing paradigm mix which proved sufficiently flexible to accommodate food security concerns and at the same time continue to take steps toward further liberalization of world food trade. The two conditions enabling the resilience of a mixed paradigm regime are: (i) Containment: the adaptability of the mixed paradigm in terms of the opportunities to legitimize inclusion of exceptionalist-inspired food security measures on the negotiating agenda despite their counter-productive effects on market liberalization; and (ii) Flexibility: the ability to facilitate pragmatism and compromises to reduce disagreements on the calibration of these measures within the paradigm mix. This explains why a post-exceptionalist policy regime can be a relatively robust institutional arrangement despite internal tensions between contradictory ideas.

A number of agricultural policy studies have already demonstrated the utility of the concepts of ideas and paradigms in understanding domestic, EU and international agricultural policy regimes (e.g., Alons [2014]; Coleman *et al.* [1997, 2004]; Daugbjerg and Swinbank [2009]; Langhelle *et al.* [2014]; Skogstad [1998]). Recent studies have demonstrated that agricultural policies can be based on a mix of paradigms (Alons and Zwaan [2016]; Erjavec and Erjavec [2009, 2015]; Feindt [2010]; Skogstad [2008]) but there has been no analysis of the resilience of agricultural policies and regimes based on mixed paradigms when challenged, for instance, as a result of altered power relations and policy agendas.

Ideas, paradigms and regime change

Ideas are causal beliefs (Béland and Cox [2011]: 3), or more specifically, narratives linking events in causal order and thereby providing meaning to certain situations (Béland [2009], Berman [2013]: 232; Hall [1993]: 289). By defining the nature of policy problems and what caused them, ideas constitute the deep layer of public policies, providing a foundation to think about the way in which problems can be addressed and which challenges are likely to be faced in resolving them. Hence, ideas also provide guidelines for policy-making since having causal theories about which factors or conditions created a problem leads policy designers toward certain courses of policy action (Béland and Cox [2011]: 3; Blyth [2002]; Daigneault [2014]: 458).

In addition to this cognitive function, ideas also include a normative dimension which relates to appropriate standards of behavior or desirable outcomes. While the cognitive dimension of ideas refers to how the world is, the normative dimension refers to how it ought to be (Béland [2009]: 705–7; Campbell [2002]: 23–5; Skogstad and Schmidt [2011]: 8–9). Finally, ideas are the basis of power when actors have the capacity to influence other 'actors' normative and cognitive beliefs through the use of ideational elements' (Carstensen and Schmidt [2016]: 320).

The related, but not always easily distinguishable, literature on policy paradigms has developed in parallel with the ideational literature (see Skogstad and Schmidt [2011]). Frequent cross-referencing and interchangeable use of the concepts of ideas and paradigms blurs the boundaries between the two literatures. Hall's (1993) seminal article introducing the concept of paradigms in the policy literature can be used to make a distinction between ideas and paradigms. He defines a policy paradigm as

> a framework of ideas and standards that specifies not only the goals of policy and the kind of instruments that can be used to attain them, but also the very nature of the problems they are meant to be addressing. (Hall [1993]: 279)

In other words, a policy paradigm consists of a deep layer and an operational layer. The former refers to the basic understanding of how the world is and/or how it ought to be – the idea. The operational layer sets out the policy objectives and strategies to achieve them. These are defined by the idea underpinning the policy regime (Hall [1993]: 290; see also Daigneault [2014]: 461). Hall (1993: 280) assumed that a policy regime in which more than one paradigm exists will be inherently unstable (see also Carstensen [2015]: 305; Princen and 't Hart [2014]: 472; Princen and van Esch [2016]: 357).

There is now a growing recognition that different paradigms may not be as incommensurable as originally assumed. A new policy paradigm does not necessarily replace the old one; 'rather it comes to constitute the reference point in relation to which these older structures must adapt' (Surel [2000]: 508). Re-analysing the paradigm shift from Keynesianism to monetarism in British macro-economic policy (which Hall [1993] used to support his argument about paradigm change), Oliver and Pemberton (2004: 432–4) find that the shift was gradual and incomplete. Some Keynesian measures were maintained and additional ones reintroduced later on. The recent developments in the paradigm literature highlight that different paradigms can co-exist within the same policy regime. Princen and 't Hart (2014: 472) suggest that unless the 'underlying philosophical ideas are … incommensurable, … a wholesale shift from one set [of ideas] to another is not necessary, as various kinds of hybrids between the two sets are conceivable and yield internally consistent perspectives' (see also Campbell and Pedersen [2014]: 11). This is a likely outcome in situations in which policy-making is characterized by negotiation and compromise between actors with competing interests and different world views (Princen and van Esch [2016]: 360).

To form a majority supporting paradigm change, reform advocates favoring a particular paradigm often have to compromise. For the policy broker, forming a majority coalition matters more than paradigmatic purity (Carstensen [2011]: 153–60). Despite logical inconsistencies of such policy compromises, 'viable mixes between policy paradigms can exist, in different forms and with different emphases' (Princen and van Esch [2016]: 372). This may not necessarily lead to inconsistencies in practice (*ibid.*). Whether or not a particular paradigm mix is inconsistent depends on whose lens one is applying. As Wilder (2015: 1009) points out, the perception of inconsistency is relative as it must be recognized by policy actors and it is subject to ongoing reconsideration. This need to emphasize pragmatism over abstract logical consistency becomes even more profound in consensual policy institutions such as the WTO. In comparison with some, particularly the earlier writings on policy ideas, the recent paradigm mix literature seems to allow considerable room for political settlement and compromise on specific measures. However, regimes cannot be reduced to a purely interest-based compromise. Following Krasner (1982), regimes rest on ideas and paradigms ('principles, norms, rules') – sometimes in the form of a mixture.

The concept of resilience originates in the natural sciences but has found its way into the social sciences (Schmidt and Thatcher [2013]: 14). In their study on neo-liberalism, Schmidt and Thatcher (2013: 1) define the resilience of neo-liberal ideas as 'their ability to endure, recur, or adapt over time; to predominate against rivals; and to survive despite their own many failures'. However, neo-liberalism is broadly defined and comes in many different versions with components imported from other ideologies. A number of countries (e.g., the Scandinavian countries and Germany) have adopted variants of neo-liberalism that might be characterized as paradigm mixes. As Schmidt and Thatcher's definition of neo-liberal resilience also covers such versions of neo-liberalism, it can be adapted to the study of the resilience of mixed paradigms. It is particularly the 'ability to endure, recur, or adapt' which is relevant in this context, provided that the analyst allows for some rebalancing between the paradigms. Since the inclusion of rival ideas is a defining feature of paradigm mixes, this aspect of resilience is less relevant in the study of paradigm mixes. We believe that 'survival despite … failures' is already included in the first aspect of the definition ('endure, recur, or adapt') and therefore should not necessarily be analysed as a separate dimension of resilience. This use of the concept is closely aligned with Schmidt and Thatcher's (2013: 14) notion of a resilient (neo-liberal) policy paradigm which is characterized by 'its adaptation to new circumstances … , its capacity to respond to challenges, and its ability to change while maintaining key elements so that the result is continuity in the set of ideas as a whole' (*ibid*: 14).

We argue that paradigm combinations can indeed be rather resilient even if they are constituted by paradigms based on ideas and a mix of policy instruments and goals that are logically contradictory. In policy regimes based on a single paradigm, policy controversies can develop into a conflict over the ideational foundation of the regime in which different positions cannot easily be reconciled. This can threaten the viability of the policy regime. Paradigm mixes allow controversies to be contained within the regime as ideational statements, and policy proposals inspired by these can be legitimized and thus contained within the regime. Further, paradigm mixes can provide a high level of flexibility in policy revision processes as new measures can be accommodated without challenging the ideational underpinnings of the regime. They can be justified by referring to ideational remnants of the old paradigm or by framing them as improvements, logical extensions or updates of existing operational measures. While this may lead to a rebalancing of the paradigm mix, it is less likely to undermine it. Rather it provides flexibility to rebalance concerns within the policy when circumstances change. At the same time, they constrain actors as the ideational underpinning of the paradigm mix sets limits for what is considered within or outside the negotiating agenda. This ideational power motivates actors to frame their policy preferences within the paradigm mix (Carstensen and Schmidt [2016]).

We suggest that the ability to contain conflict and the flexibility embodied in a paradigm mix explains the resilience of the international food trade regime. To test this proposition, we firstly establish the specific paradigm combination of the WTO Agreement on Agriculture. Secondly, we identify the new challenges to the regime. Thirdly, we explore the conditions enabling the resilience in a situation in which the focus on food security has steadily increased during the ongoing Doha Round and in which the developing countries have become powerful players. We undertake a longitudinal qualitative case study applying some historical background evidence published in two previous research projects (Daugbjerg and Swinbank [2009] and Langhelle et al. [2014]). The analysis of how the issue of food security and changing power balances have influenced the Doha Round agricultural negotiations from 2008 to 2015 is based on official WTO documents and statements/proposals released by the negotiating partners.

Exceptionalism and normalism in the food trade regime

As argued above, a paradigm consists of a deep ideational layer and an operational layer setting out the objectives and policy strategies to achieve them. Daugbjerg and Swinbank (2009: 5–14) distinguish between two fundamental ideas in agricultural policy: *agricultural exceptionalism* and *agricultural normalism*. Based on Grant's (1995), Skogstad's (1998) and her associates'

(Coleman *et al.* [1997]) work, they define agricultural exceptionalism as an idea which assumes that agriculture is a unique economic sector with special market and production conditions, deserving special treatment in terms of government policy. This idea underpins a distinct *state-assisted agricultural policy paradigm* in which the price mechanism is seen as 'a suboptimal means of achieving an efficient and productive agricultural sector' (Coleman *et al.* [1997]: 275).[2] This paradigm dictates a crucial role for governments in maintaining farm incomes through a myriad of revenue increasing (including restricting imports) and cost-reducing policy measures (Daugbjerg and Swinbank [2009]: 5–14). In *agricultural normalism*

> agricultural markets are perceived to be basically stable and capable of provid-ing society's desired outcomes. Imbalances and instability in agricultural markets are the consequence of government intervention, not the result of imperfec-tions in agricultural markets. Both agricultural markets and production operate in a similar fashion to those of other economic sectors. (Daugbjerg and Swinbank [2009]: 12)

This idea underpins *the market liberal agricultural policy paradigm* in which 'market allocation takes precedence over state intervention, and efficiency over equity' (Coleman *et al.* [1997]: 275–6) and in its pure form 'the role of the state is simply to correct for market failures or imperfect markets' (Daugbjerg and Swinbank [2009]: 13).[3]

In the GATT era, the food trade regime was based on an agricultural excep-tionalist underpinning which was particularly evident in articles XI and XVI of the GATT. Article XI allowed the use of import restrictions in agriculture. The waiver of unlimited duration granted to the US in 1955, allowing it to use quantitative import controls, legitimized other countries' measures to restrict imports (Hillman [1994]: 31). Article XVI allowed the use of export subsidies for primary products and legitimized the EU's extensive use of them. Importantly, the lack of disciplines on domestic support and the EU's use of variable import levies were perhaps even more forceful expressions of agricultural exception-alism in the GATT.

The AoA agreed in the Uruguay Round changed the ideational underpin-ning of the international food trade regime by setting the direction toward trade liberalization. The agreement stated that the 'long term objective … is to establish a fair and market-oriented trading system' and that the aim of 'substantial progressive reductions in agricultural support and protection' is to result in 'correcting and preventing restrictions and distortions in world agricultural markets' (WTO [1995]: 43). Articles XI and XVI of the GATT 1947, formally still remaining in the GATT 1994,[4] have been overridden by Article 21 of the AoA.[5] The agreement had a built-in agenda. Article 20 stated that farm trade liberalization was 'an ongoing process' and that 'negotiations for conti-nuing the process' would be initiated before the end of 1999. With its agricultural normalist foundation, the agreement set the course for gradual trade liberalization.

However, substantial components of agricultural exceptionalism remained. Article 20 also stated that 'non-trade concerns, special and differential treatment to developing-country Members, and the objective to establish a fair and market-oriented agricultural trading system, and the other objectives and concerns', including food security, should be taken 'into account' in the reform process. This reflected the preferences of member states holding agricultural exceptionalist views. Further, substantial components of the state-assisted policy paradigm remain at the operational level, i.e., the specific disciplines of the agreement. The creation of special agricultural safeguards (SSGs) for agriculture which allow importing countries to charge an additional duty on imported produce when imports surge or import prices decline below a trigger price; 39 members reserved the right to use the SSGs. While capping tariffs, the agreement still allows comparatively high tariff levels. Though it did impose disciplines on the most trade-distorting forms of domestic support, the farm sector continues to receive substantial subsidies. Finally, the agreement allows continued use of export subsidies but has disciplined them in relation to budgetary outlays and subsidized export volumes. With these substantial components from the state-assisted paradigm, the international food trade regime can best be characterized as a paradigm mixture with agricultural normalism as the dominant ideational underpinning but with some exceptionalist components. The agricultural exceptionalist legacies are more profound at operational level which allows member states' continued, but disciplined, use of policy measures which are associated with the state-assisted paradigm.

Challenging the market liberal paradigm?

Margulis (2017: 27) argues that almost every GATT trade round that involved agriculture included 'some sort of food security dimension'. Food security was codified 'into the rules and practices of the multilateral trade system' in the Uruguay Round negotiations. Nevertheless, the 'extent to which the provisions of the AoA set out rules and commitments that applied specifically and directly to food security is underappreciated' (Margulis [2017]: 49). In addition to being recognized as a non-trade concern, food security concerns were addressed in relation to the three main pillars of the AoA, i.e., domestic support, export competition and market access (Margulis [2017]).[6] Food security was never explicitly defined in the AoA, but the international community agreed on a definition at the Food and Agriculture Organization's (FAO) World Food Summit in 1996: 'Food security exists when all people, at all times, have physical and economic access to sufficient, safe and nutritious food to meet their dietary needs and food preferences for an active and healthy life' (FAO [1996]: 3–4). The Declaration emphasized that 'overall trade policies are conducive to fostering food security for all through a fair and market-oriented world trade system' (*ibid*: 20).

Food security has been one of the most contentious non-trade concerns in the WTO Doha Round negotiations (Farsund *et al.* [2015]; Margulis [2017]). Already in the process leading up to the commencement of the Round, stark differences in the relationship between trade and food security were emerging. In the Analysis and Information Exchange (AIE) process, India, supported by other developing countries, stated that it should be allowed to provide domestic support to address food security concerns, arguing that the 'hypothesis that liberalization alone will improve food security does not take into account the problems faced by a number of developing countries' (WTO [2000]: 3). The US, on the other hand, stated that trade liberalization 'will be beneficial to food security', and that food self-sufficiency 'is not food security. Real food security is enhanced by having many sources of supply, not dependence on only one source' (WTO [2000]: 8).

The Doha Declaration (WTO [2001]) pursued the built-in negotiating agenda of the AoA which outlines an ambitious agenda for further agricultural trade liberalization. However, it also stated that developing countries should be able to 'effectively take account of their development needs, including food security and rural development' and that 'non-trade concerns will be taken into account' (WTO [2001]: 3). The issues of Special Products (SP) and Special Safeguard Mechanisms (SSM) soon became focal in the discussions and resembled the exceptionalist legacy of the regime. The former would allow developing countries to maintain high tariffs on agricultural products which are critical for national food security. The SSM is a border measure that would allow developing countries to raise tariffs temporarily in order to neutralize the trade effects of import surges or declining import prices as such developments could threaten food security and rural livelihoods. The main motivation for introducing the SSM 'begins in the belief that the Uruguay Round Agreement on Agriculture … was a bad deal for developing countries' (Wolfe [2009]: 521). The SSM dominated the agenda before, during and after the game-changing WTO Ministerial Conference in Cancún, Mexico in 2003.

Four weeks before the Conference, the EU and the US had agreed on a 'joint text' which provoked many developing countries as they saw this as a repetition of the Uruguay Round in which these two major agricultural trading powers, when finally agreeing, dictated the terms of the AoA. This attempt by the EU and the US to set the terms again had a substantial impact on the agricultural negotiations (Langhelle *et al.* [2014]: 38–9). In particular, the emergence of the G20 and G33 developing country coalitions significantly altered the power balance within the Doha Round farm trade negotiations.[7] The G20 coalition was initiated by Brazil in the run up to the

Cancún Ministerial (Langhelle *et al.* [2014]: 39). It comprises developing countries advocating market opening and reduction of domestic support in developed countries while maintaining special and differential treatment for developing countries – in other words, market liberalism in developed countries and state-assisted agriculture in developing countries. Brazil, India, and later on China, became the leading members of this increasingly influential group. The G33 coalition was initiated by the Philippines and Indonesia. The main objective for Indonesia was to ensure that the issue of food security, rural livelihood and rural development became an integral part of the negotiations (Wolfe [2009]: 519). Although all negotiating parties in principle supported the SSM, there was no agreement on the specific design of this border measure. This was one of the reasons why the Cancún Ministerial ended in failure.

Explaining the resilience of the food trade regime

The Doha Round negotiations pursued the liberalization agenda set out in the AoA and have achieved significant progress in the deliberations on how to reduce farm subsidy and tariffs ceilings. The growing food security concerns have been reflected in an increased focus on policy measures associated with the state-assisted paradigm. The discussion in particular revolved around three such measures: a special safeguard mechanism (SSM), a special product (SP) category and public stockholding programs for food security in developing countries. However, the existence of a mixed paradigm in the food trade regime enabled negotiators to address the food security concerns without reopening debates on the very nature of the trading regime. Hence, the conditions enabling the resilience of the mixed paradigm regime are firstly containment, i.e., the opportunities to legitimize inclusion of state-assisted food security measures on the negotiating agenda despite their counter-productive effects on market liberalization. Secondly, flexibility in terms of pragmatism and compromises at the operational level, which is necessary in order to reduce disagreements on the calibration of these measures. These two conditions can be identified in the Doha Round negotiations.

The changed balance of power meant that food security became a high-priority issue in the Doha Round. A mini-ministerial conference in Geneva in July 2004 brought the negotiations back on track after the failure in Cancún. The parties agreed on a negotiating framework which stated that 'a Special Safeguard Mechanism will be established for use by developing country Members' (WTO [2004]: 7). The Hong Kong Ministerial Conference in December 2005 delivered agreement on some issues in the agricultural negotiations. A framework for sensitive and special products was agreed, allowing developed countries to list a number of sensitive products and the developing countries a number of special products and impose higher tariffs on these products. The Hong Kong Declaration also included a market-liberal statement on the elimination of export subsidies by the end of 2013 (WTO [2005]). However, since the Doha Round is a single undertaking 'nothing was agreed until everything was agreed'.

There was little progress in 2006 and 2007 as a result of disagreements on the SSM and the extent of liberalization in developed countries. However, there was some progress in the negotiations in the first part of 2008 which motivated the WTO Secretary General to summon a mini-ministerial in Geneva in July. The negotiating parties came close to reaching agreement on an agricultural package, but differences remained over a new SSM. Developing countries, with India spearheading, demanded a strong SSM, which the US opposed, arguing it would affect normal agricultural trade (Langhelle *et al.* [2014]: 42–3). The disagreements were on the specific trigger prices at which the safeguards could be put into force, not on whether or not developing countries' use of SSM should be allowed. India argued for a low threshold for import surges (15 per cent increase in import volumes) 'for the SSM to fulfil its objective of protecting farmers' not least 'from potential floods of subsidized farm imports' (Bridges [2008]: 2). The United States supported a safeguard mechanism, but only with a high trigger (i.e., above 40 per cent increase in import volumes). As Susan Schwab, the United States Trade Representative, explained: 'You can imagine any number below that turning into a free-for-all where developing countries were raising barriers every year' (Schwab [2008]). As the mixed paradigm regime allowed legitimization of trade measures contradictory to the liberalization agenda, disagreements on SSM could be contained and limited to discussions on the specific disciplines for this measure.

The SSM controversy indicated that the balance between the developing country coalitions had changed. Since the Cancún Ministerial, the G20 had been the most powerful developing country coalition, exercising considerable veto power in the negotiations. The power of G20 rested on the ability of Brazil and India to co-ordinate their positions. However, strongly influenced by the 2007–2008 food crisis, India's farm trade policy preferences increasingly aligned with those of G33. As Narlikar and van Houten (2010: 162) noted, 'India, a founding member of the G20, has become a full member of the G33 and has been showing considerably greater interest in the latter'. The controversy over the SSM proved unresolvable and triggered a long stalemate.

The most recent developments in the Doha Round negotiations are additional indications of the food trade regime's resilience. These provide further support for our argument that the paradigm mix has enabled negotiators to maintain and even strengthen components from the state-assisted paradigm in the trade regime and at the same time move further toward market liberalism. In November 2012, the G33 put forward an informal proposal on public stockholding as a food security measure in developing countries (WTO [2012]). Public stockholding is already covered by the AoA (WTO [1995]),[8] but 'the difference between the acquisition price and the external reference price is accounted for in the AMS [Aggregate Measure of Support]' (i.e., amber box domestic support which is considered trade-distorting and subject to a ceiling). G33 argued that 'acquisition of stocks of foodstuffs by developing country Members with the objective of supporting low-income or resource-poor producers shall not be required to be accounted for in the AMS' (WTO [2012]), effectively categorizing public stockholding subsidies in developing countries as green box support (defined as domestic support with no, or at most minimal, trade-distorting effects or effects on production).[9]

Initially, the proposal met with considerable opposition. As, for instance, the US Ambassador to the WTO, Michael Punke stated:

> No one in the WTO, and certainly not the United States, is saying that food security is not a legitimate concern, or that the Uruguay Round Agreement does not already allow for purchases for public stockholding. What many in the WTO are saying is that this proposal, which would effectively lift limitations on trade-distortive purchases, is not the appropriate way to deal with it. (Punke [2013])

Nevertheless, the G33 presented a proposal in October 2013 (WTO [2013a]), requesting a decision at the Bali Ministerial Conference in December 2013. The coalition succeeded in having an interim decision adopted which allowed developing countries to exceed their ceilings on production-linked domestic support (amber box) spent on public stocking of food staples until the end of 2017 when a permanent solution had to be agreed (WTO [2013b]). This enabled India and other developing countries to provide support for public stockholding of food staples acquired at administered prices from low-income or resource-poor farmers. Unexpectedly, India backtracked on the Bali Agreement in early 2014 and demanded a permanent settlement of the stockholding issue before ratifying it. The United States and several other countries opposed this. Illustrative of India's veto power in the WTO, the solution agreed in the General Council in November 2014 allowed developing countries to maintain their public food stockholding schemes until a permanent solution is agreed.

The Nairobi Ministerial Conference in December 2015 again demonstrated the influence of India and its developing country allies and how the mixed paradigm enabled political settlement reflecting different preferences in relation to trade liberalization. The ministerial declaration stated that 'the developing country Members will have the right to have recourse to a special safeguard mechanism (SSM)' (WTO [2015a]) and reaffirmed the intention to reach agreement on a permanent solution on public stockholding (WTO [2015b]). However, these recent developments did not occur at the expense of the course set by the AoA toward normalized trade in agriculture. An indication of this is the decision on immediate elimination of export subsidies applied by developed countries.[10] Developing countries were also required to phase out export subsidies but by end of 2018[11] (WTO [2015c]). One of the first assessments of the Nairobi Ministerial highlights the ability to negotiate within the paradigm mix:

> The Nairobi outcome in agriculture represents a significant step forward, even though it is only a partial attempt to address the much bigger agenda of outstanding issues related to trade in food and agriculture. Among other things, it demonstrates that negotiators at the WTO are capable of making incremental progress in developing meaningful global disciplines on policies that affect global markets for food and agriculture – and that these disciplines can respond, at least in part, to concerns expressed by some of the world's poorest countries. (Bellmann and Hepburn [2016]: 16)

Two decades after the AoA came into force, the Doha Development Agenda negotiations remain *within* the paradigm mix. Despite disagreements and shifting power balances, there are further moves toward liberalization and at the same time continued maintenance (and for the public stockholding of food staples even further strengthening), of components from the state-assisted paradigm.

Conclusion

Our analysis demonstrates that the international food trade regime is constituted by a combination of two paradigms which are logically contradictory. The current regime was established during the Uruguay Round and carefully balanced the market liberal and state-assisted paradigms. The former paradigm is based on agricultural normalism which assumes that the farm sector essentially operates in a way similar to other economic sectors, while the latter is founded on an exceptionalist view in which farming is understood as an economic sector with exceptional market and production conditions. This delicate balance between the two paradigms has been challenged during the Doha Round by the rise of developing countries in the WTO farm trade negotiations, in particular after 2003, and the increasing importance of food security concerns. These altered circumstances brought policy measures associated with the state-assisted paradigm, most notably public stockholding of food staples, the SSM and SP, into the negotiations.

The international food trade regime has proved resilient and able to respond to these new challenges, though there is still a long way to go before a Doha Round agreement on agriculture can be agreed. The paradigm mix has enabled policy controversies to be contained within the policy regime by legitimizing different ideational positions and allowing considerable room for pragmatism and political compromise on specific measures. The negotiations have been conducted within the existing paradigm mix which has proved sufficiently flexible to accommodate exceptionalist food security concerns such as increased, but disciplined, use of trade-distorting subsidies for public stockholding of food staples in developing countries, and continued negotiations on SSM. At the same time, the paradigm mix has enabled negotiators to continue to move toward further liberalization of world food trade, so far, by agreeing on elimination of export subsidies. This indicates that the food trade regime is a relatively robust institutional arrangement despite logical tensions between contradictory ideas and paradigms. More generally, our analysis suggests that a policy regime based on a blend of paradigms may be able to absorb challenges arising from a change in power relations and new agendas.

With its exceptionalist legacy from the GATT era, the international food trade regime can be characterized as a post-exceptionalist policy arrangement. This paper argues that such arrangements can indeed be relatively stable and resilient to challenges even when they have built-in tensions resulting from the existence of a logically contradictory paradigm mix. Such built-in tensions may enable containment of conflict which, in turn, is a condition for regime resilience. The international food trade regime is characterized by two dimensions of tensions. Firstly, two logically contradictory ideational underpinnings co-exist. Agricultural normalism constitutes the dominant idea setting the direction for further trade liberalization. At the same time, exceptionalism legitimizes non-trade concerns, such as food security. Secondly, there is a considerable discrepancy between agricultural normalism as the dominant ideational underpinning and the specific disciplines of the AoA which allow comparatively high levels of agricultural protectionism and support. This reminds us that inconsistency is a relative concept which may not necessarily lead to policy conflict but can indeed facilitate compromise and pragmatism as it allows policy actors to accommodate various and sometimes contradictory concerns. Hence, inconsistency can be an asset which can contain conflict between members of a policy regime and contribute to its resilience.

Though policy ideas and paradigms have been a longstanding research agenda, our knowledge of the dynamics of mixed paradigm policy regimes is limited. We know relatively little about the conditions affecting their stability and resilience. The way in which the paradigms complement each other, the extent to which they allow scope for negotiation and adjustment within the paradigm mix, and how they affect the preferences and strategies of the regime members are crucial factors influencing resilience. To achieve more systematic knowledge on the conditions explaining variance in resilience, we suggest a comparative research strategy analysing how different types of paradigm mixtures affect resilience. Such research could improve our understanding of policy change and continuity.

Notes

1. The General Agreement on Tariffs and Trade (GATT).
2. Also phrased the *dependent agriculture paradigm* (Moyer and Josling [2002]).
3. Moyer and Josling (2002) use the term *competitive agriculture paradigm*.
4. GATT 1994 is substantially identical to GATT 1947 but legally distinct.
5. It states that 'The provisions of GATT 1994 and other Multilateral Trade Agreements in Annex 1A to the WTO Agreement shall apply subject to the provisions of this Agreement [on Agriculture]'.
6. The most important negotiating outcome relating to food security in the Uruguay Round according to Margulis' analyses was the side agreement addressing the concerns of net-food importers in Article 16 of the AoA, known as the Marrakech Decision. For an overview of the food security provisions in the Uruguay Round, see Margulis (2017: 50).
7. A third coalition, the G10, also emerged in Cancún. It consisted of developed food-importing countries advocating that non-trade concerns should be taken into account by the trade regime.
8. In the Agriculture Agreement: Annex 2's articles 3 and 4 and footnotes 5 and 6.
9. The idea was originally proposed by the African Group in 2002. See WTO (2014): https://www.wto.org/english/tratop_e/agric_e/factsheet_agng_e.htm
10. End of 2020 for processed products, dairy products and pork.
11. End of 2022 for already-notified export subsidies.

Acknowledgements

An earlier version was presented at the International Conference on Public Policy (ICPP), Milan 1–4 July 2015. We would in particular like to thank the four anonymous reviewers and the editors of this journal for constructive comments on earlier versions.

Disclosure statement

No potential conflict of interest was reported by the authors.

Funding

This research has been supported by the Sustainable Innovation in Food and Bio-based Industries (BIONÆR) Program [Grant Number 216007], The Research Council of Norway.

References

Alons, G. (2014) 'Farmers versus ideas: explaining the continuity in French agricultural trade policy during the GATT uruguay round', *Journal of European Public Policy* 21(2): 286–302.

Alons, G. and Zwaan, P. (2016) 'New wine in different bottles: negotiating and selling the CAP post-2013 reform', *Sociologia Ruralis* 56(3): 349–370.

Béland, D. (2009) 'Ideas, institutions, and policy change', *Journal of European Public Policy* 16(5): 701–718.

Béland, D. and Cox, R.H. (2011) 'Introduction: ideas and politics', in D. Béland and R.H. Cox (eds.), *Ideas and Politics in Social Science Research*, New York: Oxford University Press, pp. 3–20.

Bellmann, C. and Hepburn, J. (2016) 'Overview', in *Evaluating Nairobi: What Does the Outcome Mean for Trade in Food and Farm Goods?* Geneva: International Centre for Trade and Sustainable Development (ICTSD), pp. 10–17.

Berman, S. (2013) 'Ideational theorizing in the social sciences since "policy paradigms, social learning, and the state"', *Governance* 26(2): 217–237.

Blyth, M.M. (2002) *Great Transformations: Economic Ideas and Institutional Change in the Twentieth Century*, Cambridge: Cambridge University Press.

Bridges Weekly (2008) 'Doha: Close, but Not Enough'. Volume 12(27): 1–8. Geneva: International Centre for Trade and Sustainable Development.

Campbell, J.L. (2002) 'Ideas, politics, and public policy', *Annual Review of Sociology* 28: 21–38.

Campbell, J.L. and Pedersen O.K. (2014) *The National Origins of Policy Ideas: Knowledge Regimes in the United States, France, Germany, and Denmark*, Princeton: Princeton University Press.

Carstensen, M.B. (2011) 'Paradigm man vs. the bricoleur: bricolage as an alternative vision of agency in ideational change', *European Political Science Review* 3(1): 147–167.

Carstensen, M.B. (2015) 'Bringing ideational power into the paradigm approach: critical perspectives on policy paradigms in theory and practice', in J. Hogan and M. Howlett (eds.), *Policy Paradigms in Theory and Practice: Discourses, Ideas and Anomalies in Public Policy*, Basingstoke: Palgrave MacMillan, pp. 295–318.

Carstensen M.B. and Schmidt V.A. (2016) 'Power through, over and in ideas: conceptualizing ideational power in discursive institutionalism', *Journal of European Public Policy* 23(3): 318–337.

Coleman, W.D., Skogstad, G. and Atkinson, M.M. (1997) 'Paradigm shifts and policy networks: cumulative change in agriculture', *Journal of Public Policy* 16(3): 273–301.

Coleman, W., Grant, W. and Josling, T. (2004) *Agriculture in the New Global Economy*, Cheltenham: Edward Elgar.

Daigneault, P.-M. (2014) 'Reassessing the concept of policy paradigm: aligning ontology and methodology in policy studies', *Journal of European Public Policy* 21(3): 453–469.

Daugbjerg, C. and Feindt, P.H. (2017) 'Post-exceptionalism in public policy: transforming food and agricultural policy', *Journal of European Public Policy*. doi:10.1080/13501763.2017.1334081

Daugbjerg, C. and Swinbank, A. (2009) *Ideas, Institution and Trade*, Oxford: Oxford University Press.

Erjavec, K. and Erjavec, E. (2009) 'Changing EU agricultural policy discourses? The discourse analysis of Commissioner's speeches 2000–2007', *Food Policy* 34(2): 218–226.

Erjavec, K. and Erjavec, E. (2015) 'Greening the CAP' – Just a fashionable justification? A discourse analysis of the 2014–2020 CAP reform documents', *Food Policy* 51: 53–62.

Farsund, A.A., Daugbjerg, C. and Langhelle, O. (2015) 'Food security and trade: reconciling discourses in the food and agriculture organization and the world trade organization', *Food Security* 7(2): 383–391.

Feindt, P.H. (2010) 'Policy learning and environmental policy integration in the common agricultural policy, 1973–2003', *Public Administration* 88(2): 296–314.

Food and Agriculture Organization (1996) Rome Declaration on World Food Security, 13–17 November, Rome.

Grant, W. (1995) 'Is agricultural policy still exceptional?', *The Political Quarterly* 66(3): 156–169.

Hall, P.A. (1993) 'Policy paradigms, social learning, and the state: the case of economic policymaking in Britain', *Comparative Politics* 25(3): 275–296.

Hillman, J.S. (1994) 'The US perspective', in K.A. Ingersent, A.J. Rayner and R.C. Hine (eds.), *Agriculture in the Uruguay Round*, New York: St. Martin's Press, pp. 26–54.

Krasner, S.D. (1982) 'Structural causes and regime consequences: regimes as intervening variables', *International Organization* 36(2): 185–205.

Langhelle, O., Farsund, A.A. and Rommetvedt, H. (2014) 'The global trade agenda', in O. Langhelle (ed.) *International Trade Negotiations and Domestic Politics: The Intermestic Politics of Trade Liberalization*, London: Routledge, pp. 23–48.

Margulis, M. (2017) 'The forgotten history of food security in multilateral trade negotiations', *World Trade Review* 16(1): 25–57.

Moyer, H.W. and Josling, T.E. (2002) *Agricultural Policy Reform: Politics and Policy Process in the EC and the US in the 1990s*, Aldershot: Ashgate.

Narlikar, A. and Van Houten, P. (2010) 'Know the enemy: uncertainty and deadlock in the WTO', in A. Narlikar (ed.), *Deadlocks in Multilateral Negotiations – Causes and Solutions*, Cambridge: Cambridge University Press, pp. 142–163.

Oliver, M. J. and Pemberton, H. (2004) 'Learning and change in 20th-century British economic policy', *Governance* 17(3): 415–441.

Princen, S. and van Esch, F. (2016) 'Paradigm formation and paradigm change in the EU's stability and growth pact', *European Political Science Review* 8(3): 355–375.

Princen, S. and 't Hart, P. (2014) 'Putting policy paradigms in their place', *Journal of European Public Policy* 21(3): 470–74.

Punke, M. (2013) 'Statement at Asia-Pacific economic cooperation ministers responsible for trade meetings', Surabaya, Indonesia, April 20 2013, available at https://ustr.gov/about-us/policy-offices/press-office/speeches/transcripts/2013/april/amb-punke-statement-apec-mrt (accessed April 2017).

Schmidt, V.A. and Thatcher, M. (2013) 'Theorizing ideational continuity: the resilience of neo-liberal ideas in Europe', in V.A. Schmidt and M. Thatcher (eds.), *Resilient Liberalism in Europe's Political Economy*, Cambridge: Cambridge University Press, pp. 1–52.

Schwab, S. (2008) 'Press briefing United States trade representative, Geneva, July 30, 2008', available at https://ustr.gov/archive/assets/Document_Library/Transcripts/2008/July/asset_upload_file786_15046.pdf (accessed 17 February 2017).

Skogstad, G. (1998) 'Ideas, paradigms and institutions: agricultural exceptionalism in the European Union and the United States', *Governance* 11(4): 463–90.

Skogstad, G. (2008) 'Canadian agricultural policy programs and paradigms: the influence of international trade agreements and domestic factors', *Canadian Journal of Agricultural Economics/Revue canadienne d'agroeconomie* 56(4): 493–507.

Skogstad, G. and Schmidt, V. (2011) 'Introduction: policy paradigms, transnationalism, and domestic politics', in G. Skogstad (ed.), *Policy Paradigms, Transnationalism, and Domestic Politics*, Toronto: University of Toronto Press, pp. 3–35.

Surel, Y. (2000) 'The role of cognitive and normative frames in policymaking', *Journal of European Public Policy* 7(4): 495–512.

Wilder, M. (2015) 'Ideas beyond paradigms: relative commensurability and the case of Canadian trade-industrial policy, 1975–95', *Journal of European Public Policy* 22(7): 1004–1021.

Wolfe, R. (2009) 'The special safeguard fiasco in the WTO: the perils of inadequate analysis and negotiation', *World Trade Review* 8(4): 517–544.

World Trade Organization (1995) 'The uruguay agreement on agriculture', available at https://www.wto.org/english/docs_e/legal_e/14-ag.pdf.

World Trade Organization (2000) 'Non-trade concerns. Issues raised by members in AIE papers and pre-seattle submissions. A compilation by the secretariat', *G/AG/NG/S/17*.

World Trade Organization (2001) 'Ministerial declaration. Ministerial conference. Fourth session. Doha, 9 –14 November. Adopted on 14 November', *WT/MIN(01)/DEC/1*.

World Trade Organization (2004) 'Doha work programme: decision adopted by the general council on 1 August 2004', *WT/L/579* 2 August 2004.

World Trade Organization (2005) 'Ministerial conference sixth session. Hong Kong, 13 – 18 December 2005. Doha work programme. Ministerial declaration. Adopted on 18 December 2005', *WT/MIN(05)/DEC* 22 December 2005.

World Trade Organization (2012) 'G-33 proposal on some elements of TN/AG/W/Rev.4 for early agreement to address food security issues', *JOB/AG/22*.

World Trade Organization (2013a) 'G-33 non paper: committee on agriculture special session', *JOB/AG/25*.

World Trade Organization (2013b) 'Public stockholding for food security purposes. Ministerial decision of 11 December 2013', *WT/MIN(13)/38, WT/L/913*, Geneva: WTO.

World Trade Organization (2014) 'Agricultural negotiation fact sheet', available at https://www.wto.org/english/tratop_e/agric_e/factsheet_agng_e.htm (accessed February 2017).

World Trade Organization (2015a) 'Special safeguard mechanism for developing country members. Ministerial decision of 19 December 2015', *WT/MIN(15)/43, WT/L/978*, 21 December 2015, Geneva: WTO.

World Trade Organization (2015b) 'Public stockholding for food security purposes. Ministerial decision of 19 December 2015', *WT/MIN(15)/44, WT/L/979*, 21 December 2015, Geneva: WTO.

World Trade Organization (2015c) 'Export competition. Ministerial decision of 19 December 2015', *WT/MIN(15)/45, WT/L/980*, 21 December 2015, Geneva: WTO.

Index

For Product Safety Concerns and Information please contact our EU
representative GPSR@taylorandfrancis.com
Taylor & Francis Verlag GmbH, Kaufingerstraße 24, 80331 München, Germany